THE
C.H.E.E.S.E.
FACTOR

Why You Are the Way You Are

and Help for Overcoming
Life's Common Problems

BY DONALD L. TOTTEN, PH.D.
and JOAN E. TOTTEN, M.A.

Unless otherwise indicated, Bible quotations are
taken from The New International Version of the Bible.
Copyright © 1992 by Life Publishers International.

Published by

CitadelBooks

A division of VMI Publishers
Sisters, Oregon
www.vmipublishers.com

ISBN: 1-933204-05-2

Library of Congress Control Number: 2005927698

Author Contact:

totten@tottenpsych.com

Dr. and Mrs. Totten have written a very clever, practical and insightful book on how to draw upon the Spirit of Christ at all times and in all relationships. A must read for every pastor engaged in pastoral care or counseling. This book will bless you in ways you cannot imagine.

—**Rev. Sueann K. Hagan,
United Methodist Church**

• • • • • • • •

The C.H.E.E.S.E. Factor is an excellent resource for anyone who is struggling with the past or seeking a bright future full of hope and promise in Jesus Christ. Don and Joan have integrated modern psychological theory and technique with scriptural truth in a clear and practical manner. They explain how we become the way we are and the means of becoming the person God intended. The text is a wonderful blend of explanation and application, providing the reader opportunities to personally explore and experience life-changing truths. It is a powerful tool for pastors and congregations, teachers and students, and counselors and clients. Whether from the pulpit or the confines of the small group, this text will transform peoples' lives. This book aptly fills a longstanding need in the literature to understand psychological practice from a Christian perspective.

—**George Nagel, Ph. D. Communications,
Co-Founder: Critical Thinking Institute,
Ferris State University**

• • • • • • • •

As a teacher of critical thinking and reading, I teach my students that "We live in our minds." What we experience and how we perceive the world deals with our mindsets. The C.H.E.E.S.E. Factor allows us to explore our mindsets, and come to see why we are the way we are. It opens us up to reality, to change, to hope, and to our better selves in our relationship with ourselves, with others, and with Christ.

The C.H.E.E.S.E. Factor is an excellent source for personal change, for teachers, for pastors, for psychologists, and for everyday people. The guided exercises, sets of questions, illustrations, analogies, and interventions expand our mindsets. I found the Treasure Chests especially rewarding. More than

simply speaking to our minds, The C.H.E.E.S.E. Factor engages us—mentally, physically and spiritually. Faced with the stresses and common problems of life, we find we really do have choices.

Growth is the only evidence of life. Once you have experienced growth with The C.H.E.E.S.E. Factor, you will be forever changed.

—**Helen E. Woodman, Ph.D.
Assistant Professor, Reading
Ferris State University**

• • • • • • • •

It has been our experience that discipleship must be an integral part of counseling for anyone to find true healing and wholeness. Joan and Don Totten have done an excellent job demonstrating the interconnectedness of discipleship and psychology in this book. It is a great Resource.

—**Pastors Todd and Emily Boyce,
Mount Sterling, Kentucky**

• • • • • • • •

I have recently had the delight of reading The C.H.E.E.S.E. Factor. As a busy pastor, I found it extremely helpful in relating to so many areas of daily ministry in striving to help my people with their problems. Don and Joan's book is filled with fresh insights and helpful illustrations, making it a very useful tool for ministry. The book is easy to read and not just another compilation of "case studies" from a psychological viewpoint. The authors have successfully wedded both the psychological and the spiritual together to form a splendidly fresh view from a Biblical viewpoint, yet remaining grounded in sound psychological principles. The inclusion of interventions and questions is a real bonus for busy pastors, teachers, and small group leaders who may desire to use the contents for teaching purposes. This will be a welcome new collection for those involved in the realm of emotional healing, such as marriage counselors, pastors, teachers, and others. A huge thank you to Don and Joan for this much needed and useful addition to our ministry toolkits.

—**Pastor David L. Cummings,
Evergreen Baptist Church, Cadillac, MI**

THE C.H.E.E.S.E FACTOR

Joan and I want to start with you where you are and help you move along on your journey to where God created you to be. We have written this book in an attempt to share with you some of what we feel God has given to us.

Let's clear up the CHEESE and SPICE thing right off the bat. CHEESE is an acronym for Choice, Heredity, Environment, Events, and Self-Esteem. A foundation for these influences on a person's life is laid in Chapter 2. SPICE is an acronym for Spiritual, Physical, Intellectual, Community, and Emotional. These are factors that have an affect on the elements of CHEESE. SPICE factors are introduced in Chapter 4. In the first four chapters, the affects that CHEESE and SPICE have on our lives are primarily considered to be outside of Christ and not necessarily subject to God's leading. Chapters 5 and 6 form a transition where the reader is led through a consideration of the "in Christ" relationship, and the rest of the book uses SPICE in a more positive sense. Together, CHEESE and SPICE affect our mindsets – the way we interpret and respond to life. The concept of mindsets is a major theme in this book.

This is a why and how book. *THE C.H.E.E.S.E FACTOR* is written with the hope that it will be helpful for many different audiences. The general public will find a wealth of material that is practical in applied Christianity. Christian and secular schools of higher learning can use the book as a text or resource for a course dealing with Christian faith and psychological practice. *THE C.H.E.E.S.E FACTOR* is intended to be a sourcebook for those who want information for personal exploration, for sermons, for group discussion, or for professional practice. The book is intended for the edification of Christians. However, anyone interested in productive spiritual or psychological work will find a wealth of helpful material. The book is a rich resource for individuals, couples, small groups, and anyone in the helping professions. The book can be a guide for people preparing for vocations in the spiritual and emotional realms. The material in the book can generate meaningful further study including dissertation topics.

"There is nothing new under the sun" (Eccles. 1:9). This is also true in the field of psychology. Whatever is good in psychology was in the Bible long before psychologists formed any theories. For instance:

Romans 12:2 states very clearly that mental processes underlie behavior and are involved in behavior change — "Do not conform any longer to the pattern of this world, but be transformed by the renewing of your mind" (Rom. 12:2). As a theoretical base, *THE C.H.E.E.S.E FACTOR* takes a spiritual/cognitive/behavioral approach to understanding and working with human behavior. Mindset is of great importance when considering the changes that must occur when a person chooses the "in Christ" relationship.

James 1:2 counsels us to deal with vexing situations by facing them — "Consider it pure joy . . . whenever you face trials of many kinds . . ." The commandment to "face," or expose ourselves to, trials is necessary in overcoming negative spiritual and emotional states. The goal of "facing," according to James, is to become mature and complete, lacking nothing. As stated in Romans 8:37 — to "become *more than conquerors* through him who loved us."

Any part of psychology that is not supported by Scripture is most likely an Inappropriate Stress Reliever (ISR) and will result in more stress instead of healing. "There is a way that seems right to a man, but in the end it leads to death" (Prov. 14:12). "If a blind man leads a blind man, both will fall into a pit" (Matt. 15:14).

I (Don) began gathering materials and writing in the 1960s when

I was attending seminary and preaching at small churches in Indiana. During most of this time, Joan stayed in the field and probably did more work than I in serving the people. During my course work in seminary and in graduate study, as well as in sermon preparation and private reading, I have gleaned material from numerous sources. Credit goes to those, living and dead, who wrote, obeying the dictates of the Holy Spirit. Much of what is presented in this book has come from inspiration through Bible study, meditation, and prayerful consideration for people whom God has brought under our care.

Circumstances curtailed my seminary studies after four quarters and I spent the next thirty years teaching, during which time we were serving pastorates part-time for twelve years. After retiring from teaching, I began working on my degrees in counseling with the goal of becoming a Christian psychologist. Much to my surprise, I found very little in the way of coordinating Christianity with psychology. If anything, there was more literature saying that linking psychology and Christianity was an oxymoron as a great number of people working in the mental health professions are atheists or agnostics.

Many people suggested I keep my faith a secret so as not to offend potential clients. However, my advertising states "Psychology from a Christian Perspective" and most people inquiring about services state that is what they desire. I strongly prefer to work with people who welcome the use of faith, Scripture, and prayer in therapy. I see no advantage in the blind leading the blind.

Throughout my schooling, ministry, teaching career, and work as a psychologist, my wife Joan has been an intellectual and spiritual resource. Her experiences in church work, and as an educational counselor and program director at Ferris State University, have generated much helpful material. She has contributed in various ways over the years and during the last two years has spent hundreds of hours helping in the writing and editing process. We see our job as being assistant counselors. In John 14:16, Jesus said He would send us a counselor and it is our purpose to assist Him in His work in building up the kingdom of God.

There is a need to understand and obtain the available power of

Christianity in today's world. There is a renewed interest in Christ and His work. A fresh look at "How To" will be helpful. *THE C.H.E.E.S.E FACTOR* contains many new ways of looking at, accessing, and dealing with, faith issues. Also, a lot of old material is viewed in a new light. The book applies years of successful methodology to common problems in the lives of parishioners and clients.

The materials offered in this book are bathed in extensive use of Scripture. It cannot be emphasized enough that daily reading of the Bible, with meditation on its contents, is of critical importance to the life of Christians. (No matter how small the exposure, daily reading of one verse adds up to 365 verses in a year.) We have often felt the inspiration and energy of the Holy Spirit while writing. Thoughts have come that we know are beyond our abilities to formulate.

The scriptural quotes and references are from the New International Version with a few additions from The King James Version. As young Christians, we did our memorizing in the KJV and still find some of that translation preferable. We have read several other versions and find insights in all of them. We place a lot of trust in the Holy Spirit's influence on those dedicated scholars who strived to be faithful to the original texts as we have them.

Verses are quoted extensively, and often repeated, to increase familiarity. A glossary of terms for selected chapters is placed at the end of the book so that we are communicating, not just writing. Also, at the end of the book, a set of questions is given for each chapter to act as a study guide and to promote discussion of some of the important points. We don't want to derail thinking by forcing the reader to look up a reference. Therefore you will find Scripture quotes and references sprinkled throughout the book. Many concepts are repeated as they are applied to different contexts. It often takes many blows of a hammer to drive a point home.

Jesus used illustrations and parables from everyday life to get His points across so that must be the best way to get things to stick in people's minds. *THE C.H.E.E.S.E FACTOR* contains *$$ Treasure Chests $$* at the end of most chapters with dozens of illustrations, exercises, and/or interventions that give windows of understanding and aids for remembering important principles. When you see $$, look at the end of the chapter for treasure – the windows of understanding.

Illustrations increase understanding by giving a mental picture than enhances a concept. Exercises guide people through new ideas, utilizing physical activity and usually involving paper and pencil. Interventions provide mental and physical approaches to the solution of problems. An intervention removes a problem from the usual mindset, sheds light on the situation, and provides information that can be applied to the original problem.

As professionals who have dealt with people in personal relationships as well as religious and educational settings, we have found that people seek us out and express benefit from our care and counsel. As Christians for most of our lives, and Joan having been raised in a Christian home, we have an inside look at the incalculable advantages of the "in Christ" relationship. Our sons, their wives, and their children are carrying on the generational blessings promised by God. We have lived long enough to be able to say that guidelines we have followed and taught are effective and should be shared with others.

There is much of Christian theology and psychology that is not, and cannot, be covered by this book. Our approach to psychology is to couch it in a Christian perspective and design it to fit in with what we feel is God's plan for His people. It is an attempt to maximize life and bring life to the status offered by Christ. People do not necessarily have to have a diagnosable disorder to benefit from Christian psychology. They may want to see how faith in Christ is to be manifested in their world order and how to get the most out of life. We trust that the Holy Spirit was continually involved in preparation of this material and that He will guide the reader in the application of its contents to bring about a more abundant life in Christ.

TABLE OF CONTENTS WITH FEATURES

"DO NOT CONFORM ANY LONGER TO THE PATTERN OF THIS WORLD, BUT BE TRANSFORMED BY THE RENEWING OF YOUR MIND…" (ROM. 12:2). GOD CREATED US IN HIS IMAGE SO THAT HE MIGHT HAVE FELLOWSHIP WITH US AND THAT WE MIGHT ENJOY EACH OTHER'S COMPANY.

CHAPTER 1

MINDSETS

ACTIONS FOLLOW MINDSETS

Our relationship with God makes sense only if we can choose to ignore or reject it. We can have a mindset that brings us into relationship with God, or our mindset can lead us away from Him. It is critical that we understand the concept of mindset because our actions follow our mindsets. The way we are, the way we live, and the way we make decisions are primarily determined by our mindsets, some conscious and some unconscious. Without an understanding of how mindsets influence our lives, the changes necessary to bring us into healing and health in our relationship with God will be hindered. A GLOSSARY for mindsets is found at the back of the book.

(Remember to check the glossaries and chapter questions at the end of the book.)

While various descriptors such as perspective, philosophy, rules, boundaries, perception, or cognitive distortions could be used, we like the term mindset because it fits so nicely with the teaching given in Romans 12:2. "Do not conform any longer to the pattern of this world, but be transformed by the renewing of your mind. Then you will be able to test and approve what God's will is — his good, pleas-ing, and perfect will" (Rom. 12:2). The thread of mindset will surface again and again throughout the book.

"Nicky" was distraught as she came into the office. In response to my usual, "What's happening?" she responded, "I don't know how I got into my family. I seem to be the odd person out." "You don't be-long?" "No, I look different, I act different, I just feel uncomfortable when I'm around them." "What do they say?" "Oh, they say I'm just being silly. They say I'm always welcome, but I see the way they look at me. And they're always talking about me." Nicky went on to give different bits of evidence that "proved" her belief. This excerpt from Nicky's story is used because it is an example of a mindset that affected her relationships.

It seems like some people choose not to be confused with facts once their mind is made up. Nothing will budge them from their set position. This may be a good thing or it may be a bad thing. There are positive mindsets and there are negative mindsets. A large part of psychological work is dealing with negative mindsets. That is why the theme verse for my psychological practice is Romans 12:2 because it applies to mindsets (". . . be transformed by the renewing of your minds . . ."). The reason our minds need to be renewed is that, until we avail ourselves of the mind of Christ, the basis of our thinking is faulty and we will have many harmful attitudes and behaviors. Good news! Our minds CAN be renewed with God's help, as we will learn in fol-lowing chapters. When our minds are renewed, our mindsets become more and more positive and we become able to live as God intended us to live.

Our minds are transformed and renewed when we receive the in-fluence and direction of the ". . . mind of Christ" (1 Cor. 2:16) and we receive ". . . the Spirit who is from God, that we may understand what God has freely given us" (1 Cor. 2:12). "Then," as it says in Romans 12:2, and only then, God's will becomes tested, approved, and active in our lives. We can now begin to think, as God wants us to think. Before we receive the mind of Christ, we are not able to think in a godly fashion: "The man without the Spirit does not accept the things that come from the Spirit of God, for they are foolishness to him, and he cannot understand them because they are spiritually discerned" (1 Cor. 2:14).

Taking a peek ahead to Chapter 5, which explores the "in Christ" relationship, it should be obvious that we must be "in Christ" in order to have the ". . . mind of Christ." In Chapter 5 we will examine the "in Christ" relationship in depth.

MINDSETS ARE A FILTER

An important thing to remember about mindsets is that our mindsets serve as filters for incoming information. Our filters accept information that confirms a mindset and block information that denies it. Our mindsets are our reality. Regardless of the truth, we operate within the bounds of our mindsets. There may be many arguments against our mindset and only one weak argument that supports it, but we tend to focus on the one that supports it. We grasp at straws to support our position even if it flies in the face of reality. Scripture tells us, "As a man thinks in his heart, so is he" (Prov. 23:7). This works for both good and bad mindsets. On the bad side we find, time and again in the Bible and in our lives, that people have eyes but do not see and ears but do not hear (Ezek. 12:2). Blind eyes and deaf ears relate directly to mindsets.

MINDSETS AFFECT COMMUNICATION

Many times we do not hear what is said; we hear what comes through our mindset filters. Conversations often become destructive when we respond to what we think we heard.

A great amount of communication is nonverbal. Within the family environment the non-verbal "family look" develops many mindsets. Many behaviors are caught, not taught. Clients often say it was very clear that their behavior was or wasn't acceptable even if they didn't receive verbal messages. Other mindsets are spoken: "Children should be seen, not heard." "You're not hurt." "If you want to cry, I'll give you something to cry about." "It's okay," when it is not okay. Messages that conflict with children's emotions twist their minds into pretzels.

Family environments include behaviors, some positive, some negative; some are obvious, while others are hidden. These behaviors are
often the result of mindsets of parents. Parents' mindsets may exist in
the form of unwritten rules. All of these mindsets get communicated
to their children. Even verbal communication is affected by <u>how</u> it is
said. A snarled "thank you" communicates an entirely different message from a sweet "thank you."

MINDSETS AFFECT RELATIONSHIPS AND VICE VERSA

Many mindsets are shaped in the first two years of a person's life.
A lot of bonding and boundary work is done in early relationships
between parent and child. We gain understanding about what goes
on in an infant's mind by how he or she reacts to stimuli. If she or he
looks up and sees a smiling face, she or he smiles back and a nice reciprocal relationship begins. The feeling is, "You're nice, I'm nice, and
the world is nice." If he or she sees a sad, angry, alcoholic, depressed,
anxious, etc. face, anxiety is present and he or she will actually turn his
or her face away — "The world isn't a safe place and I'm not safe."
While an infant cannot be interviewed, observation and later experience tell the tale. $$ Relationship Rings $$ (Look to the end of the
chapter for treasure.)

Mindsets are continually forming in relationships. If appropriate
bonding has occurred, a child is safe to explore, to develop feelings
of control, and is able to form appropriate boundaries for behavior.
Given appropriate bonding, positive coping behaviors, mindsets, and
habits are formed.

There are transition periods in people's lives where mindsets are
formed that affect relationships — the infamous terrible twos, the
troubled transition teens, and the energetic elder-years, among others.
Transition periods occur when certain maturation processes occur in the
brain or body, or when attitudes change. Healthy parents and healthy
children, who bond appropriately, are not threatened by the challenges

of life. Healthy bonding promotes positive self-esteem and can prevent the turmoil that often happens during times of transition.

Again, once a mindset is established, we tend to accept evidence that confirms it and ignore evidence that opposes it. For instance, when we like someone we tend to ignore the negative; when we dislike someone we tend to ignore the positive.

"Mike" smoked pot, was unemployed, and had lost his driver's license after three convictions for drunk driving. "Dora" wanted him anyway. He was a lot of fun, he made her laugh, and he was good-looking. Dora's parents tried to warn her but she defended Mike, married him, had two children with him — and he continued to smoke pot and was unemployed. Eventually they were divorced. Her mindset had drawn her into a relationship that had little chance of succeeding. His mindset allowed him to continue his destructive behaviors. When harmful mindsets are formed, acting out and conflict occurs. Destructive relationships are the product of faulty mindsets.

MINDSETS INFLUENCE ACTIONS

What drives or motivates us to perform the wonderful and terrible things we do? Paul wrote, "I do not understand what I do. For what I want do I do not do, but what I hate I do" (Rom. 7:15). He was influenced by mindsets from his past.

This chapter deals primarily with negative mindsets so we will focus on the negative side of human nature. People have a natural tendency towards evil. (You may have noticed we don't have to teach children to misbehave.) The modern term for this tendency is "predisposition." It is a nice way of saying original sin. Whether it is a predisposition to alcoholism, obesity, lifestyle choices, or risky behaviors, if we take time to look, we can find predispositions to variant behaviors in every person. But no one holds a gun to our head and makes us act on a predisposition.

So where does the evil in mankind come from? The prophet Jeremiah wrote, "The heart is deceitful (desperately wicked — KJV) above all things and beyond cure. Who can understand it?" (Jer. 17:9).

Jeremiah says evil comes from a "deceitful heart" — living a lie. As I hear about some of the terrible things my clients do, and what other people have done to them, I find myself agreeing with Jeremiah's analysis of human nature.

God has given us the awesome gift of choice. Some people use the freedom of choice to hurt others. "All have sinned and fallen short of the glory of God" (Rom. 3:23). We have made our own harmful choices and others may have sinned against us. Mindsets influence choices. Don't go past this thought without grasping its significance in man's inhumanity to man. Some actions are, plainly and simply, sinful. (*$$ Funnel $$*)

As we will examine in more depth in a later chapter, much of what is defined as sin is activity that was entered into as a means to relieve stress. Usually, those activities create even more stress and are termed Inappropriate Stress Relievers (ISRs). Faulty mindsets lead us to harmful choices that are ISRs (See chapter on stress).

Some argue that we have no choice. They say, "God made me this way and if He wants me to change, it's His responsibility." They quote Psalms 139:16 to support their position and disclaim responsibility — "Your eyes saw my unformed body. All the days ordained for me were written in your book before one of them came to be." However, the Bible clearly indicates that people make choices and are held responsible for them. Joshua said, "Choose this day whom you will serve" (Josh. 24:15). While God knows our choices, He does not force us to act on them. We need to obey God's word to ". . . not be conformed any longer to the pattern of this world but be transformed by the renewing of your mind" (Rom. 12:2). Part of the renewing is a mental housecleaning that deals with painful memories.

OLD STRAY CATS

Many of us have done things in the past that haunt our memories and often erode our joy and peace. We need to leave these things behind, using them only to help us make better choices in current decisions. Negative memories are like "old stray cats." Harmful temptations are like "cute cuddly kittens."

Various illustrations, exercises, or interventions are presented in this book to clarify a point that is to be examined and/or used for future reference. The following illustration is one of the "windows" that helps us look deeper into a concept. Keep in mind that we like cats, but people find this illustration helpful and refer to it often. In my practice I tell about old stray cats and cute cuddly kittens early in the treatment process because it is so powerful in dealing with mindsets.

If an old stray cat shows up on your back porch and you feed it and pet it, what will happen? You have a friend for life. Or, you may choose to chase it around the backyard with a broom, which is great fun for the cat because now it has somebody to play with. Unfortunately, it uses up your time and energy. Negative mindsets and bad memories are like old stray cats. We have to decide not to feed them, or pet them, or chase them around with a broom. We just send them over to God's porch as He has forgiven us and cleansed us of all unrighteousness. On the other hand, there will be new temptations — cute cuddly kittens. Such things as affairs, dabbling with substance abuse, or some other inappropriate stress reliever that seems innocent at the time, grow up to become old stray cats. Very seldom do we plan on the grief that results from our "best thinking" that seemed reasonable at the time.

THE DILEMMA OF MINDSETS

Mindsets are necessary because they give a sense of control in our lives; unfortunately, the processes by which mindsets are formed can produce erroneous thinking. Few people carefully examine how their mindsets are formed. They go through life without a great deal of thought about why they do what they do.

It makes sense to realize the environment and events of our developmental years affect how we think and act. In addition, hereditary factors contribute to our physical self and some of our personality traits. In many families the differing personalities among siblings indicate there is something more than environment going on. We need to investigate the forces that shape our thinking and actions.

$ $ $ 🗝 $ $ $

Treasure Chest #1
Resources for Renewing Mindsets

RELATIONSHIP RINGS INTERVENTION

MATERIALS NEEDED: ten or more 6-inch diameter metal rings, available in your local craft department. Usage: To illustrate how bonding progresses into boundaries, place one ring overlapping another to show that in the beginning the rings are almost one. Then gradually pull one ring away from the other to demonstrate individuation (the development of an independent personality). Use as many rings as there are members in the family to show all the interacting relationships.

After bonding, the formation of boundaries is necessary. The toddler begins to separate and becomes aware of "me." "I am a separate being." The rings now overlap with "you," "us," and "me" sections. Boundaries of the self begin to emerge. Boundaries help us form our identity and our responsibilities. Inside our boundaries is our control and safety zone. Outside is a world of hurt.

FUNNEL INTERVENTION

MATERIALS NEEDED: an 8-inch diameter funnel and a 6-inch diameter funnel. (This intervention is especially powerful for teenagers.) The tapering of the funnel represents the effect of choices on further choices. We should make choices that expand our choice possibilities. When we make good choices we move towards the lip of the funnel, which illustrates expanded choices. If we make bad choices we decrease our future. We move towards the neck of the funnel, which demonstrates restricted choices. When using the funnel to demonstrate suicidal thinking, the neck becomes a point signifying the perception that there are no other choices.

Look through the big end of the funnel and see what life will be like with restricted choices. Look through the small end of the funnel to see what life will be like with expanded choices. Insert the small funnel's neck into the large funnel's neck, making an hourglass shape. Even if bad choices have brought us to the neck of a funnel, we can begin a new funnel as new creations in Christ. While we may have lost some future choices, a new and wonderful life is still possible. We can't change the past but we can begin a new future.

"TRAIN A CHILD IN THE WAY HE SHOULD GO, AND WHEN HE IS OLD HE WILL NOT TURN FROM IT" (PROV. 22:6). THERE ARE MANY PITFALLS FOR THE UNTRAINED CHILD.

CHAPTER 2

WHY WE ARE THE WAY WE ARE

THE SOURCE OF MINDSETS

We are the way we are according to how we use our God-given ability to choose. While we are in process, gaining all that God has available for us, it will be helpful to look at influences that bring about the way we are. Perhaps you are like many hurting people who come to us in our professional and personal lives who want to be heard, helped, and healed. They feel that something is blocking the fullness that they know God is offering them. Or, you may be a person in the people business who wants to increase your ability to help others. In any event, it has been our experience that most hurting people believe that something in their past has had a negative influence on their present circumstances. They want to identify and resolve possible issues that are undermining their health and happiness. We have found that the best way to answer their questions is to help them understand how mindsets are formed and to appreciate the powerful influence these mindsets have on their choices and behaviors.

The usual procedure in my practice is to examine mindsets that influence choices and behaviors that conform us the world (Rom. 12:2). Conforming factors are explored using tools that are called the CHEESE Factory and the SPICE Rack. The CHEESE Factory deals with conditions that influence our lives while the SPICE Rack deals with factors that influence the elements of the CHEESE Factory. As we will see, the SPICE flavors the CHEESE. In each intake session with a client I draw a keyhole-shaped tree and say, "There are issues in the tree and there are roots to the issues." After the issues are stated, unless the client prefers otherwise, we discuss the roots to the issues using a CHEESE/SPICE model. Using the word CHEESE is a way to remember Choice, Heredity, Environment, Events, and Self-Esteem. Using the word SPICE is a way to remember Spiritual, Physical, Intellectual, Community (social), and Emotional.

In this chapter, we introduce the CHEESE Factory. In Chapter 3, we take a closer look at self-esteem. In Chapter 4, the SPICE Rack is added and the use of the CHEESE/SPICE model is explained in more detail. Using this model, along with the theme of mindsets throughout the book, we investigate the causes, continuance, care, and cure of spiritual and emotional problems. (While there are times the physical, intellectual, and community areas are affected as well, we realize that many physical illnesses have other causative factors.) First, let's describe what we mean by the CHEESE Factory.

CHEESE FACTORY ACRONYM

Mindsets that conform us to the world are developed in our CHEESE factory. Our Choices, or Character, are a product of a combination of Hereditary factors, the Environment in which we grew, significant emotional Events, and the resulting Self-Esteem — hence, CHEESE — Choices, Heredity, Environment, Events, Self-Esteem. It will be helpful if you take a moment to memorize these items.

Now, let's take a look at what each letter means and see how the word it represents helps develop our mindsets.

CHOICES/CHARACTER

When we are young, the choices of others have an impact on our mindsets. When we are dealing with decisions that are made later in life, our choices are not only influenced by our mindsets, they also continue to shape our mindsets. Our choices are an expression of our character whether it is one of integrity or one of inferior motives. Depending on the context of application, the words Choice or Character may be used for the C in the CHEESE factory acronym. $$ Pain/Joy Choice Charts $$

HEREDITY

The CHEESE approach to the formation of mindset takes into account both genetic and cultural forces that help shape us. As can be seen in family members, we inherit physical and emotional traits. "George looks just like his father." "Mary acts just like Grandma Ruth." Our heredity provides a mold into which the rest of the cheese is poured. Part of the human side of our heredity is an inclination to sin. We also have an inherent desire for relationship with God. Heredity, combined with environment and watershed events, influences the direction of our lives.

ENVIRONMENT

If two seeds, taken from the same pinecone, are planted in different environments, one in a lush valley and one high on a mountain, the resulting trees will have entirely different growth patterns, grain structure, and other characteristics. Likewise, our environment may have been enriched with encouragement, intellectual stimulation, and material goods, or we may have grown up lacking these things. Family relationships are an important part of our environment that may encourage or discourage factors that fundamentally affect the formation of mindsets.

The way we perceive our environment is important. Our mindset, or perception of our environment, can be based on reality or on imagination. Especially with children, a wish, a dream, a movie, or a story can create a vivid picture in the mind that may create a false memory. We sometimes need a reliable outside source to help gain accurate information about our backgrounds.

EVENTS

In addition to the influences of environment, significant emotional events blend with heredity to help form our mindsets. Moves, deaths, illnesses, accidents, etc. are Significant Emotional Events that influence how we SEE things in a different way, sometimes good, sometimes bad. How we view events can cause turning points in our lives. Some events are in our conscious memory. They may serve as markers and we make statements like, "After my folks divorced . . .," "When I graduated from high school . . .," and others. Many individuals refer to specific occurrences that helped shape their lives and mindsets. (Other events may have been forgotten or repressed but they still affect our mindsets.) $$ Events Map $$

SELF-ESTEEM

Our choices, heredity, environment, and events affect Self-Esteem. Self-Esteem is established early in life and is strongly influenced by the attitudes of significant others. We find in Matthew 3:17 that God affirmed Jesus when He said, "This is my Son, whom I love; with him I am well pleased." This incredible affirmation started Jesus on the road to His ministry and sets an example for all parents in esteeming (validating) their children. Especially when we are children, if someone we love esteems us and thinks we are wonderful, then wonderful we are. However, if they see us as "human doings" instead of "human beings," that is, if they try to make us be what we aren't or try to make us do what we can't, low self-esteem often develops. Self-Esteem is such an important element in our CHEESE Factories that the next chapter will explore it in greater depth.

$ $ $ 🔑 $ $ $

Treasure Chest #2
Resources for Understanding the Way We Are

PAIN/JOY CHART FOR CHOICES

Many issues are disputable (Rom. 14:1). While we haven't always realized it, we have used a mental Pain/Joy T-chart to help resolve issues. We have chosen between what we think of as pain or joy. Sometimes, the choice was the lesser of two pains. Quite often the choice was an Inappropriate Stress Reliever (ISR).

We now need to bring the process into conscious thought with an exercise much like listing pros and cons. The act of thinking through the possible outcomes of behavior is often a start to making better choices. This decision-making tool can be applied to any problematical choice.

Make two large T-shaped crosses on a sheet of paper. As an example, label the top of one T "Losing Weight." Label the top of the other "Eating Too Much." Label the sides of each T "Pain" and "Joy." Then ask each question several times. For example ask, "What is the pain of eating too much?" until you run out of answers. Then, "What is the joy of eating too much?" "What is the pain of losing weight?" "What is the joy of losing weight?" Then ask, "Which side wins?" Sometimes one item on one side is a big enough factor to overrule everything on the other side.

Losing Weight

PAIN	JOY

Eating Too Much

PAIN	JOY

EVENTS MAP

Starting before you were born, if there were events in your parents'
lives that affected you, continue through your life and draw a straight or
crooked path with "towns" representing SEEs (Significant Emotional
Events) in your life. You may wish to write a short explanation for each
event. Process how these events affected your CHEESE factory.

"THEN GOD SAID, 'LET US MAKE MAN IN OUR IMAGE, IN OUR LIKENESS . . .'" (GEN. 1:26). A GREAT PART OF RENEWING OUR MINDS IS THE CHANGE IN SELF-ESTEEM BROUGHT ON BY KNOWING THAT GOD LOVES US AND THINKS WE ARE WONDERFUL.

CHAPTER 3

DEVELOPING SELF-ESTEEM

RAISING CHILDREN WITH A MINDSET OF POSITIVE SELF-ESTEEM

God esteems — values — validates us by wanting to spend time with us. People with low self-esteem tend to come from families where they did not feel valued or wanted because appropriate time wasn't spent with them. In healthy marriages and family relationships, people are held in high esteem. We esteem that which has high value in our lives. That esteem is validated by actions, and, fundamentally, is measured by time spent with the valued person. The type of activity is not as important as the actual time spent together. We have an inherent sense of the value of time because any segment of time represents a part of our life. When we esteem God, we spend time with Him. When we esteem our children, we spend time with them. We are "telling" them they are important, hence their self-esteem grows.

We need to enter their world from time to time and play by their rules. This helps us understand them and helps them to grow to enter our world. It is especially enjoyable for them to give us guidance as we struggle with their world. This struggle increases empathy for both parties. They gain self-esteem by succeeding in following the rules of their games. Once they understand that rules are important in their games, they can be helped to see the necessity of rules in our "game" and gain self-esteem by following the rules of society.

While children get a strong positive message when parents spend time with them, they get a strong negative message if their parents do not spend time with them. They feel emotionally abandoned and de-valued. Children, and adults, seem to have a little scale balance in their heads. They weigh excessive time at work, substance abuse, something on TV, the dog, the newspaper, etc. against their own importance. They know when they are worth less than others' alternative choices of where or with whom time is spent. Young children don't under-stand the difference between "quality time" and "quantity time." To them, a lack of quantity is a lack of quality. Ten minutes of a rushed activity just doesn't cut it.

SACRIFICING CHILDREN

There are several references to the fire god Molech in the Old Testament. In times of extreme hardship, people would sacrifice their children to appease this god in the hope that they would be relieved of their suffering. Obviously, this practice was an offense to God and rules were put in place. "Do not give any of your children to be sacri-ficed to Molech, for you must not profane the name of your God. I am the Lord" (Lev. 18:21). In today's society, the high incidence of rage among young people, and the increasing suicide rate among teens and preteens, are testimony to the trend that many parents are responding to stress in their lives by sacrificing their children to the gods of money, activities and other personal interests. We would not be so crass as to offer our children to a fire god; no, we are more subtle, we sacrifice them to selfishness. Nevertheless, they are still sacrificed, which pro-fanes the name of God.

MINDSETS AND LOW SELF-ESTEEM

Once a person has developed a mindset of low self-esteem, it is difficult to overcome; she or he will find evidence to support the mindset. If a child believes he or she is of little value, lack of parental attention may cement that belief in his or her mind. Low self-esteem is reinforced when the action of love is missing. This is not to say that people with low self-esteem weren't loved; it may be that the action of love was lacking.

When we strive to build one another up, we become encouragers and we focus on each other's needs. "Where our treasure is, there will our heart be" (Matt. 6:21). This verse usually refers to material goods but it can also apply to relationships. If a person highly esteems another, that other person will feel treasured and self-esteem will increase. If people have high self-esteem they will treasure themselves more and they will see themselves as having greater worth. They usually make wiser decisions. People with low self-esteem feel they have little value. Beliefs that we aren't valuable often lead to mindsets that result in making bad decisions and keeping bad company.

Positive relationships require that we first love ourselves and then extend that love to others. To increase our spouse or child's self-esteem, we must first esteem ourselves and then treasure them as an extension of ourselves. An example of this is embedded in Paul's message to husbands in Ephesians 5. A husband is to love his wife as he loves himself. If he despises himself, he will project this emotion onto his wife and children. If a man mistreats his family, it is a good bet that he has serious issues of low self-esteem.

The higher the honor and esteem we have for one another, the stronger our relationships. Very few, if any, divorces occur in families where Mom and Dad hold each other in high esteem and practice that esteem daily. Very few children who are highly esteemed by their parents make the negative, restricting choices that so many of today's young people make.

EFFECTS OF SELF-ESTEEM ON MINDSETS

Self-esteem helps determine how we experience our environment and events. Low self-esteem has a tremendous impact on our mindsets. People with low self-esteem tend to give themselves negative names such as "Dummy." People with high self-esteem usually make good choices and have energy, warmth, and goodness, giving themselves positive messages such as "I can do this."

One of the most serious blows to a child's self-esteem is when a parent abandons the marriage and family for reasons that are not understood by the child. The child believes he or she is not as important to the parent as the reason for leaving. In addition, the child learns a lesson about selfishness from the example set by the parent. After being worth less than other things for a long enough time, many children put worth and less together and conclude they are worthless. They find no value in themselves and may even consider or complete suicide.

CHILDREN'S CHEESE FACTORIES

Those who have been blessed by having children find them to be one of God's many wonderful gifts. Raising children should be an enjoyable process. Part of this enjoyment is raising them in an environment that instills positive mindsets at an early age. This means their self-esteem should be a foundation for healthy growth. Good parent/child relationships provide a safe setting for establishing, and implementing, helpful rules. Covenant, as seen in Genesis 18:18-19, came before the commandments given to us in Exodus 20:1-17. Relationships should be in place before rules are given. God loves us so much that He gives us rules to keep us safe. A child's environment should include the sure knowledge that she or he is loved and then provided the security of healthy boundaries. *$$ Family Rules Rule $$*

One of the best things you can do for your children is to enjoy them. God created us to enjoy fellowship with us. That is a strong clue that we should have the same experience with our children. Children will know they are human beings instead of human doings if you rejoice at their presence instead of their presents.

One of the worst things that can happen to children is physical, sexual, and/or emotional abuse. Children often sense abuse or neglect when a perpetrator exhibits abnormal emotions but children lack power to ward off the abuse. If the abuse is physical, they sense the abuser is demonstrating anger, not appropriate discipline. If the abuse is sexual, they sense the abuser is satisfying his or her needs, not theirs. If the abuse is emotional, they may feel a sense of shame. With any abuse, children may feel confused and uncomfortable but, without experience, accept abuse or neglect as the norm.

Abuse is often made worse when there are feelings of isolation and/or abandonment. Isolation may be brought about by the abuser as he or she physically distances the abusee from social support. Isolation may be reinforced by threats that enforce silence. The victim may seek isolation because of a sense of shame or the belief that there is no one who can help.

If abuse comes from people other than the child's parent(s), the child may feel doubly betrayed. Children think parents have "eyes in the backs of their heads" so parents "must know what is going on." Children may feel they have given a clear message by acting out or by saying they don't want to be with the perpetrator (perp). When the parent doesn't protect her, the child feels betrayed and abandoned. The child believes the parent is allowing or promoting the abuse. "Oh, don't be silly. Go with Perp, he just wants to help you have a good time." After all, an "all-knowing" caregiver allowed the abuse so what good would it do to tell. Hence, the child feels abandoned and confused by conflicting emotions. In any case, the abused child is prevented from learning what normal life is. As victims grow older, they talk with others, observe others, read, and realize that their life may not have been what it was supposed to be. Irritability and sleep problems are often signs that abuse may have occurred at some time, present or past. Counseling with a competent therapist will often bring troubling issues to the surface. To help prevent or uncover abuse, ask clear questions. Ask if the child has been told to keep secrets. Ask if he or she feels uncomfortable with Perp. Be careful not to give nonverbal or metaverbal messages that make the child apprehensive.

What you teach your children develops their mindsets and helps determine what you get back from your children. More lessons are caught than taught. That is, children learn more from the nonverbals in their environment than they do from what they are told. If your actions teach selfishness to your children when they are young, you will reap selfishness from them when you are old. Love them, spend time with them, enjoy them, use appropriate discipline, and their self-esteem will be a constructive part of their CHEESE Factories. $$ Four-step Rule Process $$

Spiritual, physical, intellectual, community, and emotional factors play a significant role in developing our self-esteem, along with other parts of the CHEESE Factory. It is time to see how SPICE adds flavor to our CHEESE.

$ $ $*   *$ $ $

Treasure Chest #3
Resources for Renewing Self-esteem

FAMILY RULES RULE

Take time to write answers to the following questions. This is an especially thought-provoking exercise when completed with a spouse.

1) What rules, positive and/or negative, were present in my family of origin? 2) What mindsets did I develop to fit in with these rules? 3) How have those mindsets affected my work, play, and children?

FOUR-STEP RULE PROCESS

A simple four-step process should be built into your children so they can use it throughout their lives.

1) What is the rule? 2) What did I do? 3) How did it work out for me? 4) What did I learn to help next time?

"YOU ARE THE SALT OF THE EARTH" (MATT. 5:13). AS SALT
AND OTHER SEASONINGS ADD FLAVOR TO OUR FOOD, SO WE
ARE FLAVORED BY THE WORLD AND THOSE AROUND US.

CHAPTER 4

THE SPICE RACK

INFLUENCES ON CHEESE

In accord with the major theme of this book — healing and health from a Christian perspective — we need to recognize the strong role that spiritual, physical, intellectual, community, and emotional factors play in shaping our mindsets.

In Chapter 2, the CHEESE Factory (Choices, Heredity, Environment, Events, and Self-Esteem) that influences our mindsets, and conforms us to the world, was presented. In this chapter, the SPICE Rack is presented and the CHEESE/SPICE model is completed. We will consider how SPICE flavors our CHEESE in the formation of mindsets, and how SPICE is used in the transformation of our minds (Rom. 12:2). Improper use of SPICE factors conforms us to the world and promotes unhappiness and even illness. Proper use of SPICE factors aids in healing and maintaining health in every aspect of our being. Positive SPICE factors flavor our lives in new and wonderful ways when we begin the "in Christ" relationship discussed in chapters 5 and 6.

The Ten Commandments provide a logical basis for the SPICE approach to life. Contrary to worldly opinion, God's rules are given for our healing and health.

THE GREAT COMMANDMENTS

Dr. Luke (the author of the New Testament books of Luke and Acts) quotes a two-part summary of the Ten Commandments. In his first letter to Theophilus (Lover of God), Luke writes, "YOU SHALL LOVE THE LORD YOUR GOD WITH ALL YOUR HEART AND WITH ALL YOUR SOUL AND WITH ALL YOUR STRENGTH AND WITH ALL YOUR MIND" (Luke 10:27). This Summary Commandment combines the first four of the Ten Commandments (Exod. 20).

Heart, soul, strength, and mind correspond to emotional, spiritual, physical, and intellectual. In the following analysis the order of the elements in Luke has been changed to fit the SPICE acronym.

WITH ALL YOUR SOUL

(Spice — Spiritual) The soul is our control center. When we choose to obey God, we have power, gifts, and the fruit of the Spirit. When we place something else in control before Him, we lose His power, gifts, and fruit. If God is not at the center of our lives, something else will control us. We are created in the image of God and are incomplete without Him. We will have a god.

WITH ALL YOUR STRENGTH

(sPice — Physical) Our strength is our action center. It has to do with the physical, biological, and sexual aspects of our lives. The body is the vehicle that allows the soul, mind, and heart to carry out their manifestations. Our outward physical actions display the condition of our inward spiritual self.

WITH ALL YOUR MIND

(spIce — Intellectual) The mind is our thinking center. It deals with the intellectual and cognitive, i.e., psychological, aspects of our lives. The intellect involves our mindsets. As a person thinks in his or her mind, so is he or she — mindsets. We need to be transformed by the renewing of our minds so that we have the mind of Christ (1 Cor. 2:16b).

(spiCe — Community) The Second Summary Commandment, "YOU SHALL LOVE YOUR NEIGHBOR AS YOURSELF" (Luke 10:27b), combines the last six of the Ten Commandments and gives us the community (sometimes the word social is used) element in SPICE. Second to loving God, we are to love ourselves so that we can love and care for the community of others. If we dishonor our parents, commit murder, commit adultery, steal, give false testimony, and/or covet, we do not love or care for our family and neighbors as we should. Note: the self must be loved before we can love others. Those who hate others hate themselves first. The order of loving is: God, self, others. If we reverse the last two, others can come between God and us.

WITH ALL YOUR HEART

(spicE — Emotional) The heart is our emotional center. Because the heart rate responds so quickly to adrenaline, it is described as the seat of our emotions. Emotions deal primarily with feelings.

The Ten Commandments, and many other passages of Scripture, emphasize the importance of love in our lives — "You shall love . . ." God created us, in His image, to be loving people — we are to love Him, ourselves, and others. People who love God have joy and peace in their lives. The opposite of joy and peace is rage. The opposite of self-love is self-hatred. We propose that people with low self-esteem would measure very high on scales that test for the emotion of rage.

If we love God with all our heart, soul, strength, and mind, and our community as ourselves, our lives will be in accordance with His plan for us. If these aspects of our personalities are misused, our lives will be dysfunctional. $$ SPICE Horses $$

THE CHEESE/SPICE CONNECTION

We need to realize how our CHEESE is polluted when God's rules are ignored or disobeyed. Negative Spiritual, Physical, Intellectual, Community, and Emotional (SPICE) conditions cause most mental health problems, and thus need to be considered in problem resolution. We need to get a direction that will help us analyze those factors that have shaped our mindsets. After examining some possible negative SPICE factors in more detail, a 5X5 matrix combining CHEESE and SPICE will be presented with instructions for its use.

The elements of SPICE can affect us in many ways, some of which are not obvious on the surface. Harmful actions result from harmful mindsets that come from negative SPICE items that have polluted our life. Many of these actions are listed in various scriptural references. "The acts of the sinful nature are obvious: sexual immorality, impurity and debauchery; idolatry and witchcraft; hatred, discord, jealousy, fits of rage, selfish ambition, dissensions, factions and envy; drunkenness, orgies, and the like." (Gal. 5:19-21b). "But now you must rid yourselves of all such things as these: anger, rage, malice, slander, and filthy language from your lips. Do not lie to each other . . ." (Col. 3:8-9b). These actions are violations of God's commandments and contrary to the SPICE effects He wants in our lives. As you consider the following sections, think of different ways SPICE may have contributed to polluted mindsets that affect your emotional health and life. The following examples describe harmful effects in each of the SPICE areas. $$ Neglect/Abuse Exercise $$

SPIRITUAL

Children who hate themselves, others, or God, or who have warped mindsets about relationships, have usually been raised in homes where parents spiritually abuse or neglect them. These parents may show a public face of spirituality and good citizenship but have a private life that gives their children negative mindsets. Those who claim to be atheistic or agnostic, or who indulge in witchcraft and idolatry, have often been raised in a spiritual void.

Some parents don't teach spiritual values to their children because they want their children to make their own decisions about God. Without training, children often substitute some other "god," such as sex, substance abuse, or a cult in their lives. Thus, the mindsets of both parents and children are faulty.

People who try to please God by their actions may have been raised in homes where they were taught that they must be human do-ings (instead of human beings) in order to be accepted by God. Those who feel that God is angry at them may have been raised by parents who punished them to work out the parents' anger instead of helping children grow with appropriate guidelines and discipline.

Clearly, the lack of spiritual health in our lives as children pro-duces warped and ungodly mindsets.

PHYSICAL

Negative mindsets in the physical realm are formed in many ways. An example of physical influences on life could be one of the reasons people have problems with weight control. They may have been raised in an environment where there was either inadequate or excessive food. Food may have been used as punishment or reward. The feeling that we need to eat more food than our physical body needs is one of the hardest mindsets to break. (The issue of problems with weight is treated in greater depth in another chapter.)

Those who have an obsession with things may have been deprived of material goods or they may have learned to use material things as a substitute for love. People who physically abuse themselves or others may have experienced similar abuse as a child and may be attempting to resolve inner conflict or may be extending their rage onto others.

Children's physical habits are often formed by watching the ac-tivities of adults around them. Habits take actions out of the thought mode and place them into a mindset mode. Habits become activities that don't require thought. We consciously or unconsciously form hab-its to simplify our complicated world. Some habits are good. Exercise is an example. Unfortunately, habits of abusing substances, gambling, overeating, or excessive shopping are sustained by harmful mindsets.

INTELLECTUAL

Intellectual development and opportunities can have a tremendous influence on mindsets. Many times, our "best thinking" may lead to unplanned pregnancies or legal difficulties preventing those involved from getting an adequate education. If the mindset of an individual is that a social relationship or illegal activity is more important than gaining an education, the results are often negative.

People who have been deprived of formal education may have been raised in families where learning was not valued. Also, some families have a gender bias and do not feel that women need or deserve the same educational opportunities as men. Parents often categorize their children — "This is my athlete, this is my scholar, this is my dumb one." These names may cause mindsets that can stick with a person for life.

On the other hand, some people rebel against schooling because it becomes a source of conflict or failure. Parents may have a mindset of unrealistic expectations for their children, causing the children's self-esteem to suffer because they cannot reach the academic goals that are set.

Negative thoughts are commonly called "stinking thinking." For instance, a person may have a mindset of denial and not face a problem. Another example is when we blame others or circumstances for our negative mindset. Blame becomes a mindset that makes change difficult.

COMMUNITY (SOCIAL)

The community made up of our family, relatives, neighbors, state, country, and world affects our mindsets. People who have social problems may have been isolated or, on the other hand, exposed to too much of the world around them. If they have not experienced loss, such as the death of a loved one, they may not be inoculated against the realities of life. If there has been too much exposure, such as to pornographic materials, harmful mindsets about the value and use of other persons may be formed. Parents may have been keeping children apart from society to protect them from the world or to avoid the exposure of family secrets.

Those who feel they have to be perfect in order to be accepted in society usually come from families where they didn't feel they fit in. Somehow they had to earn their worth. They believe they will never be good enough to function in the world.

Social involvement has a tremendous influence on our mindset and on our behaviors. Modern media has marvelous benefits, information and instant communication. However, it has also extended the sin industry into individual homes. Pornography, gambling, and drugs are available, in privacy, at our fingertips and, if used, can erode our spirituality.

Some media outlets echo the hedonistic motto of today, "If it feels good, do it." Children see destructive messages thousands of times in their developmental years and form negative mindsets that lead to social errors. Our destructive activities may begin out of curiosity or just availability, but we do not expect to become controlled by them. We may not see that pornography, gambling, and/or drugs could become our downfall. Internet providers don't tell of broken communication, broken homes, broken marriages, and broken lives. The motive of the sellers is their own god — money.

In 1 Corinthians Chapter 6, the writer, Paul, quotes a saying that was circulated amongst the Christians in Corinth — "All things are lawful for me." What an interesting mindset! Paul had come to them with a message of grace. The Corinthians came to the conclusion they could have lives of corruption, and a benign God would smile on all their indiscretions. However, Paul added to the saying, "Not all things are helpful." Only God's rules are helpful. They help us avoid the consequences of sin. Paul went on, "All things may be lawful for me, but I will not be brought under the power of anything."

"Not all things are helpful." This is a much better mindset; our choices should be helpful to others and ourselves. "I will not be brought under the power of anything." The only mindset acceptable to God is that we have our minds set on Him. "Then" we will prove the perfect will of God.

EMOTIONAL

Finally, let us consider the importance of our emotional condition in developing mindsets. There are many wonderful rules (mindsets) that are developed in families. There are also negative mindsets that are instilled early in life. In many families, children are encouraged to think and voice opinions. In other families, children's ideas are belittled and a mindset of shame may be instilled. When children learn that their opinions and ideas are not important, they develop a mindset of mistrust of their abilities. If a person has a mindset of low self-worth, he or she may have come from a family that did not esteem and affirm him or her. Children may question their value if they are denied the gifts of praise and affection. Many children are emotionally scarred by the names they are called or the ridicule they receive from family members.

In functional families, children are free to express their emotions when they feel hurt. (God gave us tear ducts for a reason). In other families children are told, "You're not hurt; only sissies cry." If a hurting child is told that he or she is not hurt, the child will question his or her sense of reality.

Little children don't know for sure whether or not their environment is healthy. Even then, negative rules engender strong emotions that conflict with what is intuitively sensed to be right. Children have to work very hard to develop ways to live within negative rules in order to feel a sense of belonging in the family. Powerful negative consequences force them to violate their feelings and develop "acceptable" behaviors. They learn either not to trust others or not to trust themselves. Children usually don't trust themselves. If feelings have been denied for a long period of time, talking about them usually raises such fear that wounded children hesitate to find or utilize help even when they become adults.

All of these family interactions create mindsets that come into play in teenage and adult life. According to the extension of the first commandment (Exod. 20), the "sins of the fathers" are passed on as parents verbally and nonverbally encourage children's maladaptive behaviors. The behavior of parents develops mindsets in their children that the children carry into their adult relationships and pass on to their children.

WHAT ARE YOUR MINDSETS?

Whether we can put them into words or not, we are all operating according to mindsets that we have accepted as personal truth. Our actions demonstrate our conscious or unconscious perceptions — what we think — our reality. Whatever else you know about yourself, know that your perception is your reality and it is how you operate. Regardless of what we say, our actions demonstrate mindsets. Hopefully, our perceptions are true, but whether they represent truth or error, our perceptions are our reality and direct our thoughts and actions. *$$ Puzzle $$*

When the CHEESE/SPICE matrix is used, clients are asked to think about how each element of the matrix has formed a mindset that helped them become who they are and why they do what they do. First they consider the elements of CHEESE — that is, how have choices, heredity, environment, events, and self-esteem affected their life? Then they take each element of SPICE and see how it has polluted or flavored their CHEESE. Quite often, the decisions made by their parents must be accounted for in the matrix.

It is now time to put the entire CHEESE/SPICE model to use. You may wish to go back and briefly review the CHEESE Factory chapter to assist in integrating the SPICE Rack into your personal experience. The CHEESE and SPICE examples that are given are not meant to be exhaustive, or exclusive, but to serve as guidelines for each person's individual investigation. (Not every cell may apply.) Here we go.

THE CHEESE/SPICE MATRIX

Choose a topic to investigate — something about your life that you want to work on. Draw a 5X5 grid on a sheet of paper as shown in the diagram below. Write the five elements of CHEESE across the

top. Think about how significant factors of each one have influenced
your life and write down what comes to mind in the appropriate cell,
depending upon what element of SPICE has flavored your CHEESE.
Each CHEESE element is potentially influenced by each SPICE element and vice versa. We have up to fifty potential interactions to consider. Each cell is examined by asking what affect its components have
on each other. As examples:

- Choice/Spiritual—what affect do my Choices have on my
  Spiritual life?
- Spiritual/Choice—what affect does my Spiritual life have on
  my Choices?
- Choice/Physical—what affect do my Choices have on my
  Physical being?
- Physical/Choice—what affect does my Physical being have
  on my choices?
- Heredity/Spiritual—what affect does my Heredity have on
  my Spiritual life?
- Heredity/Physical—what affect does my Heredity have on
  my Physical being?

	C	H	E	E	SE
S					
P					
I					
C					
E					

Jason was enthusiastic as he came into my office. He said: "I used the CHEESE/SPICE approach to an analysis of my anger and I am beginning to see why I explode the way I do. The Environment/ Emotional cell really made sense. I grew up in an environment of anger. I was totally frustrated because I was always trying to please my dad but I could never do anything right. Now I feel my kids' mistakes are my mistakes and I take my anger out on them. I always vowed I'd never be like him and now I am him." He looked a bit apprehensive as he asked, "Where do we go from here?"

Where we went was an examination of God's ability to transform minds and relationships. God had been waiting for that significant emotional moment for Jason to grow in fellowship with Him. "Here I am! I stand at the door and knock. If anyone hears my voice and opens the door, I will come in and eat with him, and he with me" (Rev. 3:20).

In Chapter 5 we present God's place in our lives through the "in Christ" relationship. Once our relationship with God has begun, we can give up negative mindsets and begin thinking as He wants us to think. According to Romans 12:2, the way we change is to be transformed by the renewing of our minds.

$$$ &—↗ $$$

Treasure Chest #4
Resources for Renewing SPICE Effects on Our Lives

SPICE HORSES

Think of the five elements of SPICE as horses pulling your mindset wagon. Draw five ovals with a lead oval followed by two pairs of ovals. Label each oval with one SPICE element, according to its present importance in your life. What is the lead horse that directs the rest? If you aren't happy with this arrangement, label them the way you feel it should be. Discuss how to change priorities.

NEGLECT/ABUSE EXERCISE

The negative affects of neglect and abuse must be considered because of the effect they have on our mindsets. Examples of neglect and/or abuse are given and you can circle or fill in what you feel was neglectful, good, or abusive about your childhood experience. You may not have been neglected or abused in some areas but neglected or abused in others. This exercise is an information collector and is helpful in examining how mindsets are formed. Neglect is too little of a good thing. Abuse is any amount of a bad thing.

NEGLECT	FUNCTIONAL	ABUSE
(Too little)	(Appropriate)	(Any)

SPIRITUAL

Void		Occult
No nurture		Atheism
Not raised up into Christ		Misinterpretation

PHYSICAL

Food		Sexual abuse
Clothing		Punishment
Shelter		Overfeeding

INTELLECTUAL

Promote truancy		Unrealistic expectations
Denigrate learning		Be who you aren't
Deprive of learning experiences		Do what you can't

COMMUNITY

Isolate		Poor role model
Exclude		Promote codependency

EMOTIONAL

No hugs		Shame
No praise		Name-calling
Frustrate		Negative desires
Don't talk or feel		Need for attention

The neglect or abuse may be inflicted by other(s) initially but, tragically, we tend to pick up the pattern and continue to neglect or abuse ourselves after we leave home.

PUZZLE INTERVENTION

To begin to understand the way we approach life, we need to articulate
our principles. Think of it as putting a picture puzzle together. This
is a fascinating and helpful therapeutic technique. A 100-piece puzzle
with a well-chosen picture will work fine. I have one of a cat and a
dog. The puzzle should take about 25 minutes to put together. Each
aspect of the puzzle intervention represents something about life. The
pieces are dumped out on the table representing a life that may be in
shambles. If we can't or won't talk about some aspects of our lives,
some pieces are missing and the puzzle will be incomplete. It is best not
to give the picture of the finished puzzle because we don't know how
our lives will turn out.

Ask what the approach to puzzles is. Usually a person says they
put the frame together first. So in life, what is your frame? The frame
not only includes the rest of the puzzle, it excludes many things. The
inside of the puzzle represents our comfort zone. The area outside
of the puzzle represents the many things we exclude or never experience—quite often a world of hurt. A good frame, or set of boundaries,
excludes bad choices.

We sort out the pieces and use the ones with straight edges to put
the frame together. The frame represents basic principles of belief and
behavior, determines our boundaries and sets up the rest of the puzzle.
There are several "frame sides" we can consider for our lives. There is
love for self in accordance with the second commandment, "You should
love your neighbor as yourself." Another frame side could be forgiveness. Do not sabotage yourself or pollute yourself with bitterness. If
the purpose of your life (a frame side) is to hold another's abuse against
him or her, you will live in bondage and perpetuate that abuse upon
yourself even if the event is in the past. God will deal justly with them.
Release yourself from this self-imposed, impossible responsibility.

If the frame of our puzzle is made up of self-deprecation, bitterness, fear, and depression, our social life will be a sorry picture. If the
frame is made up of trust in God, love of self and others, joy, and
peace, we will have a picture that is a wonder to behold.

After the frame of the puzzle is put together, we usually find some
pattern somewhere that is distinctive — a boat, a house, a tablecloth,
or something. The aspects of the puzzle can represent relationships in
our lives — family, church, friends, etc. As we understand our social interactions, we can fill in around the edges, using the frame as a guide.

After putting the puzzle together, and the ensuing discussion, ask
how long it will take to destroy the completed picture. If they choose to

wreck the puzzle, they see this as a powerful application to mistakes in life. Years of work can be destroyed by a single wrong decision. Some people do not want to destroy the puzzle. If so, their desire to keep the puzzle whole can be basis for further discussion.

"THEREFORE, IF ANYONE IS IN CHRIST, HE IS A NEW CREATION; THE OLD HAS GONE, THE NEW HAS COME!" (2 COR. 5:17). THE WORK OF CHRIST AND THE HOLY SPIRIT IS TO BRING US INTO THE RELATIONSHIP FOR WHICH WE WERE CREATED. WHEN WE ARE "IN CHRIST," WE ARE ENABLED BY THE SPIRIT TO ENJOY FELLOWSHIP WITH GOD.

CHAPTER 5

THE "IN CHRIST" RELATIONSHIP

LIFE'S MOST IMPORTANT QUEST

Our relationship with God is the most important quest of our lives. It is not only imperative that we establish a proper relationship with God, it is the most delightful thing we can do. Therefore, we need to have a perfectly clear understanding of how to achieve this relationship. We need to understand that God makes the relationship possible through His work "in Christ." "Therefore, if anyone is 'in Christ,' he or she is a new creation; the old has gone, the new has come" (2 Cor. 5:17). A GLOSSARY for the salvation relationship is found at the back of the book.

In order to stop conforming to the world and to be transformed by the renewing of our minds we have to be "in Christ." Once we are "in Christ" we have the mind of Christ, a radically new mindset, and the powerful assistance of God's Spirit to help in the transformation.

In order to achieve the "in Christ" relationship, we need to "believe," "confess," "receive," and "obey." The order of salvation (deliverance) activities may vary according to each person's CHEESE factory; however a logical approach is first to believe, then to confess, then to receive, and then to obey. Let's take a few moments to consider these vital life-giving acts.

BELIEVE

"If you confess with your mouth that Jesus is Lord and *believe* in your heart that God has raised him from the dead, you will be saved" (Rom. 10:9-10). To "be saved" is to be delivered — to be "in Christ." To believe is to exercise the faith that is given to us by God ". . . faith is not from yourselves, it is the gift of God . . ." (Eph. 2:8-9). Because faith to believe is a gift from God, we know it is a perfect and sufficient faith. There is no need to doubt it; just accept your faith and exercise it.

CONFESS

"If we *confess* our sins, he is faithful and just, and will forgive our sins and purify us from all unrighteousness" (1 John 1:9). To confess is to admit that we are conformed to the world, separated from God, and that our nature and our choices require repentance and forgiveness. Then the Holy Spirit, with our invitation, begins to transform us into the persons God created us to be. $$ MUD PUDDLE $$

RECEIVE

"To all who *received* him, to those who believed in his name (nature), to them he gave the right to become children of God" (John 1:12). To receive is to accept His sacrifice as the necessary and sufficient act of atonement and to yield or submit ourself to Him as an act of reasonable thanksgiving and worship. The simple but profound solution is to accept Christ's atoning work and ask for the Holy Spirit to enter into our lives with power, gifts, and fruit. It is of paramount importance that we know that we can receive just as we are. "But God demonstrates his own love for us in this: While we were still sinners, Christ died for us" (Rom. 5:8).

OBEY

In Jesus' teaching He said, "If you love me, you will *obey* what I command. And I will ask the Father, and he will give you another Counselor to be with you forever — the Spirit of truth" (John 14:15). The "in Christ" relationship is a life of obedience to Jesus. To obey is to yield our lives to Christ; then He gives us His Spirit and we are enabled with His power, fruit, and gifts to be transformed. It is through the indwelling Holy Spirit that we have the ability to carry out God's intent for our lives.

THE PARABLE OF THE WINESKINS

"And no one pours new wine into old wineskins. If he does, the new wine will burst the skins, the wine will run out and the wineskins will be ruined. No, new wine must be poured into new wineskins. And no one after drinking old wine wants the new, for he says, 'The old is better'" (Luke 5:37-39). Grace was the new wine — a relationship with God based on laws was the old wineskin. In Christ, all is new. In order to hold the bursting power of the Holy Spirit, we must be new creations, ". . . the old has gone, the new has come!" (2 Cor. 5:17). Our minds must be transformed so that we have an entirely new mindset. ("The old is better." What an interesting comment about a mindset that is conformed to the patterns of the world.)

WE ARE NOW IN GOD'S FAMILY

If we believe, confess, receive, and obey, we are adopted into God's family (Rom. 8:15-18) and have a new beginning in Christ (2 Cor. 5:17). We now live in Him and He lives in us. We are ready for a radically different mindset. He works within us to form this mindset through the person of the Holy Spirit, if 1) we obey Jesus' commands (John 17:20-26), and 2) we ask for the Holy Spirit to be active in our lives (Luke 11:13). God will not force Himself upon us; He waits for our invitation.

The "receive" aspect of entering Christ seems to be a problem for many Christians. They believe, confess, and try to obey in their own power but have questions about whether any real transaction has been accomplished in their lives. They may feel a lack of joy and peace or they may feel empty and powerless, and quite often end up frustrated in their walk with God. They get into Christ but feel Christ is not in them. They agonize because they find that sin is still a part of their lives. They have accepted Christ but they have not accepted their acceptance, i.e., the fullness of what it means. It is difficult to leave the mindset that we must do something other than simply receive God's grace. Grace is forgiving the unforgivable. God gives His grace to us; we accept it for ourselves and extend it on to others. Once we have received God's forgiveness, we need to finish the work by forgiving ourselves. If we don't forgive ourselves, God's forgiveness is not effective. Because grace is God's action, it is futile, counterproductive, and a continuance of sin not to forgive ourselves. If you have not forgiven yourself, you block the work of the Holy Spirit in your life and you will not experience joy and peace.

Many possessing, as opposed to professing, Christians wonder why so few of their siblings in Christ share the Gospel. Well, we can't share what we don't have. We may believe and confess, but if we haven't received, we have little to give. Receiving the forgiveness of God into our lives is the fundamental and essential key in sharing God's fullness.

"Marla" hadn't attended church or her fellowship group for weeks. "I believe God has forgiven me and I can forgive others but I can't forgive myself. I just haven't found any joy in Christianity. People keep asking me what is wrong. I saw others around me in church who seemed to have "it," whatever "it" is, but it's too depressing to come away empty all the time. I just gave up."

If you haven't forgiven yourself, repent the sin of not forgiving yourself and enter the joy of the Lord. ". . . we (can) set our hearts at rest in his presence whenever our hearts condemn us. For God is greater than our hearts, and he knows everything" (1 John 3:19b-20). He knows everything — and does not condemn us. Hallelujah!!

Thankfully, once we are "in Christ" we have the mind of Christ

(1 Cor. 2:16) and the Bible opens up to us in new and exciting ways. At first our life expression may be entirely the same but as we begin to obey Him, we experience the effects of our new mindset — we change as He begins a good work in us (Phil. 1:6).

ACHIEVING THE "IN CHRIST" RELATIONSHIP

We know from our discussion in chapters 2 and 4 that CHEESE Factories (Choices, Heredity, Environment, Events, and Self-Esteem) and SPICE Racks (Spiritual, Physical, Intellectual, Community, and Emotional) have a significant influence on mindsets that are conformed to the world. This brings the question of transformation to center stage. How are we to be transformed? We are told in Scripture that if we are "in Christ" we will have the mind of Christ (1 Cor. 2:16). If we have the mind of Christ, we must certainly be able to have a Christ-like mindset. As we continue the "in Christ" relationship, negative mindsets will be transformed by God working in our new mind.

Reconciliation brings us into a new relationship with God that is called the "in Christ" relationship. If we are "in Christ" we have reconciliation, salvation, redemption, atonement (at-one-ment), etc. The "in Christ" terminology (2 Cor. 5:17) is a powerful descriptor of our new condition. If any person be "in Christ," that person is a new creation. The old is gone; the new has come. We can have a new beginning; that is the Good News of Jesus Christ!

Note this is NOT an "in church" relationship, nor an "in other Christians" relationship, nor an "in Bible" relationship, nor an "in theology" relationship, nor an "in anything else" relationship. Our relationship is with God and begins when we believe, confess, receive, and obey the elements of His gift of grace.

The process of coming into Christ has to be uncomplicated because it is available to everyone, delighting even the simple. However, salvation, next to creation, is one of God's most profound acts, amazing the wise and offending the haughty. Out of chaos He created an orderly universe (Gen. 1). Out of the chaos of our lives He creates a right relationship with Him, with our self, and with others (John 1).

THE GLORY OF GOD

One definition of sin is "falling short of the glory of God" (Rom. 3:23). We fall short by not enjoying a relationship with Him. We fall short by not enjoying the benefits of His body, the church. We fall short by not obtaining His power, gifts, and fruit in our lives. We fall short by having polluted mindsets.

Too many people focus on "falling short." We need to shift our focus to the "glory of God." The glory of God is His holiness, His wisdom, His power, His grace, His bestowing on us the power, gifts, and fruit of the Spirit, and the relationship that reconciliation brings — the awesome realization that His glory is beyond human description. We are not to fall short of His glory; we are to attain to the glory of God. The most glorious thing about God is that He wants a relationship with us. He wants to share His glory with us through the work of Christ and the Holy Spirit. He wants us to lose our negative mindsets and grab on to the "glory of God." How could anyone cling to his or her negative mindsets, knowing that God's glory is theirs just for the asking? $$ NUMBER SET ILLUSTRATION $$

In order to attain the "in Christ" mindset we first need to be delivered from our sinful nature, our "deceitful hearts," and our negative mindsets. We need to submit to the authority of God. The deceitful heart is directed away from God but if we are "in Christ" we are new creations. We now "set our hearts on things above" (Col. 3:1). What we pursue diligently will possess us. The psalmist says, "Create in me a new heart . . ." (Ps. 51:10). God was making heart transplants long before medical science used the process.

Secondly, we need atonement for our sinful acts. We need to accept Christ's atoning (at-one-ing) work as the necessary and sufficient act of God to bring us into relationship with Him. In our sinful nature we made choices that violated God's laws and His intent for our lives. We need to be forgiven for specific sinful acts. Because we are helpless to save ourselves, Jesus took our sins upon Himself. "He himself bore our sins in his body on the tree, so that we might die to sin and live for righteousness; by his wounds you have been healed" (1 Pet. 2:24). If we confess our sins, through His grace we are forgiven and His forgiveness is complete. "Therefore, there is now no condemnation for those who are in Christ Jesus" (Rom. 8:1).

THE POWER OF CHOICE

Our desire to live "in Christ" still leaves us with the power of choice. We still have the ability to sin. However, this does not disqualify us from God's family unless we intentionally and deliberately continue on a sinful path (Heb. 6:4-6). "If anybody does sin, we have one who speaks to the Father in our defense — Jesus Christ, the Righteous one" (1 John 2:1b). Christians are often grief-stricken when they sin and may feel they never had salvation (deliverance) in the first place. However, it is clear (1 John 2:1) that Christians sin. It is important to note that we can feel safe to confess sin, and get back on track, because we are assured of forgiveness. As the psalmist says, "He restores my soul" (Ps. 23). Access this grace immediately. If we do not believe we will be forgiven, we will try to hide our sin(s) using a defensive mindset and live in mental garbage dumps. It does no good to beat ourselves up before re-entering the joy and peace of Christ. In our Christian walk we pursue righteousness until it possesses us. We may feel shame but it doesn't help to wallow in it. Shame is to direct us to Christ. Take the focus off sin and place it on the grace that God has extended. Repent, re-enter, and resolve to let Jesus answer the door the next time temptation knocks.

IMMEDIACY AND CONTINUITY

Entering the "in Christ" relationship is like getting married. As soon as we say, "I do," we are totally married but the merging of two lives is a lifelong process. As soon as we accept Christ as the necessary and sufficient means of becoming a child of God, our position is "in Christ." Becoming a child of God is like lighting a candle. When the candle is lit, it gives off light immediately but it burns throughout its life. The "in Christ" relationship matures over time. When God created the world, He did it in steps. After each step He said, "It is good." When finished He said, "It is very good." God told Joshua that the process of conquering the Promised Land would not be accomplished all at once or ". . . wild animals will become too numerous for you. Little by little I will drive them out before you, until you have increased enough to take possession of the land" (Exod. 23:29-30). Perhaps the "wild animals" are negative results of trying to change too fast. Salvation takes care of our sinful nature. Growth and maturity are directed by the Holy Spirit and we "increase" over time in relationship with God.

When we say yes to Christ, we are "in Christ" and our lives should show evidence of our new condition. If we are accused of being Christians, there will be evidence to convict us. It should not surprise nor confuse anybody who finds out we are Christians.

Many people feel they are saved by grace but then feel they must maintain their salvation by their own efforts. Accepting Christ and staying "in Christ" are both grace relationships. In our love response to God's grace we, "Work out your salvation with fear and trembling for it is God who works in you to will and to act according to his good purpose" (Phil. 2:12-13). The Word doesn't say, "Work *for* your salvation . . ." it says, "Work *out* your salvation . . ." Once you have it — allow God to work in you. Accept your new relationship, the rest will come. By faith we step forth and He makes a way for us. "We are his workmanship created in Christ Jesus to do good works, which God prepared in advance for us to do" (Eph. 2:10). If we are "in Christ" we will keep His commandments and have a mindset shaped through forgiveness and grace.

Receiving Christ, that is, attaining the Christian mindset, will continue throughout the rest of our lives. "He who has begun a good work in you will carry it on to completion until the day of Christ Jesus" (Phil. 1:6). Even the apostle Paul said, "Not that I have already obtained all this, or have already been made perfect, but I press on to take hold of that for which Christ Jesus took hold of me" (Phil. 3:12). The KJV translation says, "I have not yet apprehended that for which I was apprehended." *$$ BARREL OF ROCKS $$*

DON'S STORY

John 1:12 is my salvation verse. When I was eleven years old I responded to an altar call in a Methodist Church in Stanwood, Michigan, and received Christ as my Savior. Then I spent several troubled years reacting to my parents' divorce, my father's death, and poverty. When I was nineteen, a friend, Chuck Rhodes, led me in a Bible study of the Gospel of John and upon reading Verse 12, I accepted Christ as my Lord. I "got" Him when I was eleven; He "got" me during a service at Grace Bible Church in Ann Arbor, Michigan, when I was nineteen. I marvel at the protection He gave me during those "tweenage" years. This protection has continued as I ". . . increase to take possession of the land."

JOAN'S STORY

I yielded my life to Christ when I was sixteen years old. I had been brought up to attend church and Sunday school every week and knew the importance of reading the Bible. I read my Bible every day, regularly attended youth fellowship meetings, and sang in the choir. A couple of years before I accepted Christ, on a Sunday morning after church, I was taking off my choir robe when the minister's wife, who had befriended me, asked me if I had accepted Christ. I was quite taken aback by the question and after hesitating a few seconds said, "Yes." A year or two later, that minister and his wife were transferred to another congregation and a new minister came who had eight children, among whom were some daughters just a few years older than I. The daughters were so much fun to be around.... they were "released and radiant!" Much to the dismay of my mother, I spent as much time with them as possible, mostly on weekends when they were home from their jobs in other cities.

It was during the summer that I went with Pauline, one of the daughters, to hear an evangelist at a church camp meeting near home. When the invitation was given for anyone who wanted to accept Christ to go forward to the altar, to my amazement, Pauline went forward.

I knew that Pauline had accepted Christ because of her testimony in other church meetings. It was then that I began to think about my own relationship with Christ. I thought, "If Pauline has responded to the altar call and I know she's a Christian, what could this mean? Have I ever really made that commitment?" I didn't go forward that night but within the next few days, I went to the Lord in prayer and asked forgiveness for my sins and committed my life to Him.

God had used Pauline to speak to me that night about my need to make a conscious commitment to Him. I had never done anything terribly wrong in my life; I attended church and read the Bible, so I felt I was a "Christian." When I saw Pauline taking care of her spiritual business (whatever that might have been) that night at the camp meeting, I was convicted that I had never really asked for God to take charge of my life.

What happened with that very simple time of asking forgiveness and allowing God to take control of my life is a mystery; it cannot be described adequately in words. I, too, became "released and radiant" and the joy that welled up in me was beyond belief. I was happy and at peace like never before. The joy that bubbled up within me caused people to take notice. Not only did I have a newer and brighter smile, I soon began to exercise God's love in all of my relationships. Now I hope people are drawn to me because they feel accepted and that someone cares about them. Sometimes it creates challenges for me with the types of people who come into my presence. What I now know and experience is the fact that God is with me in everything.

In both our salvation events, God used another Christian. We first had faith in them, then we had their faith, and then our own faith developed. God was working every step of the way. I came to Christ primarily because of my sin. Joan came primarily to receive the ". . . glory of God" (Rom. 3:23). *$$ SUIT OF CLOTHES PARABLE $$*

Complete this sequence by writing about your own salvation experience.

YOUR STORY

Praise the Lord!! In the next chapter, we look at some of the many advantages of being "in Christ."

$ $ $ &—★ $ $ $

Treasure Chest #5
Resources for Renewing Our Life "in Christ"

MUD PUDDLE ILLUSTRATION

Suppose you are standing by a large mud puddle by the side of a busy road. A car is coming at you and will hit the puddle. You may choose to let it happen, you may be oblivious of the situation and get splashed, or you may be trapped by the crowd or some device and can't avoid it. Now, suppose you are the driver of the car. You may intentionally splash the person, you may be oblivious to the situation and never know what happened, or you may be hemmed in by traffic, unable to avoid splashing and deeply regret it. Whether you have been splashed or are the splasher, you get mud on you. The "all" of purification includes what we have done to others, what we have done to ourselves, and what others have done to us. "All" includes what we remember and what we have forgotten. "All" includes sins of commission and sins of omission. "All" includes forgiving ourselves. We are purified of all unrighteousness.

NUMBER SET ILLUSTRATION

God is infinite; therefore any human attainment, theory, or knowledge about God is incomplete. We cannot understand the totality of His ways. The whole numbers are unending, i.e., 0, 1, 2, 3,... The even numbers are also unending, i.e., 2, 4, 6,... They are both infinite sets. There are only half as many even numbers as whole numbers, but each set is infinite. While our grasp of God is only a part of all of Who He is, we become infinite in Him while being less than Him. While we don't understand the wholeness of God, we can still work within that fantastic subset of our understanding of the whole. Parenthetically, God is more like the set of real numbers; His existence is complete and goes both ways. For you mathematicians, God is not imaginary.

SUIT OF CLOTHES PARABLE

Consider a parable of a suit of clothes. Each one of us has a suit of clothing that is free and easily available. It is our choice to receive it or reject it. The suit is a perfect cut, is perfect in color, is wash-and-wear, AND is guaranteed never to wear out. Truly, it "makes the man." Each person knows about his or her suit. Some people forget or ignore the message that they have a suit. Others plan on accepting the suit but never get around to it, while still others drive past the store and don't go in. Some people even go in and look at the suit, but for one reason or another, decide against acquiring it. They may even try it on but reject the suit. A select few, amazed that it is free, rejoice at how it makes them look and feel, wear the suit out of the store, and enjoy an eternity of flexibility and durability. Jesus is that suit that perfectly fits every person.

If you haven't picked up your suit yet, pause a moment and claim it now. Remember, God does not condemn us; He gives us salvation. We choose condemnation or salvation.

BARREL OF ROCKS INTERVENTION

Those factors that hinder us from receiving the "in Christ" relationship need to be examined and removed. "It is for freedom that Christ has set us free. Stand firm, then, and do not let yourselves be burdened again by a yoke of slavery" (Gal. 5:1). Think of your life and activities as a barrel of rocks of different sizes that keep you under a "yoke of slavery."

Draw a barrel containing rocks of different sizes. The rocks represent areas of life that need to be transformed. Between the rocks is empty space. Give this empty space to God so He can fill the barrel to the top with His Spirit. Allow Him to help you identify rocks that prevent further filling by the Spirit. Label the rocks that can be removed to make more space. Sincerely ask God to fill this additional space with His Spirit. Continue throughout your life. NOTE: We now have the mind of Christ and the power of the Spirit to help us identify and throw out rocks. Some rocks might be:

__ having accepted God's forgiveness but not forgiving myself.

__ not feeding my spiritual self with Bible, fellowship, prayer, etc.

__ continuing in some activity that I am convicted is contrary to God's intent.

__ pursuing an Inappropriate Stress Reliever.

__ failing to really accept the fact that God's grace is sufficient for all my sin.

__ pride, i.e., "My sin is so great that God can't forgive it."

__ continuing to keep myself on the throne of my life.

__ incorrect modeling and teaching from parents and others.

__ resentment towards my mind or body for getting me in trouble.

__ a sense of need to punish myself.

__ a sense of shame for things that have happened in my life.

__ feeling God does not respect me.

__ other: _____

Mother said the church was like Noah's Ark. The only reason you could stand the stink inside was because of the storm outside.

"IT IS FOR FREEDOM THAT CHRIST HAS SET US FREE. STAND FIRM, THEN, AND DO NOT LET YOURSELVES BE BURDENED AGAIN BY A YOKE OF SLAVERY" (GAL. 5:1). BELIEVE AND RECEIVE. WE MUST BELIEVE THAT JESUS IS WHO HE SAYS HE IS – THE SON OF GOD, AND THAT HE CAME TO EARTH TO BE OUR SAVIOR.

CHAPTER 6

ADVANTAGES OF THE "IN CHRIST" RELATIONSHIP

FREEDOM FROM THE NEED TO SIN

When we are "in Christ" we are no longer slaves to sin (Rom. 6:17). We can change our mindset about who is our master. We have a new SPICE Rack — our Spiritual, Physical, Intellectual, Community, and Emotional flavorings are now directed by the Holy Spirit, not Satan. We don't have to continue in old, harmful practices. We don't have to live in the septic tanks and garbage dumps of past destructive habits. We will no longer be conformed to patterns of the world but we will be transformed by the renewing of our minds (Rom. 12:2). We can be content. Note that Paul said, "I have learned to be content." You can read about the course work of Paul's PhD in contentment in 2 Corinthians 11. He tells us the "secret" of contentment when he says, "I can do all things 'in Christ' who strengthens me" (Phil. 4:13). The secrets, often mentioned in Paul's writings, are secrets only to those outside of Christ. *$$ SPIRITUAL ARMOR $$*

DON'T BE CONFUSED BY LINGERING HABITS

"I don't understand the things I do. What I want to do, I do not do; what I hate, I do. The evil I do not want to do — this I keep on doing. I find this law at work: when I want to do well, evil is right there with me. What a wretched man I am! Who will rescue me from this body of death? Thanks be to God — through Jesus Christ our Lord!" (The Apostle Paul, Rom. 7:14-25, excerpts — And a whole lot more of us.) As we read Romans 7:14 – 8:1, we agonize with Paul in that we sometimes do the things we don't want to do and we don't do what we want. The significant thing is that we now know when we are wrong and regret it. While our actions are to reflect the image of Christ, we must remember that it is our hope in Christ that purifies us, not our actions (1 John 3:3) and God gives us hope (Jer. 29:11). Each day we need to press on, "Forgetting what is behind and straining toward what is ahead . . ." (Phil. 3:13-14). We pray with Paul, "Oh, wretched man that I am . . ." but remember, "There is now no condemnation to those who are in Christ Jesus" (Rom. 8:1) — not God's condemna-tion, not man's condemnation, and not self-condemnation. We need to repent of self-condemnation if it exists in our lives; that is, we need to forgive ourselves. Self-condemnation is a tool of Satan to prevent the work of the Spirit in us. Do not despair in the process; remember, it is a process.

"IN CHRIST" MINDSET

When we are "in Christ" we have the mind of Christ (1 Cor. 2:16). SPICE influences become positive. Our mind now works the way God intended it to work. God can now speak to us through His word. The Bible now makes sense. "The man without the Spirit does not accept the things that come from the Spirit of God, for they are foolishness to him, and he cannot understand them, because they are spiritually discerned" (1 Cor. 2:14). We now understand the Spirit, Who inspired the Word, translating the Word into our minds and hearts.

WE HAVE A NEW FAMILY

When we are "in Christ" we have the body of Christ, the church, which is all those who confess, believe, receive, and obey Him. We have brothers and sisters who love to help us. In Luke 2 we read that Mary went to her cousin Elizabeth and told her the preposterous story that she was pregnant by the Holy Spirit. Elizabeth was joyous and supportive. God will give each of us an Elizabeth to support us when we share the preposterous news of Christ's birth in us. Later, we can be Elizabeths for someone else. (As we fulfill our role as Elizabeth, people won't leave our church without having been graciously greeted and warmly welcomed.)

ATTRIBUTES OF THE SPIRIT MINDSET

We can meditate on Ephesians 1, where several "in Christ" attributes are listed. When we are in the Kingdom of God we experience ". . . righteousness, peace, and joy in the Holy Spirit . . ." (Rom. 14:17). Once we are "in Christ," we have wonderful attributes of His Spirit: the power of the Spirit to be witnesses (Acts 1:8), gifts of the Spirit to fulfill His purposes as God distributes (1 Cor. 12, Rom. 12, Ephesians 4, and 1 Pet. 4), and the fruit of the Spirit (Gal. 5:22-23).

POWER TO WITNESS

One of the great metaphors for being "in Christ" is found in John 15 where we are told that He is the vine and we are the branches. We are taught that when we are in the Vine, we will bear fruit. We don't have to think about bearing fruit; we simply need to abide in the Vine and fruit will happen. The fruit may be others led into the Kingdom. The fruit may be productivity in personal or business life. For sure, the fruit will be the fruit of the Spirit — love, joy, peace, etc. (Gal. 5:22-23). Don't pray for fruit; pray to be in the Vine and fruit will be produced.

SPIRITUAL GIFTS

When we are "in Christ," we have Spiritual gifts. Spiritual gifts are different from talents. We all have talents that are a result of our CHEESE factories. In addition to our talents God also gives specific gifts for His specific purposes. Many people restrict God's work in them because they have the mindset that they have "a" gift and can work only in that vein. Pray that you will be open to whatever gift God would use in you for any time or location according to the leading of the Holy Spirit. Let Him direct you according to His purpose. Seek first the kingdom of God, that is, to be "in Christ," and let Him be in you, and the rest will be given you.

SPIRITUAL FRUIT

When we are "in Christ" we have ". . . love, joy, peace, patience, kindness, goodness, faithfulness, gentleness, and self-control" (Gal. 5:22-23). "Fruit" is singular. It comes as a package. It is important to know that we have this fruit when we have God's Spirit in us. The fruit of the Spirit is not fruit of our efforts, our prayers, or our desires; it is fruit of the Spirit. We have it; we simply need to USE it. Have the mindset that you have the attributes of the Spirit and you will find them present in your life. For example, if you feel the lack of peace, don't pray for peace; pray to be filled with the Spirit and you will find that you have peace. If you feel you lack love, don't pray for love; pray to be filled with the Spirit and you will have love.

The angels sang of good news — a Savior, joy to the world, and peace on earth to those of good will (Luke 2). The second we are born "in Christ," we begin to bear the fruit of His Spirit within us. This fruit is not of our effort but of our submission. In John 17:24b Jesus said, "May they be brought to complete unity to let the world know that you sent me and have *loved* them even as you have loved me." In John 15:11, He said, "I have told you this so that my *joy* may be in you and that your joy may be complete." In John 14:27 Jesus said, "My *peace* I give you, not as the world gives." Love, joy, and peace are marvelous fruit. They are supernatural gifts from God that are not attainable by those who are not children of God, nor are they attainable by our effort. These are not virtues that we work to attain. We have them as fruit of the Spirit within us. The fact that we have them is to be a mindset. We have love, joy, and peace. Let them reign in your life.

Love—First Corinthians 13 describes love as never failing or ending. This passage is often used in wedding ceremonies and quoted when defining the meaning of love. Love is to be the mark of relationships among Christians. We are to be 1 Corinthians 13 personified. The word "charity" (KJV) reflects the giving nature of love and helps define love as an action word. In Ephesians 3:19 we find that this gift of love "surpasses knowledge."

Joy—Joy is mentioned in 1 Peter 1:8 and defined as "inexpressible." Our faith helps us smile in what seems to be terrible circumstances. "In this you greatly rejoice, though now for a little while you may have had to suffer grief in all kinds of trials" (1 Pet. 1:6). In a companion verse James says, "Consider it pure joy when you face trials . . ." (James 1:2). This is not a suggestion. This is "pure joy," that is, the joy Jesus talked about — the fruit of the Spirit.

Peace—Peace is mentioned twice in Philippians 4:7 and 4:9 and ". . . transcends all understanding . . ." — ("Peace that passes understanding," KJV). Paul gives us a formula for peace:

1. "Do not be anxious about anything" — To be anxious is to have a mindset that our circumstance is beyond God's control. Anxiety is the opposite of faith.

2. "In everything give thanks" — No matter what the circumstance, be thankful. God will deliver us from the circumstance or use it according to His purpose.

3. "And seek God's provision" — God's provision beats the world's best.

4. Then the peace of God, in a process that is beyond our ability to comprehend, "will keep our minds in Christ Jesus." The response to our prayer is peace, "the peace of God," the opposite of anxiety. We can have His peace in the midst of

chaos. We are to be thankful "in" everything, not necessarily "for" everything. Again, this is not a suggestion. If we obey this verse, ". . . the peace of God, which transcends all understanding, will guard your hearts and your minds in Christ Jesus" (Phil. 4: 6-7).

There are many things in life that we do not understand. Things happen that seem to be negative and seem to defy logic. For those times, we are given a peace that passes all understanding — a peace that cannot be explained. The passage goes on to encourage thinking about positive aspects of life. "Whatever is true, whatever is noble, whatever is right, whatever is pure, whatever is lovely, whatever is admirable — if anything is excellent or praiseworthy — think about such things. Whatever you have learned or received or heard from me, or seen in me — put it into practice. And the God of peace will be with you" (Phil. 4: 8-9). The "God of peace" gives us "the peace of God."

When we are "in Christ" we have a love that "surpasses knowledge," a joy that is "inexpressible," and a peace that "passes understanding." Praise be to God!

As you read these last few paragraphs, you may be wondering about a trial in your own life. Many questions come to mind. Are Christians immune from trials? Does God care? What is going on? We need an understanding of why there are trials in life. Read on in Chapter 7.

$ $ $ &—⚷ $ $ $

Treasure Chest #6
Resources for Renewing Growth in Christ

SPIRITUAL ARMOR

As we enter the war that Satan now wages to reclaim our lives and souls, God equips us with protective armor. "Put on the full armor of God so that you can take your stand against the devil's schemes . . . that you may be able to stand your ground, and after you have done everything, to stand" (Eph. 6:11-13). Not only is Satan a force of evil in the world, he has schemes — plans of action to be followed. When we are "in Christ" we are equipped to stand. Whatever your view of Satan, realize that Jesus knew Satan as an adversary. We find in the recounting of the temptations in the wilderness that Jesus resisted Satan's schemes by quoting Scripture (Luke 4). We are to resist in like fashion.

We are to stand. After all else, we are to remain standing — steadfast. To be forewarned is to be forearmed. With what shall we be armed? — The full armor of God. The paragraphs that follow describe this armor. Armor was designed to protect vulnerable areas. While no metaphor will stand on all four feet and walk, Paul uses armor to help us understand the defenses and offenses we have against evil. The list in Ephesians 6:14-18 will help us consider possible weak spots and how to defend against attack. Paul suggests weapons with which we can be armed — the belt of truth, the breastplate of righteousness, feet fitted with readiness, the shield of faith, the helmet of salvation, the sword of the Spirit, prayer, and an alert attitude.

Verse 14: The belt of truth (spiCe) protects our communication, verbal and nonverbal. When we tell the truth we don't have to remember what we said. Truth keeps us from having to spend energy and time backtracking and justifying.

Verse 14: The breastplate of righteousness (spicE) protects the heart and other vital organs. Because of its reactions to stimuli, the heart is called the feeling center of our emotions. Righteousness is right living – we are to hunger and thirst for righteousness. The breastplate protects the lungs, allowing air — pneuma, the Breath of God, that is His Spirit — to flow into us and energize us. If we have a "load on our chest," it keeps us from receiving the totality of the Spirit's gifts. Give the load to God.

Verse 15: Our feet (spiCe) are to be fitted with readiness that comes from the Gospel of Peace. Readiness is a defensive weapon in the fight against Satan's schemes. Ready to flee or face, quick to promote the Gospel, quick to run from sin. "How beautiful upon the mountains are the feet of those who bring Good News" (Rom. 10:15). The Gospel of Peace (spicE) allows us to live without fear and anxiety. Fear saps our energy and takes away our motivation to work. When we have the peace that passes understanding, secure and sure in our faith, we can be ready and willing to promote the Gospel in our community life.

Verse 16: The shield of faith (Spice) protects our intentions. The just shall live by faith, not observable facts nor feelings. Feelings go up and down like a barometer. God's gift of faith remains constant. When we don't ask for, or don't receive His gift of faith, we are prone to temptation. We are continually bombarded with temptations, assailed with doubt — ". . . the fiery darts of the enemy." The shield is held in the hand and is moveable to add further protection to the other elements of armor. Faith enhances truth, righteousness, readiness, and salvation. The Word, prayer, and alertness all are quickened by faith. Testings become opportunities for glorious decisions. We can beat doubt to death with the shield of faith.

Verse 17: The helmet of salvation (spIce) protects the head, the seat of intellect —our thought processes. Salvation (deliverance) is a grace-gift from God and is a reasonable and sufficient answer to our sin predicament. If we try to merit one-tenth of one percent of our salvation with our own efforts, we will be hampered by pride. Paul's message in Philippians 3 is helpful. "Not having a righteousness of my own . . ." In His grace we are free to respond in love without having to be concerned about our spiritual worth.

Verse 17: The sword of the Spirit (spIce), which is the Word of God, is a weapon of attack. What an excellent weapon the Word/word of God is. "The Word became flesh and made his dwelling among us" (John 1:14). "My word will not return to me void, but will accomplish the purpose for which it is sent" (Isa. 55:11). The Word is Jesus — God's communication in human form, and the word is the Bible — God's communication in written form. Jesus is also the "word" that accomplishes God's purpose.

Verse 18: "Pray in the Spirit (Spice) on all occasions." Prayer is a weapon of offense and defense. Jesus prayed often and effectively. We need to follow His example not only in activity but also in content. If we study how He prayed, what He prayed for, when He prayed, why He prayed, and where He prayed, we will increase our prayer power.

Verse 18: We are to be alert (we need more lerts). Alertness (sPice) is not thought of as a weapon but is very necessary in battle. Alertness has to do with physical readiness. Ezekiel has a lot to say about watchmen. Pastors and spiritual leaders have the obligation and privilege of being alert for their flock. People depend on them for guidance (Eph. 4:1).

Remember, this is the armor OF GOD:

TRUTH — "I am the Truth . . ." (John 14:6).

RIGHTEOUSNESS – ". . . righteousness . . . from God . . .by faith" (Phil. 3:9).

PEACE — "But the fruit of the Spirit is . . . peace . . ." (Gal. 5:22).

FAITH — ". . . faith . . . is the gift of God . . ." (Eph. 2 8).

SALVATION — '. . . salvation is found in no one else" (Acts 4:12).

THE SWORD OF THE SPIRIT — ". . . is the word of God" (Eph. 6:17).

About once a month we should make a serious check of our armor and see that it is in good repair. May God bless you in the mighty work to which you are called!

"My grace is sufficient for you, for my power is made perfect in weakness" (2 Cor. 12:9). The only way we know the depth of God's grace is to experience it in the depth of agony.

CHAPTER 7

WHY DO WE HAVE TRIALS?

You could see the red rising in "Hank's" face as his anger boiled to the surface. "Why 9-11? What did those people do that was so wrong that they deserved that kind of death?" "Why did my little sister get killed in a tornado? She never had a chance at life." He desperately wanted to believe in God but he seriously wondered if he could believe in a God Who could allow such terrible things to happen.

WHY AND MINDSETS

Have you ever wondered why there are trials and tragedies in life? I imagine most people have. People approach life with presuppositions, mindsets that were formed in their CHEESE Factories. Perhaps they were sheltered from some of the harsh realities that others face. As we consider the question of why there are trials in life, we need to check our mindsets. One of those mindsets may be the idea that there should be no problems in life. $$ COIN INTERVENTION $$

Worldly thinking says, "If God is good, He shouldn't allow suffering because suffering is bad. If He is in control, bad things shouldn't happen." We are conditioned to expect things to be perfect. Advertisers continually hawk wares that heal diseases, ward off aging, and cover defects. The message of some religious teachers is that if we aren't physically healthy we are spiritually sick. Later on we will see that we should pray for healing but if the healing doesn't come, we are to seek God's greater purpose.

If your mindset is that a good God will not allow any challenges in life, there is little possibility you will be content. If you have made up your mind that nothing bad should happen, you will not only be disappointed, you will miss opportunities for growth and maturity in your Christian walk. Frankly, the idea that all should be sweetness and light is an incorrect mindset that conforms to the pattern of the world. In Romans 12:2 we are told not to conform to such patterns. *$$ LIFE IS LIKE A GOLF COURSE $$*

The bumper sticker that says, "Manure Occurs," or words to that effect, is true. We need to learn how to deal with this truth. Comfort and assurance can be found in Romans 8:28: "We know that in all things God works for the good of those who love him . . ." Or, in the King James Version — "We know that all things work together for good…" No matter which Bible version you choose, you can take comfort in knowing that God is working on your behalf in all things. The words, "we know" indicate this knowledge is a mindset. When we know, our mindset will be that God allows bad things to happen but He can use them for good. Sometimes He allows painful things to happen so we can grow spiritually and emotionally (SpicE) so he can use us in His purpose for others. *$$ POTTERY $$*

Many reasons have been proposed for the existence of bad things in the world. A lot of hardship comes from the result of so-called natural forces, i.e., floods, earthquakes, storms, etc. Results of these forces raise questions about the existence, intent, or power of God. For some people, the answer is shrugged off as a throw of the cosmic dice. Others may believe in a god who is helpless or vindictive. The problem with those mindsets is that they provide little, if any, comfort and limit God's involvement in our lives. The authors' mindset is that God is good, is in control, is concerned about helping us in the deepest of suffering, and that we live in the best possible world for His purposes. That gives us the greatest peace. There are questions for which we don't have answers, at least not yet. The best answer we have is that Christ is RISEN! The single fact of the resurrection of Christ shrivels every other question. Consider this: the only way we can know the depth of God's comfort is to experience it in the depth of pain.

A lot of the trials we face are brought about by our own bad decisions, impulsive actions, and sinful behavior. We must be careful not to blame God or others for our mistakes.

CACTUS PATCH MINDSET

There was a man found thrashing about in a cactus patch. After he was de-needled and patched up he was asked what he was doing thrashing around in a cactus patch. He replied, "It seemed to be the reasonable thing to do at the time." That sounds foolish but we all have our cactus patches — things that seemed reasonable at the time — our best thinking. Hopefully, we get into fewer patches as experience increases our wisdom.

If our mindset is that God is good, that He created all that exists, and that this is the best possible world for His purposes and our lives, we have a positive answer to the question of why there is pain and suffering. For the best possible life in this best possible world we need the best possible faith, the best possible knowledge, and the best possible wisdom to deal with that knowledge. (Knowledge is what we know; wisdom is what we do with what we know.)

For you young people — cats have whiskers to tell them where not to stick their heads. If your "whiskers" haven't developed yet, talk to someone you trust who has been there or who has avoided some of the cactus patches of life. Your parents may not be perfect but you can usually trust their warnings even if they take a "do what I say, not what I do" approach. THERE ARE SOME THINGS YOU JUST DON'T WANT TO LEARN FROM EXPERIENCE. It is so much easier to learn from someone else's mistakes. And, it is so much easier to stay out of trouble than it is to get out of trouble.

BACK TO, WHY TRIALS?

There is no need for faith if there are no difficult times. God's grace is only sufficient if it is sufficient for the worst of circumstances. More difficult times call for deeper faith. Fortunately, faith is a gift from God (Eph. 2:9-10) and He has infinite resources.

There are several passages of Scripture that offer insight to the problem of suffering. Paul wrote in 2 Corinthians 12:7-10 — "To keep me from becoming conceited because of these surpassingly great revelations, there was given me a thorn in my flesh, a messenger of Satan, to torment me. Three times I pleaded with the Lord to take it away from me. But he said to me, 'My grace is sufficient for you, for my power is made perfect in weakness.' Therefore I will boast all the more gladly about my weaknesses, so that Christ's power may rest on me."

$$ VERSES TO USE AND SHARE $$

The Apostle Paul experienced great power in prayer. When he had prayed three times, as did Jesus in the Garden of Gethsemane, and the thorn wasn't removed, he did not curse God; he looked for an underlying message. Paul asked for relief and God said, "My grace is sufficient." Paul found that the thorn kept him from being conceited. The thorn showed him that he needed to be totally dependent on God and that only God's grace is sufficient. The thorn did not go away. *The thorn did not go away!* The thorn helped Paul to see his weaknesses as assets that continually turned him to God. The thorn allowed God's power to be used in him. Paul accepted the thorn, delighted in weakness, and worked with God's power.

As we examine our "thorns," our response model, as shown in 2 Corinthians 12:7-10, should be to pray three times that our thorn be removed. We expect it to be removed. If it isn't removed, we take our eyes off the thorn and focus on God's grace. His grace is sufficient. Either His grace is sufficient or it isn't. *His grace is sufficient!!* This is a mindset. Being conformed to the world, and to inappropriate stress relievers that are so alluring, turns out to be insufficient. Only God's grace is sufficient. The first commandment becomes more precious. "You shall have no other gods before me" (Exod. 20) — Him only.

An alternative mindset suggests that those who continue to struggle with trials lack faith or have something wrong in their lives. People who believe this must think they are better Christians than the writers of the New Testament letters. In 2 Corinthians 12:7-10, 1 Peter 1:6, and James 1:2 we see a much different approach and find that early Christians like Paul, Peter, and James did not live trial-free lives.

Some people have a mindset that hardships are God's payback for evil. Bible passages show this is false thinking. Jesus asked, "Or those eighteen who died when the tower in Siloam fell on them — do you think they were more guilty than all the others living in Jerusalem? I tell you, no!" (Luke 13:4), indicating sin was not a cause for their death. Sin does have natural consequences but we all know terrible people who live well and wonderful people who experience trials.

A better answer is given in Jesus' remark about a man born blind. "Neither this man nor his parents sinned . . . but this happened so that the work of God might be displayed in his life" (John 9:2-3). Trials sometimes exist so that God's power in healing, or His comfort in pain, can be revealed. God sometimes works by relieving the problem and sometimes by giving peace with the problem, all for His sovereign purposes. Peace within a problem is a greater miracle than being relieved of the problem. We have choices. We can either distress constantly over situations in which we have little or no control, or we can call upon God's power, gain peace in the midst of trials, and move on.

If we allow something to interfere with our joy and peace, it has become our god; we worship "insufficiency." God will not allow us to find sufficiency in anything else because no other thing or person is sufficient. Our best thinking and our best actions are not sufficient. We are to think of them as "rubbish" (Phil. 3:8). We can rejoice in our weaknesses, because through them we turn to God and find His strength. "And we know that in all things . . ." including our weaknesses ". . . God works for the good of those who love Him . . ." (Rom. 8:28).

Please know that by no means are we minimizing life's trying situations. Some are excruciating. But, one of the lessons from 2 Corinthians

12 is to ask that the problem be removed. Then, if it isn't removed, we are to listen and rely on God's direction and strength to work within the hardship. During Jesus' trial in Gethsemane He prayed, "Not my will but yours be done" (Luke 22:42). Although the disciples were asleep, Jesus was not alone. Just as an angel ministered to Him, God will send the help we need in our personal Gethsemanes. It is a joy to know that Jesus and the Holy Spirit advocate for us in our trials. When we don't know how to pray, as we ought, the Spirit intercedes for us (Rom. 8:16-17). When Satan or others accuse us, Christ intercedes for us (Rom. 8:34). In fact, in Hebrews 7:25 we have the promise, "He is always able to save us completely, when we come to God through him, because he always lives to intercede for us." Always, in each moment of our lives, Jesus is interceding for us.

A lot of our response to pain depends on our mindset of who God is and what His purposes are. Consider the alternatives. We can choose to be miserable. We can choose to become depressed. We can argue with God. We can shake our fist towards the sky. We can curse God or circumstance. Or, we can consider it pure joy, utilize our resources in the Holy Spirit and persevere, becoming mature and complete, lacking nothing. *$$ LESSONS FROM JAMES 1:2-4 $$*

MORE RESOURCES

Fortunately, when we encounter the need to ask why, we are not alone. God gives us others who have "been there and done that" to give us comfort. Through experience and/or training, they can help us through difficult times. Also, God comforts us. "Praise be to the God and Father of our Lord Jesus Christ, the Father of compassion and the God of all comfort, who comforts us in all our troubles, so that we can comfort those in any trouble with the comfort we ourselves have received from God" (2 Cor. 1:3-4). Sometimes we can work through the problem ourselves. More often it is better to utilize the help of others who can share God's comfort with us. Then we can pass His comfort on to someone else. Note: God is the God of "ALL comfort." If we seek comfort in anyone or anything else we are getting second-rate comfort. If we seek help in an inappropriate stress reliever we will just compound the problem. Rely on Him.

WHY ME?

Paul didn't ask, "Why me?" He wrote, ". . . I have learned to be content whatever the circumstances. I know what it is to be in need, and I know what it is to have plenty. I have learned the secret of being content in any and every situation, whether well fed or hungry, whether living in plenty or in want. I can do everything in him who gives me strength" (Phil. 4:11b-13). (This is only a "secret" to those who aren't growing in Christ.) In terms of this book, this passage might be rendered: "I have a mindset that I am secure in Christ. Circumstances don't faze me; those things that used to upset me do not bother me. I have learned that I am completely empowered for any circumstance."

We experience hardships so that we may learn to be content. Contentment is <u>not</u> a fruit of the Spirit. Paul said he "learned" to be content. See 2 Corinthians chapters 11 and 12 for the course content of his advanced degree in contentment. To be content, or happy, is something we have to learn.

While happiness is a wonderful thing, it is different from joy. Happiness is like contentment, a milder emotion than joy. The mindset of contentment is not based on circumstances but upon maturity in Christ. If we are depressed or anxious because of some circumstance, we have yet to understand and gain the fruit of the Spirit. Peter wrote, ". . . you believe in him and are filled with an inexpressible and glorious joy . . ." (I Pet. 1:8). While contentment is not a gift, joy IS a gift, a supernatural gift from God ". . . that my joy may be in you" (John 15:11) — a fruit of the Spirit (Gal. 5:22). As we are filled, more and more, with the Spirit of God, we experience more and more of His joy. We can't explain it; we just have it. We can have joy in the midst of sorrow and unhappiness.

TESTING AND TRIALS

"No temptation has seized you except what is common to man. And God is faithful; he will not let you be tempted beyond what you can bear. But when you are tempted, he will also provide a way out so that you can stand up under it" (I Cor. 10:13). Take your eyes off the "temptation" and focus on the "way out." Note carefully, it does not say, "if you are tempted." It says, "when." Many people feel they have sinned just because they are tempted. Think about it; Jesus was tempted but did not sin. Temptation is not sin. We sin only if we pursue the temptation. Remember, the first thought is Satan's work; the second thought is our responsibility. Sin comes only if we are "dragged away" by our desires (James 1:14).

We are not to manufacture a way out; we are to seek God's way. We will find the means of escape when we take our eyes off the test and focus on discerning His "way out." God's way, as found in James 1, and Philippians 4, is the way of "joy" and "contentment." He will not test us beyond our ability to endure. We must KNOW this! It is a mindset (spIce). Even though it seems better that He remove the source of pain, we know He will get us through it so we can persevere to maturity, lacking nothing. The thorn may remain but we have His power. He is more often a God of comfort than a God of altered circumstance. He may alter us instead.

In the book of Hebrews we find a powerful passage that refers to hardships as discipline:

> "Endure hardship as discipline; God is treating you as his sons (children). For what son (child) is not disciplined by his father. If you are not disciplined then you are illegitimate children . . . Moreover, we have all had human fathers who disciplined us and we respected them for it. How much more should we submit to the Father of our spirits and live! Our fathers disciplined us for a little while as they thought best; but God disciplines us for our good, that we may share in his holiness. No discipline seems pleasant at the time, but painful. Later on, however, it produces a harvest of righteousness and peace for those who have been trained by it" (Heb. 12:7-11).

THE WORDS OF ETERNAL LIFE

As we love God with all our minds (spIce), there will be decision points in our lives when we must be transformed by the renewing of our minds. Perhaps something so hideous has happened that we wonder if there is a God or if He cares. After a difficult teaching in Jesus' life, ". . . many of His disciples turned back and no longer followed Him." 'You do not want to leave too, do you?' Jesus asked the Twelve. Simon Peter answered him, "Lord, to whom shall we go? You have the words of eternal life" (John 6:66b-68). When you are beset with trials, remember Jesus is the only one Who has the "words of eternal life." Jesus is the best answer to the world situation — mindset. Accepting Jesus is not a default decision. It is choosing life in the power of God. I don't have all the answers but I know Him Who does. He ". . . has the words of eternal life."

"The righteous will live by feelings." Right? No! "The righteous will live by <u>faith</u>" (Rom. 1:17). Our mindset is called faith because we cannot prove it. The righteous do not live by facts or by their feelings, but by their faith, and faith is a gift of God. As you encounter life's challenging situations, have the mindset (faith) that God is with you, is constantly working for you, and will help see you through the circumstances of life and death.

Without the depth of pain and disaster, we would not know the depth of faith and comfort (Spice). Indeed, as has been obvious, many people allow their faith and patriotism to lie dormant until a disaster occurs. We may not even think of God when everything is working well. Praise Him for the thorns. We are really not ready to live until we are ready to die. We are not ready to enjoy the "plenty" until we can appreciate the "want" (Phil. 4:12). We have a wonderful death insurance policy.

Job said, "Shall we accept good from God, and not trouble?" (Job 2:10b). We need to take a good look at our expectations about life and circumstances.

$ $ $ 🗝️ $ $ $

Treasure Chest #7
Resources for Renewing Our Ability to Withstand Trials

COIN INTERVENTION

Life is like a pocket full of change. Take ten coins of various denominations and toss them on the floor in front of you. Every day is a throw of the coins. Different days bring different positive (heads) and negative (tails) events. That's the way life is. Discuss how each day or event seems to have positive and negative factors. There is good and bad in every day, every person, every job, etc. We choose how we react to what shapes our day. Choose a coin and ask what it represents. There is often a head and a tail to a specific thing that influences our life. We can focus on the head (+) or the tail (-). If our mindset is negative, we will dwell amongst the "tails" of life. If our mindset is positive, we will dwell amongst the "heads" — Choose. If an event seems bad ask, "Why is this the worst thing that can happen?" Then, using the same event, ask, "How could this be the best thing that could happen?" Be thankful. Usually we should focus on the heads and try to find some good in the tails.

LIFE IS LIKE A GOLF COURSE

The beginning golfer may wish for the "perfect" golf course — U-shaped fairways and cone-shaped greens. Two or three strokes will put the ball in the hole. But you won't find that course. Golf course developers know that golfers prefer a challenge. When difficult golf shots are accomplished, the golfer feels good. Just as a golfer finds satisfaction in overcoming difficult situations, you, too, will rejoice as you move through trying times. Over time, with experience, you will build a golf bag full of problem-solving devices to use for various challenges. As you read this book, you will find several clubs (skills) to use or adapt to new problems as you gain in spiritual and social wisdom.

POTTERY

Sometimes we rebel. "Why am I suffering this particular affliction?" Part of the answer is found in Paul's argument in Romans. "But who are you, O man, to talk back to God? Shall what is formed say to Him who formed it, 'Why did you make me like this?' Does not the potter have the right to make out of the same lump of clay some pottery for noble purposes and some for common use?" (Rom. 9:20-21). God allows us to ask the hard questions. But there are some unanswered questions in life — "I don't know yet." YET! For the present, we must seek a solution or rest in faith. Some people get so stuck in the "why" that they profess atheism. However it takes more "faith" to be an atheist than to be a theist. Atheists have more "I don't knows" than theists. If there is no God, something came from nothing. However, we are simply too complicated to have occurred by chance. How can "no God" be helpful? "No God" is not good news. The good news is that God IS, ("I AM"), and His grace is greater than our affliction.

VERSES TO USE AND SHARE

If you are experiencing emotional, physical, or any other kind of hardship, strength and comfort can be found in the following verses. Focus on God's grace and consider the following:

Romans 5:3-5: Working through tribulation alerts us to access the patience given to us by the Holy Spirit.

Luke 21:13: Persecution will result in our being witnesses to those who are watching.

Romans 5:3-5: Pain helps us develop character.

I Peter 1:7: Trials prove our faith to be genuine; they build assurance that we can handle further or greater stress.

Philippians 1:19-25: Some trials are meant to bring us deliverance.

Hebrews 5:7-9: Jesus learned obedience through suffering; then He became the source of salvation for all who obey Him. We are to be like Him. That means we, also, may suffer.

LESSONS FROM JAMES 1:2-4

Our perspective is generally focused on the present. God is focused on eternity. Christians are people of eternity. If you are a Christian, you are a person of eternity. This is not pie in the sky by and by; it is the knowledge that earth is not meant to be heaven. A verse that many see as an oxymoron is James 1:2-4. "Consider it pure joy, my brothers, whenever you face trials of many kinds, because you know that the testing of your faith develops perseverance. Perseverance must finish its work so that you may be mature and complete, not lacking any-thing." Don't see this as a suggestion. It is a command. As we meditate on this verse we learn several valuable lessons about trials.

Consider: con = with; side = choice. Which side am I on?

We have "pure joy," that is, Christ's joy that is fruit of the Spirit joy.

Note that it says FACE trials, not lie helplessly and whine.

We are to focus on the joy of growth, not the pain of the trial.

Issues are intended to increase intimacy.

We have God's resources to help us face the trial.

We develop perseverance.

We become mature and complete in our relationship with God.

We are prepared to help others.

We lack nothing of that which really matters.

Let it be a finished work. Don't ask to get off the fire too soon. You may say, "Right, you haven't experienced MY trials." However, God knows all about your trials. He knew about them before you were conceived and is with you now. Satan needs permission and has restric-tions for what he does to you (Job 1:12).

"Call to me and I will answer you and tell you great and unsearchable things you do not know" (Jer. 33:3 — God's phone number). Have total expectations of God, reasonable expectations of self, and realistic expectations of others and circumstance.

CHAPTER 8

EXPECTATIONS

ASSUMPTIONS

"Bill" and "Betty" had been married six months. She expected him to quit spending time with his drinking buddies. He expected her to be the same provocative sex kitten he had dated. Now he spends most of his nights with his buddies and she grows colder and colder. Both were bitterly disappointed and seriously questioned if they should just divorce and start over with someone else. (Unless they change, probably some other drinker and sex kitten.)

We assume that a person will act a certain way, or we anticipate a predictable outcome from an event. Usually, our expectations work out as we think they will. All too often however, we get the rug pulled out from under us. Expectations that are not met can have a significant impact on us. The resulting disappointment and frustration can lead to negative mental states such as depression, anxiety, and/or anger. One of the great lessons from the book of Jonah is that we sometimes elect to be anxious or depressed instead of seeking and receiving forgiveness for our wrong thinking.

Expectations are akin to mindsets. We may have such strong expectations that alternatives are not acceptable. As with mindsets, we grasp at straws to maintain expectations and ignore evidence that they are unrealistic. As with mindsets, expectations are influenced by our past and are formulated in our CHEESE factories (Choices, Heredity, Environment, Events, Self-Esteem).

Our personal expectations have their origin in, and are often influenced by, family expectations. Family expectations come to us in different ways. They may be made clear by verbal requirements. They may be veiled in smiles or frowns. We may be cast in, or take on, a family role such as scapegoat, clown, mascot, baby, pet, star, smart one, student, weasel, snitch, tattletale, teacher, hero, protector, nurturer, helper, rescuer, provider, referee, mediator, peacemaker, troublemaker, black sheep, quiet one, lost child, stupid, worthless, %#@$&*, among others. Family expectations strongly influence our self-image and self-esteem.

The roles we accept shape our mindsets and behaviors. We adapt to them so we feel accepted in the family. Positive role expectations are preferred but even positive expectations may promote anxiety or damage self-esteem if others expect us to be someone we aren't or if they expect us to do something we can't.

If we don't expect good things to happen in our lives, we often gravitate towards Inappropriate Stress Relievers (ISRs), harmful activities that generate a lot of garbage. Even if we make a resolution to get rid of garbage habits, we often go right back to them ("The old wine is better."). Many people spend their lives chasing their garbage trucks down the street, or worse, follow them into the dump and live in the garbage dumps of negative or unmet expectations. Think about that mental picture. Consider the ludicrous decisions that are made in our garbage dumps. Many ISRs are found there. How smart is it to live in the garbage dumps of our lives?

THREE TYPES OF EXPECTATIONS

We should have unlimited expectations of God, reasonable expectations of ourselves, and realistic expectations of others and circumstance.

EXPECTATIONS OF GOD

We can have totally positive expectations of God. We know that God will never disappoint us. That is an absolute truth and we should have that mindset. His mercies are new every morning. (Lam. 3:22-23). He is always with us (Ps. 139:8-10). He is true to Himself. He cannot and will not change. There may be times when you may wonder if God knows what He is doing but if you hang in there the picture will become clear. God is good. Everything should be interpreted in that light.

Expectation rule number 1: God is good. Expectation rule number 2: If in any way God appears not to be good, see rule number 1. All things are interpreted by these rules. Mindset — we can have faith in God, positive expectations.

EXPECTATIONS OF OURSELVES

We must have reasonable expectations of ourselves. We are not perfect. Perfectionists hold themselves to a higher standard than God does. Many people do not live in the joy that comes with the Spirit because they see sin in their lives. The Apostle Paul said, he had ". . . weaknesses . . ." (2 Cor. 12:9-10), but he delighted in them because they caused him to rely on God's strength. As Christians, we fight against our human nature. The very fact that we engage in the battle is proof that we have the mind of Christ. Those outside of Him simply give in to evil. We make mistakes but we try not to make them on purpose. We know from His word that God has given us a way to escape the futility of beating up on ourselves. God forgives us when we ask. If we can't forgive ourselves, we think we know something He doesn't. Some people think God wouldn't forgive them if He really knew them. That kind of thinking is a tool used by Satan to keep people trapped in the unhappy bondage of their garbage dumps. Remember God's bar of soap found in 1 John 1:9 — "If we confess our sins, he is faithful and just to forgive us our sins and purifies us from all unrighteousness." Note it says ALL — what we have done, what has been done to us, what we know about, and what we have forgotten — everything! He forgives our sinful nature and the sins that result from our nature. He even forgives the sin of not forgiving ourselves. We need to repent for not forgiving ourselves. In 1 John 3:19-20 we see that, "Even if our minds condemn us, we can set our minds at ease for God does not condemn us and he knows everything." Ask God to forgive you for not forgiving yourself. Then you can fulfill His intent that we become new creations (2 Cor. 5:17), living in love, joy, and peace. We accept the fact that we are in process and can use a simple change model.

What was my faulty mindset?

What did I do?

How did it work out for me?

What did I learn about future choices?

Our heavenly Father thinks we are wonderful and we should feel that way, too. After all, we are created in His image. We need to live in that image.

Sometimes our mindsets allow us to be victimized by reasonable expectations of others or circumstance. We can be sabotaged by reasonable expectations. Unfortunately, life isn't always reasonable. We are better off with a mindset of realistic expectations.

EXPECTATIONS OF OTHERS AND CIRCUMSTANCE

We should have realistic expectations of other people or circumstances. There are even some people or circumstances for which we have zero or negative expectations. We know there are choices and forces in this world that will harm us. We must remember that people can't be our god. No one is perfect and we can't look to him or her for power, gifts, and fruit that only God can give.

Unrealistic expectations can prevent change by creating an unhelpful mindset that keeps us from dealing with reality. For instance, consider an overconfident team that expects they will win a certain game. Even though the score may be lopsided in favor of the opponent at halftime, the overly confident team won't be able to "get it in gear"

because "this can't be happening." Overconfidence puts an extra player on the other team. Don't let Satan be that player. Don't think you can make it without God. *$$ BARRACUDA ILLUSTRATION $$*
There are reasonable and righteous expectations — things that should happen. However, there are realistic expectations — those things that probably will happen. If our expectations are not realistic, we set ourselves up a host of negative emotions. Realistic expectations take into account people's personalities and the fickle nature of circumstances over which we have little control. We need to think about our expectations and carefully choose the source of our emotional satisfaction.

TRACTOR INTERVENTION

Imagine yourself sitting on a wagon inside a circle of tractors that are all headed outwards. Label the tractors as expectations in relationships, jobs, habits, etc. Some of the tractors are new, some old, some running smoothly, some spitting and sputtering; some may be dead and beyond repair. If you hitch your wagon (expectation) to the wrong tractor, you may just sit there or you may spend more time working on the tractor than enjoying the ride. It is a good idea to make wise choices before getting hooked up because it is a lot easier to stay unhooked than to get unhooked. If you realize that you are hitched to the wrong tractor, simply hook into God. To what tractor are you hooking your wagon?

REALISTIC PRAYER

What about positive expectations of God and "unanswered" prayer? Unanswered prayer is any prayer that doesn't come out the way we think it should. This mindset is an example of stinking thinking. "God didn't do what I wanted so He wasn't listening." "Hear lord for Your Servant speaks." This mindset is that God is a slot machine. You push in 50 cents worth of prayer and expect Him to pay off in silver dollars. In reality, God always answers prayer, "Go," "No," or "Grow" according to His will. "Go" means yes and is like the go in an

Internet link — you get results. "No" means what we are asking for is not in our best interest and God is protecting us. "Grow" means our mindsets need to be transformed to agree with God's will. We need to trust that He does answer and His answers are based on knowledge that we may not have.

If our expectation (mindset) is that some good, some learning, and/or some positive results come from "No" and "Grow" answers, a measure of peace and fulfillment will come. "Consider it pure joy when you face various trials . . . for the end result is maturity" (James 1). Maturity is not a gift or fruit of the Spirit; we gain maturity by facing trials.

UNREALISTIC EXPECTATIONS OF CONTROL

A huge factor in mental health is an expectation that we have some control over what happens in our lives. When we feel that life has gone out of control we are subject to emotional distress. (An irritation is an expectation violation.) Disappointment that leads to depression, irritation that leads to anxiety, and frustration that leads to anger are common reactions to loss of control. These emotional states result, at least in part, from unrealistic expectations. These emotions are indications that we are expecting joy and peace from someone or something less than God. He has allowed us to have negative emotions so that we will know when we are on the wrong track. *$$ TRANSFERENCE AND COUNTER-TRANSFERENCE $$*

DEPRESSION FROM UNMET EXPECTATIONS

Our expectations may be wonderfully righteous but if they are not realistic under the circumstances, we are set up for reactive depression. (Depression that stems purely from neurotransmitter malfunction is outside the realm of this book.) Reactive depression comes from an actual or perceived loss, an emotional reaction to an unmet expectation. The loss may be from exterior events like the loss of a loved one or the loss of a job. Or, the loss may come from interior sources such as the loss of self-esteem when someone we respect treats us shamefully.

These losses represent a loss of control. Something happened that was beyond our ability.

We need to know that even if we are out of control, God is in control. Faith in the goodness and power of God will help us recover from difficult times.

ANXIETY ABOUT EXPECTATIONS

Anxiety occurs when we feel we do not have resources to control a perceived threat that is yet to occur. We do not expect to be able to handle what life is going to bring. Not knowing what to expect can be exhilarating in small doses but in major life events it may be overwhelming. If we perceive an event to be out of our control, the event becomes a threat, which causes anxiety. Anxiety is basically a distrust of God's ability or care. The answer to anxiety or fear is to focus on and depend on Christ. A person who expects to be able to handle the various challenges of life will not suffer anxiety. The cure for anxiety is to use our resources to deal with fear. In Christ, we have all the promises, power, gifts, and fruit that we need to handle any threat, even death. When we have control, or the faith that God is in control, our lives become manageable. Paul encourages us not to be anxious but to be thankful in all things (Phil. 3). It is hard to be anxious and thankful at the same time.

Reactive depression is linked to the past. Anxiety is a concern about the future. Depression is about loss in the past; anxiety is about expectation of loss in the near or distant future. Hopefully, lessons learned from past experience will assure us that God is in control of our past, present, and future.

ANGER AS THE RESULT OF UNMET EXPECTATIONS

Unfulfilled expectations can be a cause of anger. Anger is an adrenaline reaction caused by a threat to ourself or a thing or other person we hold dear. When a situation seems out of control, our emotions may go out of control and we react by smashing something or somebody.

It follows that anger management, along with good health habits and social support, will help decrease stress brought on by unmet expectations and enable our bodies and minds to resist invasion. Good health habits depend on personal motivation, which is based on hope for a positive return for our efforts. If it took a few months or years of an ISR (Inappropriate Stress Reliever) to get where we are, it may take an ASR (Appropriate Stress Reliever) time and the discipline to get where we want to be. Mindset. (See chapter on ANGER.)

A BIBLICAL APPROACH TO HANDLING UNMET EXPECTATIONS

The Apostle Peter said, "I will always remind you of these things, even though you know them and are firmly established in the truth you now have" (2 Pet. 1:12). Sometimes we miss something the first time. Sometimes we forget what we learned. In any case it is good to go over certain truths to keep ourselves fresh in the Word.

LEARNING TO BE CONTENT

Reactive depression, anxiety, and anger may be thought of as the opposite of contentment. The Apostle Paul said, "I have learned to be content whatever the circumstances. I know what it is to be in need, and I know what it is to have plenty. I have learned the secret of being content in any and every situation, whether well fed or hungry, whether living in plenty or in want. I can do everything through him who gives me strength" (Phil. 4:11b-13). One way to handle anxiety is to not get anxious in the first place. The secret of dealing with expectations is being "in Christ" and having access to the power, fruit, and gifts of the Holy Spirit. Paul's thinking was transformed by the renewing of his mind. He had a new mindset — contentment. When we have a mindset of contentment we find evidence to support contentment and we ignore contrary evidence. "Con" means with, a "tent" is a dwelling place — a tabernacle. To be content is to tabernacle with God.

Contentment (happiness) is an emotional goal that was reached by Paul. His achievement can help us know that God will see us through adversity. Paul went to college at good old SSEE, the School of Significant Emotional Events. He learned contentment by reacting to experiences of stress with the "in Christ" attitude.

We can have total expectations of God. When we are walking in, with, and through the Holy Spirit, we are given evidence of His indwelling presence by: His fruit—love, joy, peace, etc. (Gal. 5:22-23), His gifts (1 Cor. 12, Rom. 12, Eph. 4, 1 Pet. 4, and others), and His power (Acts 1:8). When we recognize, and actuate, the fruit of the Spirit in our lives, we are granted the gifts of the Spirit and we proceed in the power of the Spirit. This trilogy validates our "in Christ" relationship.

In our life "in Christ" we have love that surpasses knowledge (Eph. 3:19), inexpressible joy (1 Pet. 1:8), and the peace that passes understanding (Phil. 4:7, KJV). A fact that is little understood is that we HAVE these things if we have the Holy Spirit. Again, they are fruit of the Spirit, not fruit of our efforts. If you want love, pray to be filled with the Holy Spirit. If you want joy, pray to be filled with the Holy Spirit. If you want peace, pray to be filled with the Holy Spirit. "How much more will your Father in heaven give the Holy Spirit to those who ask him!" (Luke 11:13). We don't need to conjure them up or work for them. Just allow God's amazing grace to work in your life. His grace is alive and active now.

Unrealistic expectations are a source of stress in our lives. Relief from stress is important because stress is painful and we tend to seek pleasure and avoid pain. The choices we make in areas of pleasure seeking and pain relief sometimes result in Inappropriate Stress Relievers (ISRs). We need to take a good look at how ISRs come about.

$ $ $ 🔑 $ $ $

Treasure Chest #3
Resources for Renewing Expectations

BARRACUDA ILLUSTRATION

One of Don's teachers told the story of a barracuda in a large glass tank. Minnows would be put into the tank and the barracuda would do its thing, slashing about, killing minnows, and eating the pieces. One day a plate glass divider was placed in the middle of the tank. The barracuda was on one side and the minnows were placed on the other. The barracuda expected to feed. It slammed against the glass until it gave up. The glass was then removed and the barracuda starved to death with minnows swimming all around it. It no longer expected to be able to feed.

Sometimes people have pounded their heads against an unrealistic expectation so long, without satisfying results, that they have learned to be helpless. We should never give up but we do need realistic expectations about the outcomes of our endeavors. What has been, or is, the plate glass in your life? If it seems you have been pounding your head fruitlessly, you don't have to learn to be helpless. You need to look for realistic opportunities that are within your grasp. You have the choice to be a "new creation in Christ" every minute of every day.

TRANSFERENCE AND COUNTER-TRANSFERENCE ISSUES

Many people go into helping professions with conscious or unconscious expectations. Caregivers are not immune to the negative effects of their CHEESE factories. If they have unresolved personal issues, they may need more care than the people they are attempting to help. They may use those in their care instead of helping them. Some expectations may be so ingrained we aren't aware of their influence. Expectations may show up as transference or counter-transference in our dealings with people.

Transference is a term used to describe emotional involvement that is transferred from a client/patient to a caregiver. The classic example is when a counselee sees the counselor as a parent figure. Counter-transference refers to emotional reactions a counselee evokes from a counselor. People who try to help others may be subject to needs or expectations in their own lives that enter the therapeutic process. Such feelings should not be suppressed but should become part of the therapeutic discussion and process. These psychological factors can be found in any interactions between people, not just in professional offices.

The counselor has to be careful not to abuse the client by using the client to meet his or her needs. The critical question is: Whose needs are being met? Following is a list of some counter-transference characters and their characteristics:

Save the World Willie — Abused in the past, he has axes to grind and is out to save the world. The client is just grist for his mill. Willie may suffer from burnout.

Paranoid Patty — There are evil forces that block every effort in her agenda. The client is out to thwart her efforts.

Traumatized Ted — Ted was abused as a child and feels that only he can deal with similar trauma. He identifies so closely with the client that he cannot be confrontational when necessary.

Angry Angie — She doesn't like supervision or any authority figure for that matter. Any suggestion is taken as negative criticism and resented. Clients interfere with her processes.

One-way Wanda — She has the answer and is unable to adapt to individual needs.

Defended Danny — He spent such a tremendous amount of energy deflecting trauma as a child, he cannot accept the pain that victims feel. He avoids core issues. He expects the client to accept his own defenses instead of working through the problem.

Abusive Abigail — She uses inappropriate intervention techniques that were part of her caregiver's repertoire.

Compulsive Conrad — He burns out caring for others. He neglects himself and his family.

Perfect Percy — He is so anxious to please; if only he does everything right the client's problems will be solved. He believes it was his fault he was abused as a child.

Vigilant Virginia — She fears being wrong and is constantly on the lookout for signs of personal failure.

Rescuing Ralph — He crosses boundaries and tries to do the client's work. He may over-identify with a client and become inappropriately emotional or physical.

Perpetrating Peter/Pansy — He or she emotionally or sexually abuses clients.

Timid Timmy — He is unsure of himself. He may fail to confront even when he knows a situation calls for it. Bullying clients back him down. He is "sorry" and spends a lot of time apologizing.

Denying Delilah — "My parents were alcoholics, I was molested, I was starved and beaten with electric cords, but it did not affect me." "I took Psych 101 so I don't need therapy." She may encourage clients to deny problems and deprive them of appropriate help.

Magical Matthew — He may move too quickly with the rosy idea that "things will work out." His idealized solutions often fail.

Codependent Cora — She needs clients to be ill so she can work out her issues through them. She will sabotage efforts to heal. Clients will use her to validate their illness.

Vigilante Virgil — He is so angry, he wants to hang the %&#*&%. Revenge is his main goal.

"THEY SOW THE WIND AND REAP THE WHIRLWIND" (HOSEA 8:7).
INAPPROPRIATE STRESS RELIEVERS CREATE MORE STRESS.

CHAPTER 9

STRESS AND INAPPROPRIATE STRESS RELIEVERS

We've alluded to Inappropriate Stress Relievers (ISRs) in preceding chapters. Now it's time to discuss them more thoroughly. What we turn to in times of stress is our "god" — food, alcohol, etc. When people are not "in Christ" negative CHEESE and SPICE factors affect their choice of stress relievers. Quite often, these stress relievers are inappropriate. A GLOSSARY for dependence is found at the back of the book.

He said he needed to hit the porn sights on the Internet because it helped him relax after a stressful day at work. She was adding vodka to everything she drank because it dulled the pain of her shriveling marriage. The teenage children were smoking marijuana to ease the stress of hearing their parents scream at each other and the eight-year-old had been kicked out of school for the third time for fighting. What on earth was going on?

STRESS

Stress is caused by demands or pressures that push or pull us from an established state. Unmet expectations or boundary violations are often significant contributions to stress. Something upsets our equilibrium, violates a boundary, or does not meet an expectation. Stress is created when we are forced, or choose, to change. CHANGE CAUSES STRESS. It may be that change is necessary to move from a very stressful situation to a less stressful situation. Even this causes stress. Other reasons for stress are: having to do something we don't want to do, or not being able to do something we want to do. It is important to realize that any change is stressful, even positive change.

Stress is directly proportional to a feeling of lack of control. We consciously or unconsciously expect a measure of control in our lives. We may be aware of our expectations of control in a situation or they may be a submerged part of our CHEESE factory. When we are stressed, the resulting emotions of depression, anxiety, or anger, as discussed earlier, are unpleasant, so we seek a stress reliever.

INAPPROPRIATE STRESS RELIEVERS

It is a human tendency to seek pleasure and to avoid pain. The natural mind often seeks pleasure in the form of an Inappropriate Stress Reliever (ISR), causing more problems. What we thought would bring pleasure brings more pain and causes more stress. The mind of Christ, however, seeks an Appropriate Stress Reliever (ASR) from which lasting pleasure is gained.

EFFECTS OF STRESS RELIEVERS DIAGRAM

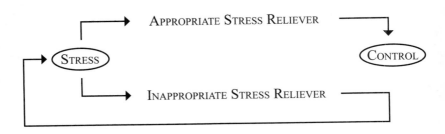

As indicated in the diagram, an ASR leads to control and emotional relief, while an ISR creates a continuous cycle of stress.

Inappropriate stress relievers clamor for more and more of our time and emotional energy until they take over and own us. Remember, if we pursue something long enough, it will possess us. Once the ISR takes over, there is fear of going back to the previous stressful state of being. Recovery is compounded by the original problem plus the results of the ISR(s).

One of the most common causes for distress is some form of sin that is loosely defined as ". . . falling short of the glory of God" (Rom. 3:23). Human attempts at a cure for stress commonly contain disobedience to God's commands. Inappropriate Stress Relievers are a futile and painful misdirected search for God. Either God will increase in our lives and ISRs decrease, or ISRs will increase and God will decrease.

There may be a genetic predisposition to ISR activities embedded in the "deceitful" nature of humans. Some people seem to be vulnerable to becoming addicted to ISR behaviors. In theological terms, the inherent inclination towards sin makes us vulnerable, perhaps willing, to partake of forbidden fruit in seeking pleasure or to avoid pain. Genetic predispositions (heredity) form a mold that environment and events fill and influence our choice of ISRs. Various factors may trigger the ISR relief cycle. Each person seems to choose the substance or activity that matches the psychological and physical needs produced by his or her CHEESE factory.

One of the strengths/weaknesses of being human is the ability to form habits. Habits are a form of conditioning. A series of repetitions, or a strong single significant event, will create neural pathways that connect emotional states and activities. Once the neural pathways are laid down, subtle cues can be triggers for the activity — sights, sounds, smells, tastes, touches, places, memories, negative feelings, etc. The earlier in one's life the connections are formed, the harder it is to break the habit. Using ABC, there is an Antecedent, a Belief about the antecedent, and a resulting Choice of behavior. Once our belief about a circumstance is set (mindset), and we practice it enough times, the belief is no longer a conscious factor. We go directly from the Antecedent to the Choice without thinking. This sometimes results in Dire Consequences. ACDC.

In order to change from destructive behavior choices, we need a "renewing of the mind" (Rom. 12:2). A new belief and alternative practice exercises are required to change behaviors. Treatment includes choosing the "in Christ" relationship, which requires thoughtful Bible reading, meditation, prayer, fellowship in the Body of Christ, and alternative acts such as relaxation, techniques of imaging, deep breathing, and muscle relaxation, among others. Most of all, we need to rely on the Holy Spirit to be our comforter and counselor. (See chapter on Appropriate Stress Relievers.)

If the world is an unhappy place for us we will develop some type of stress-relieving behavior or behaviors. If we do not seek and find God's plan as the best ASR, emotional problems such as depression, anxiety, and anger will result. God's plan for fellowship and mutual enjoyment calls for fulfillment in Him. However, many people substitute harmful behaviors for God. We try to fill a God-sized void with something less than Him, wimpy gods.

"Wimpy gods" are ISRs and are recognized because they cause more stress. AN ISR CAUSES MORE STRESS. Unfulfilled expectations may lead those who find it difficult to deal with emotional or physical stress/pain, to choose harmful stress/pain relievers such as excessive use of alcohol, gambling, compulsive shopping, street or prescription drugs, eating disorders, inappropriate sexual activities, affairs, over-involvement in athletics or work, excessive religiosity, and/or use of nicotine. The list is much longer. You can extend it to your own situation. Each of us has, or has had, our own ISRs. These ISRs can jeopardize our psychological, as well as physical health. Those who expect ultimate fulfillment from other gods will not find satisfaction.

Note carefully that we each have our own harmful or helpful methods for dealing with stress. "Helpful methods" such as sports, church activities, or food regimens intended to reduce stress, can become excessive and disrupt health or relationships. While ISR dependence is not usually the intended goal of an addict, what begins as a stress reliever can become a stress generator.

If we always do what we have always done we will always get what we always got. And if our expectation is that more intensive use of an ISR will help, we may become addicted. The problem is, too much is never enough. We still don't find relief. We need an infinite God and that need will not be satisfied by anything less than God. In addition, while we are using the ISR, we don't grow as we should in our ability to withstand and utilize stress.

How serious are Inappropriate Stress Relievers? They can be deadly. Let's consider some obvious and some subtle ISRs using the framework of the Seven Deadly Sins as an organizer.

THE SEVEN DEADLY SINS AS INAPPROPRIATE STRESS RELIEVERS

Inappropriate Stress Relief falls short of the glory of God; hence it is sin. With a little poetic license, some obvious and some obscure ISR conditions will be considered using the Seven Deadly Sins as an organizing device. Remember, no metaphor or simile will stand up on all four feet and walk, including this one, but it may help shed light on the perils of ISRs.

Seven Deadly Sins	Man's answer/ISR
Pride	Divorce
Envy	Manipulation
Anger	Substance abuse
Sloth	Gambling
Greed	Spending
Gluttony	Misuse of food
Lust	Sexual sins

DEADLY SIN # 1 — THE SIN OF PRIDE — ISR = DIVORCE

Pride — An exaggerated idea of self-importance. When applied to marriage, one or both parties may feel their personal needs are more important than the marriage.

God said, ". . . a man will leave his father and mother and be united with his wife, and they will become one flesh" (Gen. 2:24). Unity and oneness in marriage are themes throughout the Bible and are used as examples of our relationship with God. Divorce as an ISR, when adultery, abuse, or abandonment is not present, usually has a lot to do with pride. When pride interferes with that relationship and personal needs become more important than the "one flesh" relationship, the marriage will suffer. Pride in our separate flesh will undo a marriage. (If marriage makes us "one flesh," then divorce is a rending of our flesh and it is naturally and predictively painful.)

Challenges usually do not lead to divorce. Pride, on the other hand, and unwillingness to change, often do lead to divorce. A mindset that challenges are bad may submarine the marriage because people get stuck on issues and don't bend. Personal trips to Gethsemane and Golgotha are often required. If our mindset is that the marriage will work, we will make it work.

We shouldn't think of divorce as an option while working on a marriage. A "double minded" person is unstable in all her or his ways (James 1). It is confusing to try to be loving and resentful at the same time. If we choose resentment, the ISR solution of divorce may follow.

IS DIVORCE THE ANSWER?

Sometimes married couples become so immersed in their present problems that they do not consider the future pain that a divorce decision may bring. As noted in 1 Cor. 10:13, their mindset is focused on the "test" instead of the "way to stand up" to it.

If one thinks the other person was responsible for the problem that led to divorce, they are often shocked to find similar problems in the next relationship. More second marriages end in divorce than do first marriages. A realistic look at the pain of divorce may motivate spouses to work on maintaining a marriage. What it amounts to is a question of what pain and problems you want to face. The grass may look greener on the other side of the fence but it still has to be mowed.

Being realistic about the effects of divorce on children, the legal costs incurred, the possibility of spiritual, emotional, and financial devastation, violating God's commandments, and the concern about social diseases from new relationships may motivate people to take a second look at re-inventing their present relationship. Instead of beginning a new relationship with a new partner, have a mindset to begin a new relationship with the "old" partner. If it's "My way or the highway," watch out that you don't become road kill. Don't let pride ruin your marriage.

DEADLY SIN # 2 — THE SIN OF ENVY — ISR = MANIPULATION

Manipulation — to manage unfairly to meet perceived needs. "I want you, or what you've got, more than I want your well-being." Manipulation is an ISR in that it damages relationships and creates stress.

Of all the people in the world, who would you most like to be? If the answer is "MYSELF," then you probably do not have a problem with envy. Otherwise, you envy something that someone else has and may use manipulation to try to obtain it. Most people try to structure their environment so that their perceived physical and emotional needs are met. Quite often, manipulation is used as an unfair attempt to meet those needs. Manipulating another person is usually a selfish action because the other person is being used instead of being helped. It may look as if a gift is being given but the receiver's needs are not the object. Manipulators sometimes deny or fail to recognize that their actions are meeting their own personal needs. They may even convince themselves they are being helpful.

Manipulation often comes disguised as a gift. If anger is felt when the other person does not respond to the "gift" in some expected way, manipulation was being used. Resentment builds when the attached strings don't bring the desired results. Sometimes anger shows up years later. A sure sign of manipulation is the thought or statement: "After all I've done for you!" This statement means the "helpful" actions were meant for the giver's benefit. A payback of some kind was expected. As an example, if I give a hundred-dollar bill to someone and they take out a match and burn it, and I am not offended — it was a gift. If their action causes anger, there were strings attached — it was a manipulation

Flattery, threats, "poor me," guilt trips, anger, etc. are methods of manipulation. The results often go on even after the death of the manipulator. Mental "tapes" of disappointment, pain, and lack of trust often keep on playing in the backs of our minds and become baggage in new relationships.

Anger and manipulation often go hand in hand. Some people use anger to manipulate others, especially when they recognize that peace-loving people give in when they see a tantrum coming on.

We may not be able to define manipulation but we know we are being manipulated when we feel emotionally pressured to do something we don't want to do. We feel irritated and sense that a boundary has been crossed. An irritation is a boundary violation. We need to identify the boundary and, first of all, make sure the boundary is appropriate. We need to identify the irritant and see if it is a learning experience. If the boundary and/or the irritation are not appropriate, we can seek to adjust the situation. *$$ BOUNDARY VIOLATION DIAGRAM $$*

Taking a page from science, a manipulator could be described as a parasite, something that uses up its host. Once the host is killed, the parasite moves on or dies. There are two alternatives to parasitic manipulation. Again from science, a symbiotic relationship is where both participants' needs are satisfied. The gift, or act of giving, results in mutual advantage. A second alternative is when something is done purely for another with no expectations. As an example, the word "agape" takes on special meaning as described in detail in 1 Corinthians 13. Other versions of the Bible use the word "charity," which includes the idea of giving. This giving is for the benefit of another without thought of self, unconditional giving, no strings attached, with no thought of return.

DEADLY SIN # 3 — THE SIN OF WRATH — ISR= SUBSTANCE ABUSE

Wrath is intense anger. Intense anger is such an important subject that whole books are devoted to it. In this book, a separate chapter explores anger issues. In our discussion of wrath, the ISR of substance abuse as an expression of anger is suggested. The anger might be directed at the self or as resentment against another individual, a group, society in general, or even God. Angry people usually strike out against someone, something, or themselves in order to vent their emotion. Some people misuse substances because of a rebellious attitude. They do it simply because it is wrong.

An abuser may be consciously or unconsciously punishing him or herself. The harmful effects of the abuse of alcohol, cigarettes, marijuana, street drugs, prescription drugs, over-the-counter drugs, inhalants, and other mind-altering substances are widely known, so abuse may indicate a desire to punish the self.

Misuse of substances may be an indication of low self-esteem, an expression of anger directed at the self. People sometimes use substances as an expression of anger turned inward because they think they are trash anyway so, "Why not?" (As soon as you think, "Why not?" don't.)

Angry people sometimes adopt an "I'll fix you" attitude. However, "I'll fix you" more often puts the fixer in a fix, i.e., "I'll fix you; I'll drink a six-pack." Then a stop sign may be ignored and a family might be destroyed. Who got fixed?

It is often helpful to differentiate between social/recreational drinking and emotional drinking. A few beers with friends is different from "drowning sorrows." Emotional drinkers drink to alter their mental state. Their "best thinking" gets them hooked to an ISR. Of course, either social or emotional drinking can lead to dependence. Substance abuse is an inappropriate stress reliever because it causes more stress.

DEADLY SIN # 4 — THE SIN OF SLOTH — ISR = GAMBLING

The focus of the deadly sin of sloth is on gambling for those who have become dependent on gaming in its many and various forms. Some people want something for nothing. They dream that riches will fall into their laps without effort. The mushroom-like growth of the casino industry is testimony to this desire. The problem is, the house almost always wins in the long run. The owners of casinos aren't gambling. They know they will average a predictable profit per customer. Machines can be set for a given return in the long run. A variable/ratio schedule of reinforcement is used for gambling machines because it creates the greatest potential for continued play.

Like other addictions, gambling may start for many reasons. Often a person wants to get rich quickly and easily. But once the pleasurable feeling of an endorphin rush has been experienced, the person may return to gambling to avoid the "crash" feeling, which is the rebound from the high. Belief, or rational thought, goes out the window as the gambler goes immediately from the anxiety Antecedent to the gaming Choice. (ABC) Either the need for the "high" can be eliminated or some other source of pleasure can be substituted. The pain of losing must be greater than the pain of change before some people will try to change.

The increase of availability of games of chance has brought an increase in the number of people who develop dependence on gambling. As with any addiction, the forces behind dependence are many faceted — Spiritual, Physical, Intellectual, Social, and Emotional (SPICE). These factors vary from person to person and within each person over time. As there are SPICE causal factors, there are SPICE issues involved in treatment. Effective treatment requires a clear diagnosis and/or understanding of underlying problems that will lead to a helpful intervention. Otherwise, the treatment may be misdirected and may fail, causing more harm than good. Repeated failures encourage feelings of helplessness and hopelessness.

SPICE ANALYSIS OF GAMBLING

Spiritual — There is always a spiritual component to an ISR, including gambling. We really need God but we look for relief or fulfillment in a wrong activity. If a sheep wanders from the shepherd, it will eventually find trouble of one kind or another. New saying — "You can't fill a God-sized void with a slot machine." God has placed within us a need to search for wholeness and meaning found only in Him. Some people gamble to lose, believing the punishment of losing pays for some transgression. Christ paid for our sins; we do not have to lose money as an act of atonement.

Wisdom from the Bible can provide help in kicking a habit. Meditate on the following verses and let them direct your prayers.

Philippians 4:13 — I can do all things through Christ Who strengthens me.

1 Corinthians 10:13 — He will never test us beyond our ability to endure.

1 Corinthians 6:12 — I will not be brought under the power of anything.

Physical — Some people get a "rush" out of winning and/or losing. They may be adrenaline junkies. The thought of winning (someone has to win), the bells and lights (someone is winning), and an occasional win, keep the endorphins flowing and cause a pleasurable feeling. Money is a symbol of power in our society. The idea of being part of a big money event is exhilarating for some. Some want to win to increase their fortune. Some need to lose to prove they are affluent enough to afford losing.

The best physical solution to a problem with casino gambling is to stay out of casinos.

Intellectual — Some people feel they have a "system." They can outsmart the house. They gamble on a certain night, carry a good luck charm, use a technique of pulls, etc. The 20 percent of the time they win reinforces their mindset. Their mindset filter allows them to ignore the 80 percent of the time they lose.

Out-of-control gambling is a maladaptive behavior that is an attempt to treat a perceived conscious or unconscious need. To accept responsibility and admit there is a problem is to suggest the need to change. Change is anxiety producing. Unless the causal factors are removed, or new behaviors are in place, anxiety may result in further maladaptive behaviors. One addiction may be exchanged for another. With proper counseling, the white light of honesty will eventually help with the solution.

Resolution requires confrontation of defenses. Denial is a mental component of dependence. "I don't have a problem." Some say even if they lose, the money goes for a good cause — some group's needs, or a state education fund. However, if a person wishes to give to some cause, there are reputable charities that will maximize the use of a gift for special needs. Rationalization — "I don't lose that much." "I'm not like so and so." Like the cigarette smoker who empties the ashtray every few hours so he or she doesn't have evidence of the number of cigarettes smoked, the gambler does not like to keep track of losses. An occasional $500 win is remembered while the frequent $200 losses are pushed aside. These defenses may have to be exposed and broken down before treatment can be effective. The brutal honesty of group work can be helpful here.

Community — Behind most, if not all, excessive gambling is an unhappy relationship with self, parents, spouse, children, others, or God. Those who have low self-esteem (poor relationship with the self) or an inability to find fulfillment with a significant other, may seek fulfillment with a non-human object. These objects take many forms, one of which could be a gambling apparatus.

What need is being met? Social skills training may be necessary. Sometimes a broken relationship has to be healed. Problem-solving skills, communication skills, and/or assertiveness training may help. Support groups provide encouragement and appropriate confrontation.

Emotional — There are various cycles of human behavior, for instance, the roller coaster buildup-explosion-honeymoon cycle of vi-olence. Gambling may serve as a tension-relieving activity (ISR) for some. As tension/stress/anxiety build, the sufferer seeks an outlet or stress reliever. A sense of power/control offers a fantasy life that pro-vides escape from the humdrum of reality. The crowd-noise-lights-en-ergy-excitement washes away inhibitions and, once the gambler joins the setting, he or she may find it difficult to stop until resources are depleted and/or debt is incurred.

Relaxation techniques may be helpful to reduce anxiety. Meditation, deep breathing, progressive muscle relaxation, and/or imagining be-ing in a restful place are proven techniques.

All the SPICE factors presented, and more, add up to what some call dependence. However, unless a gun is being held to the gam-bler's head, he or she is making a choice. Gambling, like other areas of dependence, requires active participation.

DEADLY SIN # 5 — THE SIN OF GREED — ISR = LIVING BEYOND OUR MEANS

The credo of the greedy person is, "I want it all and I want it now!"

The phrase "living beyond our means" usually means being in financial trouble. The astounding amount of credit card debt in this country is a painful example. Often, the use of credit cards makes purchasing easy. We are lulled into a feeling that the credit card is a blank check. When the bill arrives in the mail, we are shocked into the reality that the charges have to be paid back WITH INTEREST. The resulting debt creates stress.

With the tremendous amount of purchasing power that we have, we often find we have more clothes than closets, more gadgets than garages, and more stuff than storage. The large number of storage fa-cilities is mute testimony to this problem. We are subject to the "bigger barns" syndrome as seen in Luke 12:18. Many people mortgage their futures for the satisfaction of the present. Some folks' motto is, "I'll buy until I die, and then it is someone else's problem."

Greed extends into many areas of life. A desire for excess food, too many activities, extramarital emotional or physical involvement, and abuse of natural resources are a few examples. Living beyond our means in an attempt to relieve stress causes more stress. We can eliminate a great deal of stress by living within our means. For those of us who aren't "living beyond our means," don't start. Establish boundaries and don't cross them. It is easier to stay out of stress than to get out of stress. For those who recognize they are living beyond their means, the sometimes-painful process of bringing life under control needs to begin. Cut up the credit cards; cut off the bad relationship. It is so often necessary to choose between two options rather than try to do them both. Flip a coin if necessary. Help is available if you are not able to get your life under control by yourself. Don't let your greed exceed your grasp.

DEADLY SIN # 6 — THE SIN OF GLUTTONY — ISR = MISUSE OF FOOD

The misuse of any resource can be considered gluttony, whether it is forest products, oil, or minerals, etc. Food is one of the most misused resources in many societies today. Misuse of food is an ISR because it causes social and physical stress. The misuse of food is such a complicated issue that it is relegated to a separate chapter. The misguided perception that excessive food is needed is one of the hardest mindsets to change. Many people live to eat instead of eating to live. Food is used inappropriately for stress relief, power, celebration, and comfort. Too much food is eaten for too many reasons. Some of the reasons we eat are because food tastes good, because we are conditioned to eat, to hide or enhance body parts, to defend against relationships, and because there is a low tolerance for emotional pain.

DEADLY SIN # 7 — THE SIN OF LUST — ISR = PORNOGRAPHY

Lust creates stress. When we long to have some sin that will be harmful to us, we set up a stress situation in our lives. That stress calls for relief and most often results in the choice of an ISR. We live in a fallen world that distorts normal sexuality into lust. What God meant for procreation, re-creation, and recreation within marriage has become, for many, an obsession — an addiction. In addition to fornication and adultery, another distortion of God's intent that is affecting more and more people is the problem of viewing or needing to view pornography. Those who care more about making money than the lives of their viewers make pornography readily available through the Internet and other media sources. The ISR of seeking and viewing pornography results in strained or broken relationships, lowered self-esteem in spouses and, often, financial difficulties. *$$ EXAMINE THE PLACE OF PORNOGRAPHY $$*

Some generalities — women often base their self-esteem on their appearance while men base their self-esteem on performance. Women may go to extremes to maintain their looks while men may seek sexual prowess to maintain a sense of virility. Women hate being compared to someone's ideal of shape and activity. Men don't have that problem in our culture; they have other problems. Note the explosion of virility drugs. Those who hawk such things imply that men aren't men if they can't get an erection and have prolonged sex. Of course, the advertisements show an eager female. Life takes on an impoverished meaning if men view themselves primarily as sexual beings.

Healthy parents are needed to educate healthy children. As boys watch and listen to their fathers and other male role models, they formulate their own approach to women and sexuality. Incorrect modeling portrays women as objects and sex as power. Frequently, males are conditioned to express anger and sexuality but lack emotional and relational skills, therefore, they focus on the body. Rape is a sexual expression of anger. Men who have a mindset that they need to view pornography do not have a sense of what normal intimacy is. Parents need to teach their children to integrate sex within a relational context rather than as a fulfillment of lust.

In most cases, that which can be very good can be very bad. The bad happens when the good is distorted. The sexual relationship in marriage can be wonderful and fulfilling. On the other hand, aspects of sex can be addictive or compulsive, undermining relationships.

Appropriate sexuality will help combat distorted sexuality. When our lives are rich and full, sexuality is less likely to be distorted. It's like a lawn with healthy grass — the weeds are crowded out.

.   If you have, or someone close to you has, a problem with pornography, one step towards a solution is a SPICE approach to diagnosis and treatment.

DEALING WITH MALADAPTIVE AND/OR ADDICTIVE BEHAVIORS

First Corinthians 6:9-20 gives guidelines for dealing with a variety of maladaptive and/or addictive behaviors that were present in Corinth then, and our society today. Sexual immorality, homosexuality, drunkenness, and slandering are among the list. Note that no one of these acts is emphasized above the others but a key thought is, "that is what some of you were" (v. 11). WERE! — past tense. All of these activities, and many others, can be eliminated or controlled using the steps outlined in the following verses.

First, "You were washed, you were sanctified, you were justified in the name of the Lord Jesus Christ and by the Spirit of our God" (1 Cor. 6:11b).

Washed — "Let us draw near to God with a sincere heart in full assurance of faith, having our hearts sprinkled to cleanse us from a guilty conscience and having our bodies washed with pure water" (Heb.10:22). Washing cleanses away past sin. Note, a guilty conscience calls for a stress reliever — washing away guilt removes the motivation for an ISR.

Sanctified — "May God Himself, the God of peace, sanctify you through and through. May your whole spirit, soul, and body be kept blameless at the coming of our Lord Jesus Christ" (1 Thess. 5:23). To be sanctified is to become what God intended for us to be in the first place.

Justified — "This righteousness from God comes through faith in Jesus Christ . . . For all have sinned and fall short of the glory of God, and are justified freely by his grace through the redemption that came by Christ Jesus" (Rom. 3:22-24). To be justified is to be made right with God.

When we claim these promises, a new mindset emerges. We face the future as "new creations" (2 Cor. 5:17). The passage goes on with helpful thoughts.

The Corinthians thought they were saved by grace, not activity, so they said, "Everything is permissible for me" (I Cor. 6:12). Paul responded, "Not everything is beneficial ... I will not be mastered by anything. . . The body is not meant for sexual immorality, but for the Lord." The same power that can raise the dead will help us. We do not take the members of Christ and unite them with sin. We are to unite with the Lord and be ". . . one with Him in spirit" (1 Cor. 6:17). He who sins sexually sins against his own body. We are bought with a price and we are a temple of the Holy Spirit. We are to honor God with our bodies. Spend time in prayer, uniting with the Holy Spirit, as you allow these verses to empower you in behavior change.

Using ISRs can lead to addictive, or, new word, dependent behaviors. These behaviors present their own set of problems. We need to understand dependence and how to work to resolve it.

$ $ $ $ $ $

Treasure Chest #9
Resources for Understanding Inappropriate Stress Relievers

BOUNDARY VIOLATION DIAGRAM

Draw a circle in the middle of a sheet of paper. The circle represents boundaries shaped by our CHEESE factories. The size of the circle is inversely proportional to your feeling of control. The inside of the circle is your safe zone. In your safe zone you feel in control. Outside the circle is a world of hurt. Quite often some of that hurt penetrates your safe zone, causing stress. Draw an arrow penetrating the boundary. Label the arrow as whatever threat is irritating you. Examine the boundary. Is it appropriate and realistic? If not, renew your mind. Invite the Holy Spirit into your circle. If the boundary is righteous examine the arrow. Is God using it for your personal growth? Can the "grain of sand" produce a pearl? Discuss what growth is necessary. Gain resources and draw a bigger boundary circle to enclose the irritant, which is now under control. If your boundary is appropriate and the irritant is clearly not a messenger of God, try to do something about it. If you can't change the situation, make it an old stray cat and send it to God's door.

When we are experiencing threat or loss, our circle shrinks until we redefine our self in the world. Quite often, our redefined self closes off part of the old, keeps some of the old, and adds a new area, shown by overlapping circles.

Are you in denial? No, the Euphrates.

EXAMINING THE PLACE OF PORNOGRAPHY IN ONE'S LIFE EXERCISE

Take time to write responses to the following questions or statements. It is helpful to discuss them with your spouse.

- How do you define your "self?" Do you start with the soul, the mind, or your genitals?
- Do you worship the power to reproduce?
- Is testosterone your driving force?
- We will have a god. Often it is ourself, the creature, rather than the Creator.
- How is it affecting your prayer life?
- How is it affecting communication with your spouse?
- Selfish — wife and/or kids and all else are worth less than pornography.
- Our culture extols it — am I a victim of social conditioning?
- Is masturbation used with porn?
- Is the Internet a problem?
- How do you define your spouse?
- If she or he doesn't want sex as much as you do, is she or he less of a woman/man?
- Does God love women more if they have a bigger bra size?
- Is it a way of filling a perceived need without adultery?
- Porno may be a payback for not being fulfilled — an entitlement issue.
- What does it do for you?

STRESS AND INAPPROPRIATE STRESS RELIEVERS

- Is resentment involved?
- Porno may be a threat used to manipulate your partner.
- If the threat of porn causes a spouse to buy you off with sex, sex becomes a business.
- What percent of your day is spent involved with porn? How important is it?
- What is porn doing to your marriage?
- How is porn an addictive item for you with withdrawal, tolerance, or time spent?
- Compare the high versus the crash.
- The porno performer is being paid. There is no feeling; it's a job — strictly business; she or he doesn't care for you. She or he was usually abused as a child or teen.
- Fantasizing about a wife or co-worker as a perfect partner may lead to unrealistic expectations.
- Am I stuck in puberty, arrested development? I have this plumbing, so what is it for?
- When did viewing begin? Is it a sign of something wrong?
- If you bait a trap with a picture of a piece of cheese, you might catch a picture of a mouse.

HELPFUL STEPS IN TREATMENT

Write a "dear porno" letter. Work together on it, "In that while we were yet sinners . . ." (Rom. 5:8). Forgive each other and involve your spouse in discussing the above criteria. Don't fight it; it will get stronger. Don't fight the enemy; find a new friend — that is, replace the fantasy of porn with realism and alternate activities. Cleave yourself only unto your spouse. Enter Gethsemane; partake of Golgotha. Part of us must die with Christ that we might rise again in victory.

An obsession to view pornography is not an insurmountable problem. Rather than a sense of frustration and helplessness, we need a positive spirit and knowledge of our resources. Increase your boundary circle to include power over pornography. The chapter on Appropriate Stress Relievers suggests many things we can do on the outside while God works from the inside to help overcome the issue. Seek empowerment and meaning from God, not from sex. God will create in us a clean heart and give us self-control through His indwelling Spirit.

"THE FATHERS HAVE EATEN SOUR GRAPES AND THE CHILDREN'S TEETH ARE SET ON EDGE" (JER. 31:29). IN RELATIONSHIPS WHERE ONE OR MORE OF THE PARENTS HAS AN ADDICTION, THE CHILDREN INVARIABLY SUFFER.

CHAPTER 10

ISSUES WITH DEPENDENCE

In order to find relief from some of the effects of living with a person who is dependent on a substance or an activity, it is necessary to understand some of the complexities of relationships centered on the dependent person. Those who are dependent on the substance or activity play a very subtle blame game. Those who accept the blame are caught in a web of low self-esteem as they fail to do the impossible task of fixing the dependent person.

UNDERSTANDING DEPENDENCE

The word addiction has been applied to so many vices that a new term, dependence (exhibiting tolerance and withdrawal symptoms), is now being used to describe effects of substance abuse. It is our position that we can misuse either or both substances and activities and the use of either can result in physiological and/or psychological dependence. Dependence on harmful substances or activities stems from mindsets brought about by CHEESE/SPICE factors. Therefore these factors must be considered in a comprehensive ISR/ASR approach that explores contributing and healing elements that pertain to the problem behavior.

INAPPROPRIATE STRESS RELIEVER
IDENTIFICATION*

One of the characteristics of dependence is denying that there is a problem. One of the most necessary steps in recovery is admitting that there is a problem. Denial makes it difficult to be honest. Denial is unlikely when we are completely honest with others, and ourselves, especially if we are open to the suggestions of those who love us. The following exercise will help you understand whether or not you have a dependence problem. Write down the ISR you are examining — alcohol, sports, sex, shopping, etc. — and check the items that you know are true. If three or more items are checked, you have a problem that needs attention. Remember; be honest.

1.   __ TOLERANCE: needing more of the substance or activity to have the same result until the substance or activity controls (owns) you.

2.   __ WITHDRAWAL: stopping use of the substance or activity results in physical and/or emotional discomfort when returning to a normal state.

3.   __ More money than intended is spent using the substance or activity.

4.   __ You find yourself unsuccessful in trying to cut down or quit.

5.   __ The substance or activity uses up more and more time.

6.   __ You choose companions and activities that involve the substance.

7.   __ Healthy relationships, occupation, or recreational activities suffer.

8.   __ You keep on doing it when you know it is having harmful consequences.

9.   __ You are planning the next time during this time.

10. __ You resent other people implying you have a problem.

Amended from the Diagnostic and Statistical Manual of Mental Disorders, Fourth Edition. 1994. The American Psychiatric Association, 1400 K Street, N.W., Washington, DC 20005.

Whether the problem is alcoholism, workaholism, sportaholism, or any other ism, in our counseling clients with dependence issues, we use any method or combination of methods that is effective in bringing relief. Several approaches are listed for consideration in the chapter on Appropriate Stress Relievers. We believe that mentally healthy people have the capacity for choice and they are responsible for the actions their choices produce. If poor choices have been made, the error needs to be admitted and corrected within the "in Christ" relationship.

It is interesting to note that a person who is dependent upon a substance, or any other ISR for that matter, will often find someone whose CHEESE factory has resulted in their being an enabler. Those who enable dependent people are said to be codependent.

CODEPENDENCE

There are about as many definitions of codependency as there are definers. We propose this one: If one person depends on another's dependence, there is codependency. That is, my sickness is that I need for you to be sick. If I am codependent (Co) then I need someone to have a dependence problem (Dep). My sense of well-being depends on my maintaining Dep's ISR. Co acts in such a way that Dep reacts in a predictable manner and vice versa.

Codependency is sometimes seen in relationships where one person (Dep) has a problem with alcohol and the other person (Co) supports the user's habit. The term codependency, along with the term addiction, has been extended to a variety of behaviors. Often, a person who has a problem behavior will gravitate towards someone who will support the problem just as an enabler seeks, consciously or unconsciously, a dependent person to help. A passive person will find an aggressive person who will find a passive person, and so on ad nauseam. The Dep/Co interaction is often seen in abusive relationships.

An abuser has rage to express. A person with low self-esteem or a guilt complex may find someone who satisfies their need to be punished. Codependent people are usually driven by guilt. They need to make up for something in their background that they feel will be solved by investing themselves in the problems of another person.

Co needs someone to fix. Quite often, a child who grows up with a parent who has a dependency problem will become a caregiver. The child feels important in this role and a state of equilibrium is established. Without intervention he or she will find an adult partner with a similar problem and attempt to resolve the problem or to prolong the feeling of self-worth generated by feeling necessary; hence the equilibrium is transferred to the new relationship. If the equilibrium is unbalanced by the recovery of one of the persons, the relationship may break down. Therefore Co or Dep may sabotage the healing process. One or both may complain about the situation outwardly but inwardly, psychological equilibrium requires the problem to continue. We will find, or create, a relationship that fits our dysfunction.

In treatment, an effort is made to find the roots of codependency. Then satisfactory alternative behaviors can be formulated and acted upon. Again, see the chapter on Appropriate Stress Relievers. Each person must be helped to move towards a neutral, well-balanced relationship. Hopefully, a strong conviction will motivate Dep and Co to find solutions in God instead of seeking an ISR.

Whether or not one wants to accept the labels of addiction or dependence, two questions should be asked to determine if steps should be taken to change: 1) Does "it" control me or do I control "it?" 2) Is my life, my relationship, or my job suffering because of my choices? If the answer to either of these questions is yes, GET HELP. Find and use appropriate alternative behaviors.

THE BLAME GAME

A dependent person (Dep) who chooses to blame another has to be in a position of power. Hence, he or she will surround himself or herself with weak or wounded enablers. The power position is the source of much emotional abuse. Quite often, children, women, or minorities become scapegoats for people in power who have no desire to change. The power and control offered by the position add to the difficulty in change. Once an abuser categorizes a less powerful person or group as sub-human, they can be abused without the abuser feeling guilt.

Abused people often believe it IS their fault when bad things happen to them. Part of this belief comes from the need to feel that the world is a predictable place and that they have some control over what happens. Battered women lose the ability to correctly assign blame. "I'm being punished so I must be doing something wrong." Another wrong belief occurs when children take the side of a parent who is abusing his or her spouse. The child believes the abused person must be doing something wrong or they wouldn't be punished. Rape victims will sometimes blame themselves for wearing the wrong clothes or being in the wrong place.

Children are totally dependent on adults and find it necessary to believe that adults are good and trustworthy. Parents, or other adults, cannot be blamed. "Mom and Dad can't be wrong or the world is a very scary place; therefore, I must be wrong." Often dysfunctional Deps reinforce these self-shaming messages. "If you would behave I wouldn't lose my temper." Children may be told they are provocative, uncooperative, stupid, etc. Children are subject to magical thinking. They often believe they control events by their thoughts. To make sense out of the negative events in life there has to be fault somewhere. "If I do something bad, I get punished. So, if I'm being punished I must have done something bad." "It must be me." If they think they did something wrong, there is reason and causality to events that makes abuse easier to accept.

Children, when old enough to reason, feel guilt for what they have done wrong. They understand appropriate discipline. But if they are punished when they haven't done anything wrong, they will develop shame for who they are. Guilt is for what I have done; shame is for who I am. Guilt has to do with human doing; shame has to do with human being. Abused or neglected children may develop a shame mindset that comes with being blamed when they weren't in the wrong. "I don't know of anything I did wrong but I am being blamed so I must BE wrong — damaged goods — basically trash. If I am trash, then I must deserve trash. I'll trash my education, date trash, marry trash, and may choose a trashy way to make a living." Because they think they are trash, they make trashy decisions. The trash just keeps on piling up and they live in the garbage dumps of their lives. Quite often other people's trash gets dumped on them. Children of divorce, incest, neglect, or abuse need to know that the trash in their lives is not their fault. Someone has to give them assurance that they were not to blame, i.e., a ticket out. If you are suffering because someone made bad choices against you, you are not at fault. Talk to someone who cares. *$$ LIVING IN GARBAGE INTERVENTION $$*

When Don was a teacher he used to have trouble with trash on the floor. The trashier the floor, the more the students trashed it. Then a "ticket" was required from each student to get out of the room. The ticket was something from the floor that didn't belong there. He soon had one of the cleanest floors in school. Hopefully, the students learned that life is easier to keep clean than to get clean. Our lives become clean when we realize that the faith God gives us is our ticket out of our lives, no matter how trashy.

ENABLING

Enabling is a term that accompanies codependency. Co enables Dep to continue the dependent behavior because Co needs for Dep to have the problem. Co makes excuses for Dep, makes provisions for Dep's perceived needs, and cleans up Dep's messes. If Dep gets better, Co suffers and may leave the relationship. Co's harmful mindset will often lead him or her into a vicious cycle, going from one Dep to another.

Most dependent people are intertwined with a codependent person or group, both feeding on and enabling the other. Those who are codependent also need help. Their problems come in many forms that are braided in with the problems of the dependent one. The person using an ISR will blame God, circumstances, or others for the problem so they don't have to change. The other person assumes responsibility and a relationship achieves equilibrium. Generally assigning and accepting blame are part of an ISR relationship. It is fascinating how people use blame to work for them. "You're making me crazy!" "If you wouldn't burn my toast, I wouldn't have to beat you with my fists." Generally, Deps blame others, events, or things for their habits. They won't take ownership of the problem and therefore won't change. This mindset is called denial. "I don't have a problem, you do." The dependent person will manipulate his or her spouse or children to take responsibility for the problem and expect them to fix it. The spouse and/or children may become codependent enablers. They devote a great deal of their time, emotions, and focus in life on the problem. They become dependent upon Dep's illness and they often lose themselves in the transaction. A combination of CHEESE personality traits such as sensitivity, compassion, and empathy, all good things if not abused, can be misused by a blaming dependent person to develop a deep-seated mindset of guilt in Co with long-lasting characteristics that are difficult to change. Typically, once the mindset of guilt is formed, Co will see confirming evidence to support it. *$$ THE ENABLING PROCESS $$*

Cos need to be transformed by the renewing of the mind (Rom. 12:2). The mindset has to change. The convicting power of the Holy Spirit will open the mind of Co and begin the healing process. The Spirit convicts not only of sin but also of righteousness so Co can be led from illness into health.

If any person is in Christ, that person is a new creation, the old has gone; the new has come (2 Cor. 5:17). We need a new CHEESE factory. We need to recognize and <u>Choose</u> our new <u>Heredity</u> as a child of God; develop a new <u>Environment</u> of prayer, Bible study, meditation, and fellowship with like-minded believers; and structure <u>Events</u> that confirm our new self. Our <u>Self-Esteem</u> has to come from God's esteem for us, coupled with a new attitude regarding ourself. God doesn't make us into junk.

One of the deep motivations for Cos is that they inherently realize that Dep's attachment to his or her "substance" is more important than Co is. Co may strive to become more important than the substance. When that doesn't happen, anger and acting out may occur. Without knowing why, a deep sense of abandonment occurs. A parent doesn't have to leave home to abandon a child. The alcohol, the TV, etc. will suffice.

The problem with taking ownership of Dep's problem is that Co cannot fix Dep. As Co continues to fail, a deep sense of shame and inadequacy may develop. Co's self-image may become that of a loser with a negative sense of self-worth because she or he can't fix the problem. It is a terrible thing when a child assumes blame for an adult's lack of self-control.

Not succeeding in the family of origin, Co may be driven to find Dep after Dep to fix. Co may go from one dysfunctional relationship to another. Co's addiction to Dep's problem entails an ever-increasing need to cure Dep and, paradoxically, a sense of loss if Dep gets better — a real rock and a hard place. The relationship often is broken if only one person gets better. It is best that healing for both dependent and codependent occur at the same time so the relationship isn't broken. Dep needs to replace the substance or activity with an ASR and Co needs to replace the need to rescue with a healthy, well-balanced relationship. As the problems are interrelated, the healing process is also interrelated.

The first step in overcoming the problem of being a Co of a dependent person is to realize that Dep's problem is not Co's problem. The second step is to refuse to take ownership of Dep's problem and stop enabling. Give up trying to fix people. We can't change them; we can only give them something different to react to. The decision to overcome being a Co has to be made; the rest is process. We shouldn't let someone else's problem mess up our lives.

There are many Cos in the helping professions. One of the quickest ways to burn out in the people business is to try to do someone else's work for them. We have to be careful because many clients would rather do anything than change. They will try to turn their caregiver into a Co and get them to take over responsibility for the problem. If the client can play his or her game with the therapist, both suffer. We have a duty to make clients accept responsibility for their problems.

We are SPICE people — Spiritual, Physical, Intellectual, Social, and Emotional. To change the latter four, a person's emphasis and focus needs to be empowered by the Holy Spirit so the other four can be influenced. When serving and following God becomes Dep's or Co's primary need, God's power, fruit, gifts, direction and assurance make change possible. The work of Christ and the Holy Spirit is to produce in us the image for which we were created. In that image we can fellowship with God. He gives forgiveness, power, and healing. When we are in Christ, we are new creations; we know that God's grace is sufficient, and that He is at work in all things for good.

ADULT CHILDREN OF DEPENDENT PARENTS

The acronym ACOA — Adult Children of Alcoholics — is useful for those dealing with the problems that result from having an alcoholic parent(s). However, the parent doesn't have to be an alcoholic to have a negative effect on a child. Children will demonstrate many of the same characteristics if one or both parents have a dependence on any drug or activity of choice that is more important than members of the family. The parent may be overly involved with work or sports, obsessed with a friend, another person, etc. Therefore, we feel Adult Children of Dependent (ACOD) is more appropriate.

Generally, people who have grown up in families where there was dependence on the part of one or both parents will recognize themselves in many of the following items. These lists are a take-off from the SPICE rack. The spiritual aspect will be supportive of efforts to deal with the other elements. The columns are not intended to correlate across or down.

Not all ACODs demonstrate all of the following traits. However, enough do to establish patterns. Circle items that you feel apply to you. Discuss each circled item. When did it start? What was going on at the time? Has it been resolved? Determine a solution using one of the problem-solving methods presented in chapters 12 and 13.

CHARACTERISTICS OF ACODs

PHYSICAL	INTELLECTUAL	SOCIAL	EMOTIONAL
Migraine headaches	Confusion	Distrust	Fear
Ulcers, colitis	All or nothing-	High tolerance for-	Guilt
Digestive problems	thinking	inappropriateness	Anxiety
Muscle tension	Memory gaps	Crisis orientation	Shame
Sleep disorders	Perfectionism	Hard to have fun	Depression
Stress disorders	Indecision	Over-dependent	Sadness
Eating disorders	Hypervigilance	Intimacy problems	Anger/Rage
Allergies	Self-hatred	Manipulative	Resentment
Sexual dysfunction	Self-devaluing	Controlling	Loneliness
Chemical -	Underachieving	Anxiety/Panic	Numbness
dependency	Compulsive-thinking	Over-responsible	Bitterness

ACODs often do not know what normal is. Their lives have been so subnormal that normal seems abnormal. Normal families seem strange to them. Again, not all of these characteristics apply to every ACOD. Circle or check the number of any characteristic that you have seen in your life.

1. __ They are used to chaos and either find or create chaos to use coping skills developed in the family of origin.

2. __ They don't finish jobs or frequently change jobs.

3. __ Lies and deceptions come naturally to them.

4. __ They accept blame when not at fault. They say "I'm sorry" a lot.

5. __ Life is serious. They don't play or do not enjoy play.

6. __ They feel a strong need to be in control.

7. __ Close relationships are difficult to form.

8. __ They crave affection and may perceive abuse as love.

9. __ They hunger for praise.

10. __ They feel uncomfortable around normal people.

11. __ They are perfectionists.

12. __ They defend people who mistreat them.

13. __ They spend a lot of time trying to fix others.

14. __ They have a problem with delayed gratification.

15. __ They are apprehensive bordering on paranoia.

16. __ They have abandonment issues.

17. __ They fear success and shoot themselves in the foot.

18. __ They don't respect authority.

19. __ They get upset when criticized.

20. __ Their lives and surroundings are a mess.

21. __ They are indecisive.

22. __ They go to great lengths to be accepted.

23. __ They may pester others for affirmation.

24. __ They feel they are less important than their parent's substance or activity.

SUGGESTIONS FOR ALTERNATIVE STRESS RELIEVERS

It is necessary to realize that both Dep and Co have dependence problems. Dep is dependent on a substance or activity, and Co depends on Dep to have a problem. Treatment for either one involves many of the same steps.

- Focus on the individual. Utilize CHEESE/SPICE and problem-solving models to create a program that fits the individual need. Explore the social and personal consequences of the habit. List "wet faces and wet places" (tempting people and locations). Build individual social skills and coping strategies. Develop problem-solving strategies that are alternatives to masking the problem with a substance or activity.

- Use a buddy. Learn relational skills of communication and common interests. Utilize all the social support you can.

- Pool the resources of the entire family to avoid enabling and to set boundaries of behavior.

- Involve the community in prevention and rehabilitation programs.

- List triggers for abuse. Avoid negative emotional states, i.e., HALT — Hungry, Angry, Lonely, and Tired. Depression, anxiety, frustration, or boredom should be recognized as high-risk situations and need to be dealt with before they become triggers for use. Money is a big trigger. A money manager may be required.

- Twelve-step programs are usually available and have been adapted to assist in working with different areas of dependence.

- Individual and group counseling can be helpful.

- Encourage desire. Foundational to any change is the desire to change. If either Dep or Co resists efforts to help, there is little that can be done. In Chapter 11 we look at factors involved in the process of change.

$ $ $ 🔑 $ $ $

Treasure Chest #10
Resources for Understanding Dependence Issues

LIVING IN GARBAGE INTERVENTION

Draw a picture of a dump with piles of garbage. Label the piles with ways you are living in the garbage dump of your past. The good news is that you can give each bit of your garbage to God, trusting His promises to deal appropriately with your sins and the sins of those who have harmed you. Discuss how He may be using that event for growth in your maturity and for His purpose.

THE ENABLING PROCESS

There are many steps in the Dep/Co process. Not all aspects are necessarily present in each person.

A. A person (Dep) has become dependent upon a substance or activity.

B. Dep denies having a problem.

C. Co goes through life finding people to fix.

D. Dep and Co find each other.

E. Dep consciously or unconsciously makes or allows Co to take responsibility for Dep's problem.

F. Dep enjoys the power over Co.

G. Co assumes responsibility for the problem because of some unconscious need.

H. Co makes excuses for Dep and takes the blame.

I. Dep is forgiven and not held responsible.

J. Co has a driving need to fix Dep.

K. Co wants to be more important than the problem to Dep.

L. Co cannot solve the problem.

M. Co becomes hard on himself or herself.

N. Co develops a sense of inadequacy and shame.

O. Co develops negative mindsets.

P. Co may self-medicate and develop his or her own dependent behaviors.

Q. Co may become a perfectionist.

R. Co has a gnawing sense of worthlessness because of his or her "failure" and may accept abusive behavior as justifiable.

S. Co has unrealistic expectations that are impossible to meet.

T. Anger, depression and anxiety are often present.

U. The symptoms are masked but not cured.

V. Other problems often jam up behind the need to fix others.

W. If not interrupted, the Dep/Co cycle repeats through relationships and/or generations.

CHAPTER 11

THE DESIRE TO CHANGE

"Be transformed by the renewing of your minds" (Rom. 12:2). Transformation is change. Renewal is change. But why is change so difficult? So far, we've looked at positive and negative mindsets and those things that help shape them. Obviously, our positive mindsets should be kept. But, what about the negative ones? We know they aren't contributing to joyous lives. As we shall see, the ability to change depends on the hope that change is possible, the mindset that we are in control, the mindset that change will alleviate pain, and a process that helps change to occur. First:

THE EXODUS

The book of Exodus, and the continuing saga in Numbers and Joshua, is an amazing story of change. The initial pain necessary to promote the desire to change, the years of wandering, the grumbling, the inappropriate stress relievers, and the failure to accomplish the God-given goal of reaching the Promised Land are like so many of today's personal stories. It took tremendous stress in order for the different people in the Exodus story to change. Bricks without straw for the Israelites (Exod. 5:18) and death of the first born for Pharaoh

(Exod. 7-11). Only the pain of Goshen forced the Israelites out to the promise of Canaan. Only the loss of the first-born forced Pharaoh to release the Israelites.

God gave His chosen people many opportunities to trust Him but they continually grumbled and wanted to go back to Goshen. How often we are tempted to go back to our Inappropriate Stress Relievers (ISRs). The Israelites used ISRs in that they made idols, worshipped false gods, held on to habits and customs (negative mindsets) of their old lives, and married unbelievers. All of these things kept them from receiving what was promised.

During Moses' 120-year life-span, God had him spend 40 years in Pharaoh's palace to get an intimate knowledge of Egyptian life and 40 years tending his father-in-law's sheep in the wilderness to gain an intimate knowledge of desert life, all so he could spend the next 40 years leading God's sheep out of Egypt through the same wilderness. Isn't that neat? God sees the end from the beginning.

Moses met God at Horeb (Exod. 3:1). During that meeting Moses had a conversation with God (Exod. 3:4-17). Moses asked, "Who am I?" God answered, "You are the person with whom I will be." Moses asked, "What shall I tell them You are called?" That is, "Who are You?" God answered, "I AM." No beginning, no end. Moses said, "They won't listen to me." God said, "I will give you signs and wonders." Then Moses said, "I can't talk plainly." God said, "I will help you speak and will teach you what to say."

When Moses was out of excuses, he cried out, "O Lord, please send someone else to do it." How Moses could call God Lord and refuse Him at the same time is interesting (we all do it) but God already had plan B in motion. "Your brother Aaron is on the way." We learn a lot about being stuck in mindsets and resistance to change from the book of Exodus. How many ways do we attempt to put off God's design for our lives?

God met with Moses "in the back side of the desert" (Exod. 3:1) to change his mindsets and to make him an agent of change. Have you been there? Have you met God there? He was there, is there, and is with you now in "the back side" of your present experience. We all have our own arguments with God. Have you settled yours?

When we have resentment towards God, resistance to positive change occurs. One of the reasons we fail to obtain God's promises is that we are so busy worrying about our wilderness that we don't find the Promised Land. Sometimes we see the thorns as "giants in the land," that is, obstacles. (Num. 13:38). We then see ourselves as grasshoppers, weak and ineffective. There will always be thorns (2 Cor. 12). (Remember the safety and control oval and the threat arrow.) We need to choose to live in grace amongst the thorns. God will either remove the thorn if it is harmful, or allow it if we are to gain maturity from it, and it is according to His purpose to help others (mindset). Living in grace amongst thorns is a greater miracle than thorn removal.

PAIN AND CHANGE

We will usually put up with a lot of stress before we will change. Sometimes the only thing that causes us to accept the pain of change is the greater pain of staying the same. We need to choose our pain; choose our joy. Use a Pain/Joy Chart. We either have the pain of change or the painful consequences of not changing. We need to choose the joy of new behaviors versus the joy of the familiar. Someone has to start the process; seldom is that person someone else. The change starts with a change of attitude — a mindset to change.

"Therefore, since Christ suffered in his body, arm yourself also with the same attitude, because he who has suffered in his body is done with sin" (1 Pet. 4:1). We need a powerful attitude to change — the same attitude Jesus had when He ". . . set his face to go to Jerusalem" (Luke 9:51).

We can look at Jesus' experience in Gethsemane for help in changing. His humanity really did not want to accept the pain of the cross. "Father, if you are willing, take this cup from me," but His divinity said, "Yet not my will, but yours be done . . . and being in anguish, he prayed more earnestly, and his sweat was like drops of blood falling to the ground" (Luke 22:42, 44).

We know the human side all too well. We say it's too painful to give up our mindsets about excessive food, gambling, alcohol, pornography, bitterness, gossip, blame, etc. "If there is any way possible, let me keep my ISR and remain in my misery." However, if we are "in Christ," His divinity empowers us to leave the old life. "If any person be in Christ, that person is a new creation . . . the old has gone . . ." (2 Cor. 5:17).

The results are worth the pain of change. "During the days of Jesus' life on earth, he offered up prayers and petitions with loud cries and tears to the one who could save him from death, and he was heard because of his reverent submission. Although he was a son, he learned obedience from what he suffered and, once made perfect, he became the source of eternal salvation for all who obey him" (Heb. 5: 7-9). We can become instruments of salvation for others as we submit to God. (Incidentally, the word for submission here is the same one used in Ephesians 5 where it says we are to submit one to another. Sub-mission — we submit ourselves to the mission.)

There are times that we are so subnormal that normal seems abnormal. New behaviors must be practiced until they feel normal, familiar and predictable. It takes ten or twenty repetitions of a new behavior before it starts to feel comfortable and normal feels normal. When the new behavior is set in place, the former behavior will feel uncomfortable. Arm yourself with courage and fortitude. The journey of change will be easier if you don't look back. Lot's wife looked back and turned into a pillar of salt (Gen. 19:26). We don't want to share her fate. The ISRs need to be old stray cats. Don't feed them, don't pet them, and don't chase them around with a broom

Changes in life present several problems. Some people will do anything but change. We know when a baby needs changing. Phew! The fourteen-pound diaper has reached sixteen pounds. And we know what to do. Lovingly, with a smile, we remove the old, cleanse the area, powder, and apply a new or clean diaper. Colossians 3:5-17 indicates a "diaper changing" process for a person entering the "in Christ" relationship. Put off the old man and negative habits. Put on newness that reflects Christ's nature in you. Put on your new suit of clothing.

We need to admit that what we are doing is not in our best interest, that our lives are a mess, and that a new mindset leading to change is needed. But we don't like to admit that it is our behaviors that are at fault so we play the blame game. My parents were wrong, God is wrong, something — anything else — is wrong, so it's not my fault and I don't have to change. "If I can just blame someone else, I'm off the hook." Alibis began in the Garden of Eden. However, it didn't work for Adam and it won't work for us.

HOPE IS NECESSARY FOR CHANGE

FALSE HOPES

Those whose minds are conformed to the world, hope someone or something else will change so they won't have to. They are fundamentally convinced that they are not so bad and, anyway, it is the world that is wrong. If something else changes they won't have to, so they spend their time and energy making their lives, and others', miserable by trying to force them or the world to change.

Sometimes we believe, or hope, that if WE change, the world will change. Think about it. The world resists change also. In fact, if we change, the world usually tries to force us back into its mold (Rom. 12:2). People "have our number." Change on our part almost always involves change in relationships. Change on our part upsets their mindset of us and "rocks their boat." They had us all figured out and now our behaviors are disturbing their equilibrium. Most people are reactors. They are pinballs, beaten around by the paddles of life. They are like water that takes the form of whatever environment holds it. We can't change others — we can only give them something different to react to.

The stress of change presents a huge challenge. We may have to leave our "discomfort zone," which, paradoxically, is causing us pain. As distressful as a discomfort zone may be, it offers some security simply because it is familiar and predictable. Change represents new territory and we tend to fear the unknown. We hesitate to enter "the Promised Land" because of the "giants" that occupy it.

HELPFUL HOPE

When our minds are transformed so that we have the mind of Christ, there is hope that change will make the future better. In speaking to those brought back from exile, God said, "I know the plans I have for you, plans to prosper you and not to harm you, plans to give you hope and a future. Then you will call upon me and come and pray to me, and I will listen to you. You will seek me and find me when you seek me with all your heart. I will be found by you and will bring you back from captivity . . ." (Jer. 29:11-14). "In his great mercy, he has given us new birth into a living hope through the resurrection of Jesus Christ from the dead, and into an inheritance that can never perish spoil or fade . . ." (1 Pet. 1:3-4a). "HOPE AND A FUTURE," "A LIVING HOPE."

It is hard to change even if we feel at fault. Thankfully, as Christians, we can admit our need to change because we have the "In Christ" relationship of God's grace complete with the mind of Christ. I can admit error when I feel safe, when I'm convinced I'm forgiven, and when I know that God is in control.

CONTROL AND CHANGE

Much of psychology is about control and change. Regardless of our circumstances, if we feel a measure of control, we resist change. Change may be hindered by mindsets, perceptions, expectations, and coping behaviors developed from our CHEESE factories. These factors are so ingrained that change is incredibly difficult.

Control is a huge factor in emotional well-being. Perceptions of loss of control and inadequate resources are key factors in the whole range of anxiety manifestations. When our perception of control in a situation is threatened, we go on the defensive and become reluctant to proceed with change. In order to change, we either need to feel that we are in control or have faith that someone else, or God, is in control.

If our mindset is that we have no control, very little change will be effected because we will be too busy defending our position.

> You could see the white knuckles as "Herman" clung to the arms of the chair in my office. His anger had served him well all these years. It had absolved him of blame. Very few people had ever crossed him. Other drivers, his family, God — all were scapegoats for his lack of self-control. But now his wife had left him, his children were avoiding him, and he was envisioning a bitter, lonely, and Godless end to what years he had left.

I asked him, and I ask you, the reader, if you're experiencing Herman's problem or some other ISR. Did you ever know you should change, must change, but hope beyond hope that someone or something else would change so you wouldn't have to? Why is it so hard to change? Our mindset makes us feel an ISR is working and then the ISR creates a mindset that we are in control. Our mindset won't let us see evidence to the contrary. Once we have activated an ISR, a combination of pride and the fear of returning to our former state make it difficult to release it. ISRs give a false sense of control. We want control and the natural mind seeks an ISR instead of an ASR. Our nature lies to us. Our deceitful mind makes us believe we are in control. We need the mind of Christ so that our minds can be renewed.

In Exodus 23:27-30, we are told that change will occur ". . . little by little . . ." until we increase enough to take possession of the land. These steps of change allow us to have a mindset of control, God's and ours, so we are not overwhelmed by change. This verse can also be applied to parenting. It sometimes seems like a slow process but perseverance will usually win out. *$$ YARDSTICK INTERVENTION $$*

GODLY CHANGE IS NECESSARY AND GOOD

Appropriate change is a process. The Holy Spirit convicts us to begin our Christian walk, and He convicts us of the need to change during our Christian walk. "When the Spirit comes, he will convict the world of guilt in regard to sin and righteousness and judgment" (John 16:8). Note: The Holy Spirit convicts in three areas — sin, righteousness, and judgment.

According to Jesus' teaching in John 16:9, sin is not believing in Him — stuck in negative mindsets and ISRs. Therefore, the opposite of sin is believing in Jesus — His wonderful mindset changing involvement in our lives. The Spirit of God convicts us of sin and the need to change. If change is only a whim on our part, we may not have God's assistance in the process. If the Holy Spirit is convicting us of a need to change, we can be sure that His power is available to help us change. However, God will not do for us what we should do for ourselves.

The Holy Spirit convicts us of righteousness. It is interesting to note that while the natural mind is not able to comprehend righteousness, God will reveal it to us through His Spirit. We are not like the old metaphor of the caterpillar that doesn't know what it is like to be a butterfly. The Spirit tells us what butterfly life is like. We now have a mindset of righteousness that facilitates positive choices.

The Holy Spirit convicts us of judgment. We now have a mindset that sin is wrong and we resist it. Then we know that God will deal justly with those who have offended us. Many people don't want to change because they want their lives to show that the offender should be punished. They live in their garbage dump and hope the other person is miserable. They take poison and hope the other person dies. How smart is that? When we accept God's true and just judgment (Rev. 19:2), we can release our resentment, live unfettered lives, and trust God to deal appropriately with our abusers.

We have to be convicted by the Holy Spirit in each of these three areas in the process of the renewing of our minds. (There may be times we need to determine the source of our mindset by taking a tour through our CHEESE factory to find and deal with the source.) Once we are convinced of the need to change we must repent (have sorrow about) our old ways.

GODLY SORROW LEADS TO CHANGE

As the change process continues, there must be godly sorrow as described in 2 Corinthians 7:10-11. "Godly sorrow brings repentance that leads to salvation and leaves no regret, but worldly sorrow brings death." It isn't enough just to admit sin; we need to repent. To repent is to turn to the opposite way, a "180." Sometimes people want a 179-degree turn. They want a little leeway and this 1-degree pulls them back. Repentance is an essential element in the process of changing one's mind so a change of behavior will occur. In other words, repentance results in a different mindset as seen in Romans 12:2. We need to change our mindsets because many of the consequences of sin stem from harmful thoughts — stinking thinking. Salvation means deliverance from sin and its consequences and new birth into right living — from death to life.

Worldly sorrow does not bring about a change in habits. Often, it only makes a person sneakier. A person may be sorry he or she got caught, sorry he or she has a problem, sorry things are the way they are, or sorry enough to be more careful next time, but have no desire to change behavior. The person will do it again if he or she isn't concerned about getting caught. When I (Don) was a child, I stole money from my mother's purse. I was whipped with a belt. I learned not to steal from my mother. After that, I confined my stealing to non-family members and stores. Worldly sorrow leads to resentment. "I won't do that again." Not because it is wrong, but because the price is too high. However, worldly sorrow will come out in some other way, usually in an expression of rage. Worldly sorrow involves bargaining or bartering. "I'll do this if you do that." We try to manipulate to gain more than we lose.

Godly sorrow leaves no regret. Godly sorrow is an ASR; it brings positive change. Positive change leads to enhanced self-esteem, empowerment, and enjoyment. Worldly sorrow leaves a trail of regrets and, sooner or later, leads to death.

CHARACTERISTICS OF GODLY SORROW

Recognizing what powerful forces are necessary for change to occur, Paul lists seven characteristics of godly sorrow in 2 Corinthians 7:11 — "See what this godly sorrow has produced in you":

"what earnestness" — serious intention, sincerely zealous,

"what eagerness to clear yourselves" — enthusiasm to make riddance,

"what indignation" — strong displeasure and dislike for the old behavior,

"what alarm" — fear caused by the presence of danger for self and/or others,

"what longing" — strong persistent craving for resolution,

"what concern" — distress, apprehension about the problem,

"what readiness to see justice done" — willingness to do it God's way.

Some of the characteristics of godly sorrow pertain to the past; some indicate how we are to act in the future. If we are earnest, eager, indignant, alarmed, filled with longing, motivated by concern, and ready to see justice done, there is hope for change.

In Luke 18:22, the story is told of a man who had great wealth. He also kept the commandments. Perhaps he wanted a pat on the back or maybe his life wasn't satisfactory, so he came to Jesus. When asked to give up his wealth, he went away sorrowing (earthly sorrow) because he had "great possessions." While the story says he kept other commandments, in turning away he violated the first commandment, "You shall have no other gods before me" (Exod. 20:2). It is important to note that Jesus didn't run after him saying, "There, there, it's okay, you don't have to give up your wealth."

Sometimes, our mindsets, perceptions, expectations, coping behaviors, or bitterness and lack of forgiveness for self or others are of great importance to us. They represent our emotional wealth, our "god." Jesus asks us to give up the negative and follow Him. Are you ready to give up your emotional wealth and make changes? Are you willing to change your mindsets?

THE DESIRE TO CHANGE

GETHSEMANE, GOLGATHA, GARDEN

We may need a Gethsemane experience for change to occur. Either use of the ISR will be chosen or we face Gethsemane. Often, an excruciating decision needs to be made. We often need the Gethsemane of Decision, The Golgotha of Death, and the Garden of new Direction. We need GOD. Gethsemane (The Olive Press — how fitting) was a lonely place for Jesus; His followers were sleeping. In Luke 22:40-46, we find that Jesus prayed earnestly (according to Hebrews 5:7, with "loud cries and tears") that some other way than His death on the cross might be sufficient for atonement (at-one-ment). There was none. Sin was too terrible! Then, under the conviction of the Holy Spirit, Jesus said, "Thy will be done."

Once the decision is made, the rest is process. Once our Gethsemane experience has convicted us that change is God's will, the old way will have to die — we will have a Golgotha experience. Our ISRs have to go on the cross with Christ Who "became sin for us" (2 Cor. 5:21). All of the stress-relieving compensatory activities (translation — bad habits) that we have used to deal with the pain of our guilt are no longer needed. Sinful stress relievers that caused more stress are washed away by the only stress reliever that brings joy and peace, Jesus Christ our Lord.

When the old man dies we are ready for the Garden of New Directions — the abundant life in Christ. This is like a resurrection experience. We must be sure to realize that newness of life in Christ requires our personal Gethsemanes and Golgothas — decisions and deaths of our sinful ways. As we grow in Christ, we may experience this process many times. What Gethsemane are you now in or should you now enter?

GETHSEMANE/GOLGOTHA/GARDEN EXERCISE

Gethsemane — What tough decision is the Holy Spirit convicting you to make?

Golgotha — What part of you has to die in order for this to happen?

Garden — What new, more wonderful, way of life is awaiting you?

Once the Holy Spirit convinces us to change, we need a process whereby change can occur. The next two chapters offer procedures that can be used to radically alter our lives and relationships.

$ $ $ ⚷ $ $ $

Treasure Chest #11
Resources for Helping with Change
YARDSTICK INTERVENTION

Many changes require a period of time or a series of steps. Place a yardstick on the floor in front of you. The yardstick represents the time or steps involved that are ahead of you. Push the yardstick ahead with your toe. The whole job is still ahead of you. Do it again. The whole job is STILL ahead of you. Step off a bit of the yardstick, even a little bit, bit by bit, and the job will be done "little by little." This is the principle of lapsed time. Time will pass. If I have a task that will take a year and I don't do it during that year, I still have a year to go to finish the job. If I do the job during the year, at the end of the year, the job is done. Time will pass so work during that time.

A different use of the yardstick is to let it represent the length of your life. Put your thumb where you are now in your life. Note what section denotes the length of time of your present circumstance. How will the rest of your life be affected? For instance, if you yield to one night's temptation, how many years will be affected?

"YOU WERE TAUGHT . . . TO BE MADE NEW IN THE ATTITUDE OF YOUR MINDS" (EPH. 4:22-23). ONCE WE HAVE THE MIND OF CHRIST, WE AUTOMATICALLY HAVE FEWER PROBLEMS AND HAVE A NEW ATTITUDE THAT GIVES A WONDERFULLY NEW APPROACH TO THE PROBLEMS WE STILL FACE.

CHAPTER 12

PROBLEM SOLVING

"Sarah" looked confused. She didn't have the look of desperation evident in her first session but I could tell she was troubled. She had admitted to screaming at her children, constantly arguing with her husband, and being unable to forgive herself for some hurtful decisions in her teens and early twenties. She had since accepted Christ as her Savior and Lord but lacked the peace and joy she saw in others. She desperately wanted what she felt God wanted her to have. She had hoped that once she became a Christian all her problems would be solved. Now she wanted to know how to do away with the lingering habits of her old life.

Before we have a look at solving Sarah's problems, let's get some background on problem solving. Life is filled with problems. First Corinthians 10:13 says, "when you are tested," not "if you are tested." James 1:2 says, "when you face trials," not "if you face trials." If we don't face the trial, we will find an ISR. Problems are inevitable and bring a level of stress depending on their severity. The ability to solve problems is a great stress reliever. This ability helps with one of the primary needs of our life "in Christ." Being able to solve problems enables us to be transformed by the renewing of our minds. It makes sense that we are to cooperate with the Holy Spirit in using our minds in this renewal. In order to use our minds productively, we need a logical process that brings about renewal. This chapter and the next present two approaches to problem solving. First, we deal with more straightforward problems that are not entrenched in the past. The next chapter presents a process for more complicated issues. The solutions generated by the problem-solving processes bring about new mindsets, or rules, that direct our lives on a higher level. These mindsets need to be put to the test by determining if they bring us more closely into the relationship with God that uses the power, gifts, and fruit He gives us.

PROBLEMS

A problem is something we don't know how to handle. If we know how to resolve an issue, it's not a problem; it's just a matter of taking the time and effort to take whatever steps are necessary. We just need to get up and set about fixing it. The decision is the hard part; the rest is process.

Not being able to solve problems is a source of frustration for many people and they often turn to ISRs. The anxiety caused by a threat we don't feel capable of handling gets the better of us. Sometimes the problem is ignored in the hope that it will go away. That seldom works either. Each of us needs the general ability to deal with our environment, either to change it or to be changed. When we are armed with a process that we know works, we are less likely to panic and more likely to set about finding a solution. There are three different solutions to problems — consensus, compromise, or concession, that is, we come to agreement, we give or take a little, or we accept it. Part of the process is to determine which of the three solution modes to choose.

We learn by watching others, by reading, by trial and error, by thinking, and/or through being taught. After much research, personal experience, and a desire to find a simple, productive, and applicable problem-solving method, we recommend the following four-step process for problems that don't require delving into the past to remove roadblocks to change.

THE FOUR-STEP PROBLEM-SOLVING PROCESS

1. State the problem clearly. Remember to consider it pure joy (James 1:2).

2. Brainstorm (with prayer) all solutions you can think of. Don't question them at this time. Face the problem (James 1:2).

3. Choose a new mindset based on the brainstorm and critique it. Ask for wisdom (James 1:5).

4. Implement the mindset with a time frame. Time allows the new behavior a chance to work or will encourage thought for a better solution. Persevere (James 1:3-4).

Be sure to keep accurate notes during each step of the problem-solving process. When you are getting used to the process it is easy to forget key elements. It is especially important to write down the statement of the problem. Then, in later steps, refer back to ensure the process is on track. Stick to one problem at a time. If other problems arise, write them down for future treatment. If more than one person is involved, be sure to write down any ideas that you have while someone else is talking.

Nail yourself to the solution. A cardinal rule should be that one solution cannot be discarded unless a better solution is in place. No one is allowed to be a wet blanket or just quit. Struggling with an imperfect solution will motivate seeking a better one.

The order of the four problem-solving steps isn't sacred. Sometimes in the middle of step three, another solution will pop up. Sometimes an "AHA!" solution will occur. Quite often, stating the problem clearly is all it takes to gain control of the situation.

If more than one person is involved, each one should first make a separate list of possible solutions. If this process is not followed a dominant person may stifle creativity, as quiet people don't always speak up. After lists are made, go around the members of the group or family involved and state possible solutions. Each one should write them all down for processing later. Then, each one should prioritize the list according to individual preferences. Check to see if there is agreement about a solution. Seek consensus or compromise. If neither can be reached, sometimes concession is necessary. If one person is always conceding, that could be a problem and should be processed using the problem-solving steps.

After the given time frame (step four) is up, monitor and adjust. If harm is being done, adjust immediately with a better approach. Repeat items one through four as necessary. This process is very flexible. Once you have experience with the four steps, you can change their order depending on the problem. During the process you may find that a return to step one is necessary to redefine the problem. *$$*
FAMILY COUNCIL PROBLEM-SOLVING EXERCISE $$

The purpose of problem solving is to come up with solutions that offer new mindsets — new rules for living. Once the rule has been established using the Four-step Problem-solving Process, it can be monitored using a different Four-step Rule Process as follows.

1. What is the solution (new rule)?

2. Use it for a time and ask: "What did I do?"

3. "How did it work for me?"

4. "What did I learn to use next time?" (Find an alternative rule if necessary.)

During a child's early years, parents and teachers generally make the rules. However, despite parents' wishes, children generally have their own ideas about things. They spend approximately the first eight years of their lives developing behavioral strategies; then they spend their "tweenage" years experimenting to see if their strategies work. Experience often becomes the best teacher. Hopefully they will survive. For older children the first two steps are reversed. First, what did I do? Second, what rule have I been following? Sometimes they need help in understanding that their actions show their rules. Then, "How is it working?" and if it isn't, "What adjustments can be made?"

PROBLEMS WITH CHANGE

When people are asked, "Who is in control of your behavior?" most will say, "I am." This raises an interesting question about choices. If we are in control of our own behaviors, within our sphere of influence, what we do is our choice. No matter what our genetic predisposition or environmental stressors, we have choices. When we stand before God, "the Devil made me do it" won't wash. We need to realize that every day we make thousands of mini-choices. Sometimes, a bad major choice is the result of several bad mini-choices that have a domino effect. The deeper we get into a negative or destructive behavior, the harder it is to make good choices. If what we do is a choice, we can assume responsibility for changing our behaviors. If we choose our actions, then we cannot blame someone else for the consequences. To deny responsibility would be to deny choice. When we accept responsibility we end the blame game. It is much easier, in the long run, to make a good choice than it is to make a bad choice. *$$ PRODUCER/ DIRECTOR EXERCISE $$*

Let's take a look at Sarah's problems by nesting them in the Four-step Problem-solving Approach.

PROBLEMS WITH SELF REPROACH

PROBLEM STATEMENT: Sarah had said, "I have not been able to forgive myself."

BRAINSTORM: The Second Summary Commandment directs us to love our neighbors as ourselves. If we do not love ourselves, we will not be able to love our family members. Most family discord stems from this simple fact.

We try to avoid pain and, without an understanding of God's grace, we don't like to face and confess our sinful nature and sinful acts. Hence, the sins of the parents are passed on to the children for generations. Failing to confess is an ISR because it brings on continuing distress.

CHOOSE NEW MINDSET: As we discussed the "in Christ" relationship and the ensuing power, gifts, and fruit of the Spirit, Sarah accepted God's grace as sufficient — even sufficient enough so that she could forgive herself.

IMPLEMENT: Sarah vowed to extend forgiveness to her husband and children for the rest of her life.

PROBLEMS WITH CHANGING CHILDREN'S BEHAVIOR

STATEMENT OF THE PROBLEM: Sarah had fallen into a habit of screaming at her children instead of using a rational approach to change.

BRAINSTORM: John 12:47-48 gives guidelines for parenting skills. "As for the person who hears my words but does not keep them, I do not judge him. For I did not come to judge the world, but to save it. There is a judge for one who rejects me and does not accept my words, that very word which I spoke will condemn him at the last day." When the "word" judges, God isn't being mean. Rules are in place and people demonstrate by their actions that they accept or reject the rule and choose the reward or consequence.

The Four-step Rule Process can be helpful in building healthy decision-making skills into children. When there is discord in a family, children can help establish rules. First, list everything each child enjoys. Using this list helps develop consequences and rewards that can be put in separate jars. All this can be done in a family meeting. Then, when dealing with a rule, the consequence for breaking the rule, or the reward for following the rule, is available. Just draw one out of the jar. Each time a rule is broken, help the child to stop, think, and analyze the situation using the Four-step Rule Process. You may wish to have them write down their responses and bring them to you. Ground them until they participate in the process in an acceptable manner. Younger children can be engaged in conversation.

Once a rule, "the word," is established, there should be acceptable consequences and rewards that are reasonable, affordable, and within your value system. As soon as possible let the children take responsibility for making rules. If their rule is acceptable, use it. If their rule isn't working, they are telling you to make the rule. Make sure they understand this. You have veto power because you are responsible for the child. If their consequence is acceptable, use it. Otherwise, they are telling you they want you to choose the consequence. If their consequences aren't adequate, you need to choose. Emphasize the fact that they have first choice. If their reward is acceptable, use it. Otherwise, they are telling you they want you to choose the reward. Often, the praise of a loved adult is sufficient. It must be very clear to the child that they are choosing the consequence by their behavior. Say to them, "You are telling me you want the consequence because you chose to break the rule. When you left the toy on the floor, you told me you didn't want it any more." The parent isn't being a meanie. Children know the rules and demonstrate by their actions that they choose the reward or the consequences. THE WORD RULES.

CHOOSE NEW MINDSET: The rules are clear and in place; the consequences and rewards are stated and "agreed" upon. The results are up to the child. This is how children learn responsibility for their actions. Likewise, Jesus does not condemn us. He has given us His word; we choose our consequences.

IMPLEMENT: After a discussion with her children about the problem-solving process, the family chose to apply it to chores. They decided to make a list of chores and trade off each week, being flexible about when chores were done as long as they were done in a reasonable time. They decided to work the plan for a month and see how it was going. Don't yell; let the rules rule.

PROBLEMS WITH RELATIONSHIPS

As my wife and I were flying over the Mississippi watershed one time, we were struck by the brownness of the stream systems caused by erosion. Runoff or pollutants had entered the streams from some source.

STATEMENT OF THE PROBLEM: Our lives and relationships are a lot like the streams we see. They can be polluted by bad things coming into them and they can even become cesspools if there is no outlet for waste. The Dead Sea is an interesting example. There is no outlet, so impurities build up as the water evaporates. It is also a problem when the source of water isn't sufficient. If enough water were to come down the river, it would burst through or find a path around. Like the problem with the Dead Sea, our lives may be dead because there is no outlet or because we don't have a big enough source of Fresh Water. We need streams of living water from God to feed the innermost part of our being (John 4:14).

BRAINSTORM: It may be helpful to think of life as a vessel or spa or some pleasant container with faucets and drains. First, identify the problem by checking the faucets. What is coming into our lives? Are there negative influences or habits that are polluting our lives? Are the good faucets open? Forgiveness, proper physical and spiritual rest, diet, and exercise are helpful faucets. Secondly, we need to check our drains. If the bitterness, envy, jealousy, or other drains are clogged (Gal. 5:19-21), our lives are not going to be pleasant. *$$ FAUCETS AND DRAINS INTERVENTION $$*

CHOOSE NEW MINDSET: No matter how hard we work to keep our intake faucets clean, sludge and slop keep coming into our lives. That is why we need to make up our minds to keep our drains open (grace) so the negative stuff doesn't accumulate. If we don't flush our emotional toilets, things get pretty wretched after awhile. How do we keep appropriate faucets open? How do we unclog a drain? Sometimes we can do the job with a drain snake or with drain cleaner. Sometimes we need outside help like a plumber. The Holy Spirit is a wonderful plumber. Don't live in your sewer and make other people miserable. When you do flush, don't follow it to the septic tank or sewer plant. It's no fun living in sewage. Let it go. The healthiest condition is to have a strong steady stream of living water flowing through us to sweep away any negatives that may enter our lives. "Indeed, the water I give him will become in him a spring of water welling up to eternal life" (John 4:14).

IMPLEMENT: Sarah and her husband decided that arguing was polluting their marriage. They opened a faucet of problem solving that gave a reasonable approach to resolving their differing mindsets. They committed themselves to a lifetime of a happier marriage.

MAKING PROBLEM SOLVING WORK

"Count it pure joy when you face various trials . . ." (James 1:2). In psychology, the term is exposure. As we expose ourself to the trial, we take the power out of the trial. If the cat's food is kept in the fridge, the cat will come running from the furthest reaches of the house when it hears the refrigerator door open. If the cat is fed, this pattern intensifies. This is called reinforcement. If we reinforce anxiety by letting it stop us from facing an emotional task, the anxiety will be reinforced and will intensify over time as we respond to it. Simply put, if we reward anxiety, anxiety will increase. To defeat anxiety, we need to face the trial.

"Face various trials" is not a suggestion. How can a trial or problem be faced with joy? Because we know we are in God's care and He is shaping us according to His purpose. Because we know that we can, with God's help, face it, solve it, and become mature, lacking nothing. God will help us get through the exposure to the trial.

Problem solving takes dedication to the process, practice, and a positive mindset that the problem can be solved. There will be solutions that don't work, but perseverance will increase problem-solving skills in time. To neglect an attempt to problem solve is to open the door to an ISR that can bring about even more problems. Mindset is a critical part of the process.

"If any of you lacks wisdom let him ask of God who gives to all men generously, without finding fault, and it will be given him" (James 1:5). Take all your problems to God and he will give you the wisdom to deal with any or all problems (1 Pet. 5:7).

The Four-step Problem-solving Process is powerful enough to deal with most day-to-day problems. However, there are problems with deeper roots that sometimes go way back into our CHEESE Factories. Chapter 13 deals with more difficult issues.

$$$ 🔑 $$$

Treasure Chest #12
Resources for Solving Problems

FAMILY COUNCIL
PROBLEM-SOLVING EXERCISE

A good group or family problem-solving process is first to go around the group twice and let each person state what he or she thinks the problem is. Then go around the group twice, giving each person a chance to analyze and state why he or she thinks it is a problem. Then go around the group several times giving each person a chance to suggest how to solve the problem. Do this until all participants have had the opportunity to state the what, the why, and the how. Then form a solution and set a time frame.

• We miss 100 percent of the shots we don't take.

FAUCETS AND DRAINS INTERVENTION

Draw a large tub on a sheet of paper. Draw some circles around the top of the tub to represent faucets and some pipes sticking out of the bottom to represent drains. Label the faucets with names of what is currently influencing your life. Label the drains with attitudes and beliefs that control the outflow. There are good and bad things in everyone's life so label them all. Close off faucets that are putting pollutants into your life. Add faucets for improvements that are desired. Unclog or add drains if something is clogging up your life. Jesus is the ultimate drain cleaner. "You are already clean because of the word that I have spoken" (John 15:3).

• What do you call a 4-door Yugo? A Wego.

• How do we know we've arrived if we don't know where we are going?

• If we don't know where we are going, we'll probably end up somewhere else.

PRODUCER/DIRECTOR EXERCISE

Many people have been in plays and practically everyone has seen a play. It is helpful for people to stop and take a look at their lives as though they were watching themselves in a play. All plays need a producer to supply materials and people, and a director to fit things into an effective production. God is the Producer and you are the director. You need to consider where you are and where you are going. Setting goals is the first step in attaining goals.

Who has control over your thoughts?

Who has control over your actions?

What script do you want for your life?

List major goals for **SPICE** —

• Spiritual —

• Physical —

• Intellectual —

• Social —

• Emotional —

As the director of your life would you fire yourself or keep yourself on? Are adjustments in mindsets necessary?

Railroad trains travel on tracks. What positive tracks are you on? What tracks are leading to destruction? Buses are more flexible. Both have a passenger list and baggage that is composed of everyone who has helped determine, and everything that has influenced, the script of your life. Do you need to jettison some baggage?

If you are driving the bus, you have more choice over your script. If you let someone else drive your bus, you go where they want to go. This may be disastrous. Where are you driving that you want to go? Where are you driving that you don't want to go? The latter need to become old stray cats. Don't feed them, don't pet them, and don't chase them around the yard with a broom.

Based on your life so far, make two lists of characters, characteristics, habits, events, etc. in the script of your life. We all have both.

GOOD GUYS (HEROES)   BAD GUYS (VILLAINS)

It is intermission and you have a chance to talk with each one. Is there anything or anyone you would like to fire? Some baggage may need to be discarded. One of the characters may be trying to hog the stage. You may be stuck with some of the villains but you can control your response to them. You have the power to yell, "CUT" and redirect the play. Is there anyone or anything that you want to add to your script at this time?

"COME NOW, LET US REASON TOGETHER, SAYS THE LORD. THOUGH YOUR SINS ARE LIKE SCARLET, THEY SHALL BE AS WHITE AS SNOW; THOUGH THEY ARE RED AS CRIMSON, THEY SHALL BE LIKE WOOL" (ISA. 1:18). BEING TRANSFORMED BY THE RENEWING OF OUR MINDS IS A COGNITIVE PROCESS. IN ORDER TO CHANGE OUR "SINS" (ISRs) TO "SNOW" (ASRs), WE NEED AN ORGANIZED THOUGHT PROCESS.

CHAPTER 13

A PROCESS FOR DEALING WITH DIFFICULT SITUATIONS

There are some problems that are "thornier" than those that can be handled by the Four-step Problem-solving Process. These more difficult issues require more in-depth investigation regarding each step in the transformation of mindsets.

We must be transformed by the renewing of our minds (Rom. 12:2). The text, in this case, does not spell out the process by which our minds are renewed, nor does it say who is specifically responsible for the renewal. It therefore follows that we are to work with the aid of the Holy Spirit in the process. The Bible helps, ". . . crave pure spiritual milk, so that by it you may grow up in your salvation . . ." (I Peter 2:2). When we think of getting a new mindset the model in Philippians 4:8 is helpful — "Finally, brothers, whatever is true . . . think about such things." We are to think about positive things — to replace the old mindset, not struggle with it. We contend with the enemy by finding a new friend — a helpful alternative.

We're writing about stubborn mindsets that are hard to change, habits we've fought and failed at changing many times. It is important to know that, in many cases, just finding an alternative replacement, by itself, will not satisfy like our chosen ISR. We have developed our ISR to a fine art and it is an old and dear friend. We must take an all-SPICE approach and consider every aspect of the problem to find an alternative that touches every aspect of our lives. Then, the alternative must be combined with desire.

The most powerful, and most often used, resource for changing mindsets in my practice is the NAME IT, CLAIM IT, BLAME IT, and TAME IT procedure (NCBT). This rhyming organizer has proved to be helpful in shaping appropriate alternative methods. Any issue can be examined using this technique. Before we proceed, a little ground-work needs to be laid. We need to keep in mind the passage from (Exod. 23:27-30) that teaches us that God is very active in our change process but He will not demand that we change so fast that chaos will result. "Little by little . . ." we will change until we have increased enough to ". . . take possession of the land." We also need a technique that allows us to get at the root of a problem. The lowly onion gives us a model for examining a problem.

ONION/SPICE INTERVENTION

This intervention is based on Jesus' questioning of Peter in John 21:15-17 when Jesus asked Peter three times if Peter loved Him. Peeling onions sometimes makes us cry but onions add flavor to the soup. Onions are made up of layers that protect and feed the root of the plant in the center. Tell the wounded person that you are going to "peel the onion." Then pursue a course of questioning each SPICE item. Tears or anger may come as released emotions open blocked memories. Assure the person that they are safe and it's okay to express emotion. You might say, "If your emotion could talk, what would it say?"

These are tough problems so don't be afraid to ask the tough questions. For instance, "Why would a good God allow this to hap-pen?" "I don't know" is often the first answer and represents the outer, protective shell of the onion. We all develop a mask to protect ourselves against what we can't control. Assure the person that it is normal to struggle at this point because dealing with the problem is probably a new experience. When the same question is gently asked again and again, the defensive layers begin to peel off and answers begin to come. Sometimes an exposed layer provides some "onionettes" to peel. When all of the SPICE elements are explored using the Onion Peel approach, the core of the problem will usually emerge.

A session does not go very far before I pull out a NCBT worksheet (see below).

TRANSFORMATION OF THE MIND WORKSHEET

FROM   Exodus 23:27-30   TO

_____!_____

_____

Peel each element using an ONION/ SPICE approach.

NAME IT

CLAIM IT

BLAME IT

TAME IT

If I always do what I've always done, I'll always get what I always got. Therefore, I need an alternative. Doing the same thing and expecting a different result is not productive.

ALTERNATIVE X DESIRE > PROBLEM

List alternatives   /   Write a sentence for desire

1. WHAT'S THE ALTERNATIVE RULE? (Now, live life.)

2. WHAT DID I DO?

3. HOW DID IT WORK OUT?

4. WHAT DID I LEARN TO DO NEXT TIME? (Adjust if necessary.)

ALTERNATIVE BEHAVIORS

The NCBT approach finds alternatives for each aspect of the problem. List each aspect that needs to be changed under FROM, then express a goal under TO. Sometimes it is helpful to state where you are under FROM and where you want to be under TO. Then, items on either side become grist for the NCBT mill as we devise ways to get from FROM to TO. Draw crossties on the railroad for each step.

The Name it, Claim it, Blame it, and Tame it steps are helpful in effecting change. In order for me to change, definite steps need to be taken. I must recognize and name an ISR. I must claim that my mindset is harmful to me; it is causing me pain, and I need to change. I must accept my part of responsibility for change and take ownership of the problem. When I say "I," I'm on the right track, because I am done with the Blame Game. Someone or something else may be at fault but I must take responsibility for my part for any change to occur. If I get stuck in the Name it, Claim it, or Blame it steps, the problem will never be solved. If I dally around, wishing things were different, change won't occur. I need to stop going to the offices of Rationalization, Denial, and Projection for help. They aren't helpful. Once in the Tame it stage, goals and action steps for new behaviors can be made.

ALTERNATIVE X DESIRE EXERCISE

NAME IT - Clearly identify an issue that needs to be considered. Be complete and concise. Use a SPICE approach and discuss the five aspects of the problem.

CLAIM IT - Peel the mindsets of denial, rationalization, and other defense mechanisms. Peel the onions of lack of acceptance or belittling that may be occurring. Wishing it weren't so is not claiming it.

BLAME IT - Assign responsibility for the problem. Peel where, and with whom, it began. What responsibility do you hold at the present time? Assuming the blame for someone else's responsibility is not healthy. If you don't take ownership of your responsibility, you won't progress. As long as it is God's fault, someone else's fault, or the world's fault, you don't have to change. You can just sit tight and wait for the other circumstance to change. *Failure to take responsibility is a huge road-block to change.* Unfortunately, hoping others will change will not solve the problem. They probably won't change and neither will the world.

TAME IT - The process of getting past the past involves identifying alternative behaviors and having an unwavering desire to utilize them. The alternatives used, multiplied by the desire to change, must be greater than the problem. This combination is not additive. No amount of alternatives will add to a lack of desire and change a mindset. From your math background, you will remember that anything times zero is zero. If there are zero alternatives, all the desire in the world will not result in a solution. Also, if there is zero desire, all the alternatives in the world will not result in a solution. A fractional desire will cut the legs out from under the alternatives. (See godly sorrow, 2 Cor. 7:10).

NCBT APPLICATIONS

If a diagnostic technique that lists a syndrome of behaviors is being used, such as Attention Deficit Hyperactive Disorder (ADHD), it is often helpful to apply the NCBT technique to each item that pertains to the problem. For instance, one of the characteristics of ADHD is losing track of things like keys. Using the NCBT approach, the FROM is, "I always lose my keys." The TO becomes, "I want to go immediately to my keys." After the Onion/SPICE discussion, the alternative may be, "I will always put my keys on the hook by the door." The DESIRE factor is especially important when using the alternative. I *WILL* put my keys on the hook. It'll work if you work it. Another characteristic of ADHD is distractibility. An analysis should come up with ways to control the environment.

Many mental disorders have a syndrome of behaviors. The NCBT Onion/SPICE analysis can be applied to individual elements in order to promote healing.

USING NCBT FOR MARRIAGE ISSUES

Peel each part of the NCBT process using an Onion/ SPICE approach. Ask the same question again and again in an atmosphere of safety. For instance, in the NAME IT stage, ask, "What is preventing progress?" "What is preventing progress?" "What is preventing progress?" Ask until no more ideas surface. Write down the answers and see if there are any onionettes that need to be peeled. For the CLAIM IT stage, examine every aspect of denial or reluctance to face the issue. For the BLAME IT stage, examine each partner's heredity and environment. List early memories and see if a mindset or coping behavior that was formed is being brought into the present experience. If an ISR is present, try to determine when it started. What was going on then? What was the primary stress? Resolve it "in Christ." Check for secondary stress. Resolve it "in Christ." Check for Significant Emotional Events (SEEs) and examine their emotional impact. SEEs may be being revived by subtle cues. Go through each of the senses — sight, smell, etc. to see what cues are active. Smell is especially important. Draw a family tree (genogram). List dates for significant events like deaths, moves, etc. Note significant attachments. Note family patterns of substance abuse, criminal activity, forms of physical, emotional, or sexual abuse, etc. Problems may occur at certain times of the day, week, month, or year. In an atmosphere of love and compassion, check for patterns of emotional instability.

In response to my question, "Are you here because you want to be or did you come kicking and screaming?" "Tom" tersely said, "I'm here, aren't I?" "Toni" had finally persuaded Tom that they needed an outside opinion of why they were having communication problems. Using the Onion/SPICE process under my direction, Tom asked Toni several times what he could do to please her. She listed: listen to me, pay attention to me, and act like you are interested in what I am saying. She didn't want answers; she wanted empathy. Then, using the NCBT – Alternative process, Tom claimed the situation to be real and took responsibility for change. They found out that in Tom's family of origin, the father made the decisions and the mother had little say. They also realized that Tom had an attention problem and found it hard to focus on her when the TV was on. A session on active listening skills and the alternative of turning off the TV during important discussions brought results that amazed and pleased the couple.

USING NCBT FOR LOSS ISSUES

Loss comes in many forms – death, jobs, health, etc. Even loss of weight or an ISR requires examination and redefinition of our place in life. When dealing with loss, the following adaptation of NCBT is helpful. Note especially secondary losses and redefinitions.

GRIEF WORK - A PROCESS FOR DEALING WITH LOSS

FROM   Exodus 23:27-30   TO

_____!_____

_____

NAME IT – Primary Loss – Secondary Losses (Peel the onion)

CLAIM IT – The loss must be accepted

BLAME IT – Place responsibility appropriately

TAME IT – Redefine relationships with self, others, God, and the world

NEW DEFINITION X DESIRE > PROBLEM

*If we always do what we've always done,
We'll always get what we always got.*

1. WHAT'S THE NEW DEFINITION?

2. WHAT DID I DO?

3. HOW DID IT WORK OUT?

4. WHAT DID I LEARN TO USE NEXT TIME?

There is no failure; we succeed in finding something
that does or doesn't work.

The Four-step Problem-solving Process and the NCBT —
Alternative approach provide new mindsets for handling stress appropriately. We now take a look at Appropriate Stress Relievers (ASR) in
more detail.

C H A P T E R   1 4

APPROPRIATE STRESS RELIEVERS

"Ralph" was irate. "It seems no matter how hard I try to stop using pornography, it creeps back into my life. My wife has withdrawn because she feels she can't meet the impossible standard that porn queens present. My son stuck his nose into my Websites, copied some things for his friends, and got kicked out of school. I'm thoroughly disgusted with myself but I'm like the dog that keeps returning to its vomit. I want you to help me quit." The last sentence raised a red flag in my mind. Here was another attempt to make someone else responsible. The wife isn't satisfactory, the son is nosy, and now I am supposed to take responsibility. How do I prevent Ralph from blaming me for his ISRs of pornography and blaming others while at the same time give him options for change?

Ralph made a list of things that were stressing him out. He then separated them into groups, designating what could or could not be changed. He then used the Name it, Claim it, Blame it, and Tame it process to come up with alternative stress relievers. He struggled a long time with the blame it step before he took responsibility for his problem. He was surprised to realize that his blaming others had prevented him from dealing with the problem. We invited his wife in on the process and, with her help, and the ASRs of taking responsibility, Bible verses, and exercise, he is making progress. *$$ SORTING ANXIETIES EXERCISE $$*

MORE ABOUT STRESS

Stress, or anxiety, is caused by demands or pressures that push or pull us from an established state. We can create our own unbalanced equilibrium and increase stress by lusting after an ISR. Any change in our equilibrium, positive or negative, causes stress because the change presents us with challenges that we are not sure we know how to handle. Instead of trying to resolve the problem with an ISR that causes more stress, we need to face the problem, find ASRs, and gain maturity. An ASR may eliminate the cause of stress or it may motivate us to find resources that bring the stressor into our safety/control zone.

The Apostle Paul found the only true ASR. He said he had learned the secret of being content, that is, without stress. He could do all things "in Christ" (Phil. 4:13). He truly had a new mindset, having been transformed by the renewing of his mind. The "in Christ" relationship empowers us to handle stress appropriately. This should not be a "secret" to Christians. Control is obtained by using an ASR that is enabled by the power, fruit, and gifts of the Holy Spirit.

TWO TYPES OF STRESSORS
PRIMARY STRESSORS

In the process of stress relief, two types of stressors need to be addressed. First, primary stress, the stress from the original stressor(s) needs to be addressed. All the emotions stored up during the duration of an ISR are still there. If, and when, the ISR is given up, we begin where we left off. For instance if a sixteen-year-old with relationship problems begins to drink heavily and stops when he is thirty-six, he still faces unresolved relationship difficulties essentially as a sixteen-year-old. This extends to any ISR and contributes to the difficulty of change. Facing the old stressor without the ISR is a formidable obstacle to recovery.

SECONDARY STRESSORS

Many people adopt ISRs instead of dealing with the original problem appropriately. In so doing, they add on secondary stressors. In order for healing to occur they must be convicted of the wrongfulness of the original ISR, get through defense mechanisms that prolong it, and then deal with the original problem plus any ensuing problems brought on by the ISR. The backlog of secondary stressors caused by an ISR can be disheartening. Dealing with inappropriate use of food, alcohol, drugs, work, etc. is serious business. There is fear that removal of the ISR will bring on an overwhelming surge of whatever problem the ISR has been medicating. Think of logs in a logjam. Many people have been killed when logjams were dynamited. The fear of facing all the logs at once often traps a person in the ISR. But the use of ASRs, when utilized appropriately "in Christ," will bring victory. Remember Exodus 23:29 — "Little by little I will drive them out before you until you have increased enough to take possession of the land." What a soul surge!! *$$ LOGJAM INTERVENTION $$*

STEPS TOWARD APPROPRIATE STRESS RELIEVERS

Number one — Gotta Wanna. A person has to want to quit the maladaptive behavior more than he or she wants to continue. Sometimes it helps to use a Pain/Joy T Chart to analyze the pros and cons of a decision. The pain of change has to be less than the pain of staying the same. It is difficult to get past the original causes and all the secondary factors to reclaim control. However, if there is no change, the rest of life will be less than what God intends for it to be. There is a need to get off the shame cycle and get on the try-cycle. Don't quit trying. Once the decision is made, the rest is process.

One advantage in dealing with ISRs is that we don't stay in a heightened state of arousal for very long. Our mind is designed to begin removing excess neurotransmitters soon after they are produced. A strong desire to do something usually decreases in a few minutes. An alternate activity combined with a strong desire to change can derail the urge. Alternative X Desire > Problem.

The solution is simple enough for the simple, and so profound that no one is wise enough to plumb its depths. We are new creations in Christ!! We are forgiven and we live in a state of forgiveness!! Our minds are renewed! We don't have to choose ISRs anymore. We are taught in Romans Chapter 6:16 that we are no longer "slaves to sin." We have died with Christ and risen into newness of life with different choices, among them, ASRs. Spend some time meditating on Romans 6. We are no longer slaves to inappropriate choices. Our new choice is to be a willing slave to God with all the resources He gives us. We can now face what used to overwhelm us. Once the decision is made, the rest is process.

APPROPRIATE STRESS RELIEVERS

We've taken a look at several Inappropriate Stress Relievers (ISRs). Now it's time to introduce Appropriate Stress Relievers (ASRs). We have found the teachings in the Bible to be a very important source of stress relievers. Its words of warning help us avoid some terrible causes of stress and its words of comfort relieve us when we are in distress. We have God's promise in our use of His written word. "So is my word that goes out from my mouth: It will not return to me empty, but will accomplish what I desire and achieve the purpose for which I sent it" (Isa. 55:11). A thorough foundation in the Bible with appropriate meditation on significant passages is fundamental to appropriate stress relief. $$ VERSES THAT HELP WITH HANDLING STRESS $$

Our old SPICE behaviors got us into ISRs; let's look at some new SPICE alternatives.

SPIRITUAL

One reason that people turn to an ISR is the mindset that not enough resources are available to handle the stress. Often, we look in the wrong places for resources. There is great news — God is a complete resource. His grace is sufficient (2 Cor. 12:9). Go back to when the ISR started. What was going on at that point that led to the ISR? The original problem may have been resolved and the ISR carried on as a habit (conditioned response) or dependence. If the original problem hasn't been resolved, it needs to be taken care of and we need to become independent from the ISR. If we don't dig out the root of the dandelion, it will usually grow back. The primary stressor has to be exposed and brought into the light where we can deal with it. That is where ASRs come in.

Appropriate stress relief begins with 1) acceptance and application to self of grace-forgiveness, and 2) extension of grace-forgiveness to others. Acceptance involves confession of our sinful nature and sinful acts and relief from self-condemnation. "If we confess our sins . . . we are purified of all unrighteousness" (1 John 1:9). "Therefore, there is now no condemnation for those who are in Christ Jesus" (Rom. 8:1). The disciples left all and followed Jesus. We need to leave bitterness and resentment and enter the joy of relationship with Him.

Extension of forgiveness is the ultimate stress reliever as we forgive others for the sins that have been committed against our body, mind, and spirit. We can trust God to deal justly with our abusers so we can rid ourselves of that worrisome duty. It is often more difficult for people to forgive themselves for what they have done than to forgive others. But God commands that we are to forgive everyone who has sinned against us, including ourself. Lack of forgiveness for self and others is a real stress creator. Not forgiving is like living in your garbage dump and hoping the other guy is miserable. Don't kick yourself around the block for taking so long to forgive. Just do it and rejoice that you have achieved this spiritual milestone.

Remember that the Holy Spirit is always at work convicting us of the error of our ways and our need for God. It is interesting to note the difference between the accusations of Satan and the conviction of the Holy Spirit. The accusations of Satan are lies, intended to destroy us, while the conviction of the Holy Spirit is truth and leads us into life. The accusations of Satan maintain stress; the conviction of the Holy Spirit relieves us of stress. One wonderful thing about this process is that we aren't stuck with our own resources to accomplish the work. If God is convicting, He will give power, fruit, and gifts to complete the process.

PHYSICAL

Stress causes adrenaline; adrenaline calls for action. So act, but act appropriately. Choose some physical activity that reduces stress along with all the other benefits of mental, social, and emotional health. Look at the chapter on anger and apply some of those management skills to stress relief.

INTELLECTUAL

Make some 3X5 cards using slogans or verses — James 1:2-3, James 1:13-15, Colossians 3:5, 1 John 2:16, Titus 2:11-12, Matthew 5:28, 1 Peter 2:11, 1 Corinthians 10:13, and others are helpful. Carry the cards that encourage abstinence and discourage use. When you are tempted to participate in your dependency of choice, take out a card and meditate (medicate) on the verse. Focus on the message instead of the ISR. Others have broken negative habits; you can do it to.

Medicate with the Gos-pill.

Those who try to make it on their own often find they do not have enough resources to handle the stress they find in life. God has given us the body of Christ, the church, brothers, and sisters who are willing and able to help. We not only have a living body to help us, we have an audience. "Since we are surrounded by such a great cloud of witnesses, let us throw off everything that hinders and the sin that so easily entangles . . ." (Heb. 12:1b). Christians throughout the ages witness to the power of God in our lives. Seek advice from successful people. They will share their resources with you.

We can always call upon God to help us. His "phone number" is Jeremiah 33:3 —"Call to me and I will answer you and tell you great and unsearchable things you do not know."

It helps to narrow the possibilities so that a choice is easier to make. We often need to choose between God and the world. Joshua proclaimed, "If serving the Lord seems undesirable to you, then choose for yourselves this day whom you will serve . . . But as for me and my household, we will serve the Lord" (Josh. 24:15). Choosing between God and the world cuts down the options considerably. We can then choose the ASR(s) that best fits our understanding of God's will in our lives.

Many people opt out of life without using their ability to think. Why? What prevents people from using their minds? Perhaps they think they know the answer. Maybe pride enters in. We may cling to old mindsets until it becomes too late. When it comes to the really significant questions in life, we need to be extremely careful when we arrive at a lasting conclusion.

COMMUNITY

We can avoid, extinguish, and/or find alternatives for the old ISR. If several alternatives have been tried without success, a complete lifestyle change may be required. Different strokes for different folks. It is necessary, as much as possible, to remove the negative emotional states, triggers, toxic people, places, sensory cues — smells, sounds, tastes, and feelings associated with the use. Don't go there. Extinguishing the activity may involve linking the activity to something unpleasant. An alternative helps by substituting something else that satisfies the need. Use your spiritual resources, get social support, develop stress and anger management techniques to reduce anxiety. Get appropriate rest, exercise, and diet. Avoid burnout, recreate, and get professional help if necessary.

Reduce depression by having realistic expectations. Get a spiritual perspective as you, "Consider everything a loss compared to the surpassing greatness of knowing Christ Jesus my Lord, for whose sake I have lost all things. I consider them rubbish . . ." (Phil. 3:8). A competent Christian counselor may be helpful. Helping others will help you. Be happy in earthly things but rejoice in the Lord (Phil. 4:4). Don't allow yourself to become socially isolated. Spend time with people who like you. Utilize church cluster groups. Join a group or team. Support a team. Talk to someone who cares. Attacking negative personality traits will help you gain a healthier, more positive approach to living. What do you have to lose other than your life?

EMOTIONAL

Anxiety, in its many forms, results from the mindset that adequate resources are not available to handle a perceived threat. When we are anxious, we are basically saying God is not sufficient. If God is not paramount in our life, anxiety is a given. Therefore, utilizing and/or obtaining skills to gain control are necessary to reduce anxiety.

There are many techniques for dealing with anxiety. Permanent control of anxiety is brought about by facing the trial with joy (James 1:2). The purpose of facing trials is to become "mature and complete" (James 1:4) — to be "more than conquerors" (Rom. 8:37). Once appropriate resources are available, face the threat and become more than a conqueror. Don't reinforce the anxiety by yielding to it. *$$ POPCORN — QUICK WAYS TO DEAL WITH ANXIETY $$*

The greatest stress reliever is Emmanuel — God with us. There is a great passage in 2 Corinthians Chapter 1 where it is stated that God is the God of all comfort and that we can comfort others with the comfort with which we are comforted.

How does God comfort us? With His Spirit, His word, and His people —

HIS SPIRIT:

> *John 14 - "And I will pray to the Father and he shall give you another Comforter that he may abide with you forever..." (v. 16). "But the Comforter, who is the Holy Spirit, who the Father will send in my name, he shall teach you all things, and bring all things to your remembrance, whatsoever I have said unto you" (v. 26).*

How do we get the Spirit of God within us? "How much more will your Father in heaven give the Holy Spirit to those who ask him" (Luke 11:13b). Invite Him into your life

HIS WORD:

> *Matthew 5:4 - "Blessed are they that mourn for they shall be comforted."*

Psalms 119:50 - "This is my comfort in my affliction, for your word has made me alive."

Psalms 23:4 - "Yea, though I walk through the valley of the shadow of death, I will fear no evil, for you are with me; your rod and your staff comfort me." We are not to try to jump over the valley but we do go through it.

Isaiah 49:13 - "Sing, O heavens; and be joyful, O earth; and break forth into singing, O mountains for the Lord has comforted his people and will have mercy upon his afflicted."

HIS PEOPLE:

1 Thessalonians 4:18 - "Wherefore comfort one another with these words."

Isaiah 40:1 - "Comfort you, comfort you my people, says your God."

Two of the most common ISRs brought to my office are inappropriate uses of food and anger. The next two chapters investigate roots of these problems and alternate stress relievers.

$ $ $ → $ $ $

Treasure Chest #14
Resources for Appropriate Stress Relief

SORTING ANXIETIES EXERCISE

Things I can't change	Things I choose not to change	Things I want to try to change
_____>	< _____ >	< _____
_____	_____	_____

Things I cannot change or choose not to change are destructive anxieties that need to become OLD STRAY CATS. Things I want to try to change need GAS —

<u>G</u>oal —
<u>A</u>ction Steps —
<u>S</u>incerity of Purpose —

Plan your work; work your plan. It'll work if you work it!

LOGJAM INTERVENTION

In the old days of logging beside rivers, logs would be released into the river. A log might snag on a rock or other obstruction and other logs jammed up behind it, affecting the flow of the river. We can use an understanding of logjams to help us deal with stress. The first log is some stressor that should be utilized to grow towards maturity. The log has the potential to be made into beautiful furniture but it jams against a rock. The rock is an ISR; it prevents the promise of the log from being fulfilled. The logs that jam up because of the ISR are secondary stressors. What "rocks" are jamming up the river of your life? We need to find out what they are and deal with them appropriately with God's help. Think of the time when your ISR began. Allow the Spirit to remind you of the stress in your life at that time. That was the original log. Name the rock/stressor/ISR that jammed up your growth. Write it down. Deal with it appropriately in Christ. What furniture should have been made from the original log? Consider the secondary stresses brought on by the ISR; those are the logs behind the original log. Write them down. Deal with them by accepting and extending forgiveness. Select ASRs to deal with the primary and secondary stressors. Write them down. Practice the ASRs until they become your choice of behaviors.

BIBLE VERSES THAT HELP WITH HANDLING STRESS

GOD'S PROMISE Revelation 21:3

"Now the dwelling of God is with men, and he will live with them. They will be his people, and God himself will be with them and be their God." God's Covenant is stated again and again in the Old Testament and restated in the New Testament. We are blessed that God indwells us through the Person of His Holy Spirit.

GOD'S LIVING WORD — John 17:22-23a

"I have given them the glory that you gave me, that they may be one as we are one: I in them and you in me" (John17:22-23a). "I no longer live, but Christ lives in me." (Gal. 2:20). Christ is alive and lives in us. We are "in Christ." What an incredible fellowship!

GOD'S WRITTEN WORD – Isaiah 55:11

"So is my word that goes out from my mouth: It will not return to me empty, but will accomplish what I desire and achieve the purpose for which I sent it."

PRAYER BRINGS RELIEF - Philippians 4:6-7

"Do not be distressed about anything, but in everything, with prayer and petition, with thanksgiving, make your requests to God. And the peace of God that passes all understanding will keep your hearts and your minds in Christ Jesus." Note that it says "in everything" not "for everything," nor to be rid of "everything." Pray for yourself and for those to whom you minister, with thanksgiving before, during, and after contact. Be thankful. Be careful in praying for the removal of a trial lest its benefits are lost.

ABILITY TO WITHSTAND TRIALS — 1 Corinthians 10:13

"No testing has happened to you except what is common to man. And God is faithful; he will not let you be tested beyond what you can bear. But when you are tested, he will also provide a way out so that you can stand up under it." Note that it says, "<u>when</u> you are tested," not "<u>if</u> you are tested." As a person and as a caregiver we will face "all kinds of trials" (1 Pet. 1:6).

THE RESULT OF TESTING — James 1:2-4

"Consider it pure joy, my brothers, whenever you face trials of many kinds, because you know that the testing of your faith develops perseverance. Perseverance must finish its work so that you may be mature and complete, not lacking anything." Note that it says, "whenever you face trials," not "if." We will face trials. Trials are for our joy because we have **APPROPRIATE STRESS RELIEVERS** from God to make each trial an opportunity for good decisions and victory. Paul's "contentment" (Phil. 4:11) came from positive decisions during each of the tests that are listed in 2 Corinthians 11 and 12.

POPCORN — QUICK WAYS TO DEAL WITH ANXIETY (OR ANGER)

Temporary relief from anxiety can be obtained from what we call "popcorn" solutions, which can be used on the spot. Envision a bowl of anxiety. The bowl isn't a threat if it doesn't spill over. The contents of the bowl can be reduced by quick measures using popcorn. Following are several relatively quick popcorn solutions. "All of the tempting (testing) which you are experiencing is common to man, but God is faithful; he will not allow you to be tested (tempted) beyond your ability, but with the tempting (testing) will give you a way to escape so you can stand up under it" (1 Corinthians 10:13). Look to see if any of these are God's "way to escape" for you:

PRAY	MEDITATE
AVOID THE SITUATION	TAKE A TIME-OUT
GET BUSY	EXERCISE
DO 10 PUSHUPS	DO YOUR HOBBY
TALK YOURSELF DOWN	THINK OF A FUN THING
TALK TO SOMEONE	TAKE A WALK
COUNT BACKWARDS FROM 10	TAKE A DEEP BREATH
REASON WITH THE PERSON	STEP BACK

SQUEEZE YOUR THUMB AND FIRST FINGER TOGETHER HARD

PICTURE YOURSELF AS A BALLOON SLOWLY LOSING AIR

"FOOD IS FOR THE BODY . . ." (1 COR. 6:13, KJV). "THEIR GOD IS THEIR STOMACH" (PHIL. 3:19). FOOD IS NOT TO BE USED TO FEED OUR EMOTIONS, BUT TO NOURISH OUR BODIES. GOD IS THE GOD OF ALL COMFORT (2 COR. 1:3).

CHAPTER 15

WHY WEIGHT?

Consuming more food than we need is one of the hardest ISRs to break. Weight control is a big problem for many people. The reason we weigh what we do is determined by our CHEESE factory and the SPICE rack that goes with it. Remember, our Choices come from our Heredity, our Environment, significant Events that have occurred in our lives, and our Self-Esteem, which is primarily structured by the influence of significant others during our early years (Choice, Heredity, Environment, Events, Self-Esteem = CHEESE). Within each department of the CHEESE factory there is a SPICE rack. Each area of a person's CHEESE factory is affected by Spiritual, Physical, Intellectual, Community (social), and/or Emotional factors — SPICE. These all go together to form our mindset about food. If our mindset is that we have to have more food than our body needs, we will gain weight the old fashioned way — one ounce at a time.

"Food has been my friend for years. It never judges me. Food tastes good. When I am full I feel safe and calmer. In my family, food was part of every joy and sorrow in life. There was food for every emotion. But now I'm faced with this long list of medical problems. My 'friend' is killing me. I've tried every diet on earth and I just gain back what I lose. What can I do?"

"Wanda's" complaints are typical of many responses to the problem of weight. The main reason we gain weight, or fail to lose weight when we should, is that weight loss violates mindsets formed by some elements of our CHEESE factory in combination with SPICE factors. It follows that changing our food intake will require attention to one or more CHEESE/SPICE areas and the renewing of our mindsets. Consider a pie chart (your choice of flavors). Different factors represent different sized pieces of the pie. Most often there are several contributors to a weight problem. We are holistic people so a weight problem usually has all-SPICE contributors and requires all-SPICE healing factors. We need to address each area. Many people lose weight then gain it back, plus some. Most diet plans don't attend to the underlying problems behind the excess weight so if weight is lost, the problems call it back. Behind every pound of weight there is usually a "pound of emotion" some CHEESE/SPICE factor. Of course, the simple answer is eating less, but for millions of people eating less isn't simple.

When it comes to gaining weight the bottom line is — excess weight comes from eating and/or drinking excess calorie-laden substances. Weight comes from eating too much food. People have different hereditary tendencies, different family customs, different emotions, different reasons or excuses, etc. — the whole CHEESE and SPICE thing; but excess weight comes from eating excess food. Different defensive mindsets may be formed to justify, rationalize, deny, or minimize our weight but excess weight comes from eating excess food. If we were locked in a jail cell with no food, we would lose weight. We can't eat too much and lose weight at the same time. *$$WEIGHT GAIN/LOSS DIAGRAM $$*

THE BATTLE OF THE BULGE

The mindsets that control our use of food are some of the toughest ones to renew. Hopefully, this chapter will provide some heavy artillery to use in the "battle of the bulge." We suggest a nested Name it, Claim it, Blame it, and Tame it (NCBT) battle plan (mindset). The rest of the chapter will be presented using an NCBT approach and individual issues within the problem will be subject to the NCBT process.

NAME IT – WHY I EAT "EATERCISE"

God has given us food to sustain a healthy body. However, as SPICE people with the ability to distort any good thing, we often eat inappropriately to satisfy needs. We are supposed to eat to maintain our physical bodies. If we are nurturing spiritual, physical, intellectual, social, or emotional needs inappropriately with food, we will gain weight. The following checklists are intended to help discover the inappropriate bases for eating. First, go through the checklists and mark any reasons you eat. Then, using the Name it, Claim it, Blame it, and Tame it steps, state an appropriate alternative for each item checked and use the alternative behavior whenever you are tempted to eat destructively. Remember, zero alternatives or zero desire will sabotage the process of losing weight.

CHECKLISTS

SPIRITUAL REASONS FOR EATING:

___ God wants me to be happy.

___ food has become a god in my life.

___ food is part of the "abundant life" that Jesus offers.

___ other:

PHYSICAL REASONS FOR EATING:

___ to hide or enhance my figure — I want bigger or smaller parts.

___ to look bigger and more powerful — I can literally throw my weight around.

___ to satisfy some self-image of body size.

___ because it's there — I find myself with food in my hands.

___ because food tastes good — I'll have just one more helping.

___ other:

INTELLECTUAL REASONS FOR EATING:

___ to satisfy an urge to stock up for hard times — maybe a famine will hit.

___ because one more bite won't hurt — every day, day after day.

___ because I don't want this last bite to go to waste — so it goes to my waist.

___ I'm entitled; I don't have other vices.

___ other:

COMMUNITY (SOCIAL) REASONS FOR EATING:

___ to form a cocoon against social relationships — it keeps people away.

___ because of family habits — we're big eaters.

___ because I come from a heavy family.

___ to please the cook — Cook is disappointed if I don't eat a lot.

___ other:

EMOTIONAL REASONS FOR EATING:

___ out of boredom — something to do.

___ for comfort — food is my friend.

___ to ease depression — food is a "pick me up."

___ to punish myself or others — I'll fix them.

___ to fill lack of forgiveness.

___ to relieve stress — food makes the pain go away.

___ to celebrate — I'm entitled; I've earned it.

___ to grieve — I'm burying my sorrow in food.

___ to have some measure of control in my life. It's my body.

___ other:

CLAIM IT — THE VENISON STOPS HERE

Questions we need to ask: 1) "Do I control food or does food control me?" If food controls me, it has become an addiction. 2) "Do I want the food or do I want the weight?" If I want the food, I just eat for the sake of eating. If I want the weight, I eat excess food for a purpose. 3) "Do I eat to live or live to eat?" If I "eat to live," my food intake matches my physical needs and enough is enough. If I "live to eat," I eat to satisfy an emotional need and too much is never enough. Tolerance is a factor; it keeps taking more to bring a level of relief. In short, we live to eat if we are meeting some need other than our basic physical requirements. We may not remember what drives us to overeat.

Most of us strive to live by the rule that what we do is in our best interest, according to mindsets formulated by our CHEESE/SPICE factories. Our "best thinking" determines what we eat. However, it is not in our best interest to be overweight. In I Corinthians 6:13 we find the interesting statement that, "Food is for the stomach and the stomach is for food." Food is for the stomach, not for the emotions. A major part of the misuse of food is using it as an ISR. If our mindset is that only food will satisfy as a stress reliever, then no alternative will suffice. As we have previously considered, an ISR causes more stress. Food is another one of those ISRs that causes more stress.

BLAME IT — WHO IS RESPONSIBLE?

Blaming others or circumstance will place responsibility outside ourselves and will sabotage the weight-control process. If we try to lose weight to satisfy some other person, we will make him or her responsible and blame him or her for lack of weight loss.

One of the problems in dealing with excess weight is that we are all different. One person gets fat on what would starve another. I often hear the lament, "Other people can eat more; why can't I?" We have different metabolisms and different lifestyles. Therefore, any reduction of weight has to take into consideration individual differences. My diet has to fit my needs. Your diet has to fit your needs. At the end of this chapter a diet based upon Biblical principles is offered.

We can become conditioned to eating too much. Like the cat running into the kitchen whenever the refrigerator door opens, we respond to environmental cues. Cats learn that refrigerators are associated with food. They are "conditioned to respond. Humans associate food with whatever Eatercise Factors apply (See your checklist.). We are capable of secondary (and beyond) conditioning. Secondary conditioning may be as simple as seeing a refrigerator on television that reminds us of the food we have in ours and we are cued to eat. We become conditioned to seeing a large amount of food on a plate. Seeing only the amount of food that we need is shocking and disheartening. We may have forgotten what original factors conditioned our eating mindsets. They may have begun with self-talk but the voices have faded to a muted whisper as we go from the antecedent cue to the choice of eating without examining our beliefs.

As in the use of alcohol, where a person can be an emotional drinker or a social drinker, a person can be an emotional eater or a social eater. The purpose of emotional eating is to alter the mental state and is an ISR. If a substance is misused to relieve anxiety, an attempt to cut back on misuse of the substance will release a great deal of stored anxiety. Utilize anxiety reduction skills. Lack of forgiveness creates emotional stressors that often lie behind the problem of weight gain and retention.

Food can be a substitute for finding relief in God. Food may become an idol from which we seek comfort but, God is ". . . the God of all comfort, who comforts us in all our troubles" (2 Cor. 1:3-4). If we choose food for comfort we are accepting a lesser god and will get inadequate comfort requiring more food, ad nauseum. It is important to remember that the biblical model (Phil. 4:8-9) for handling a stressor is to replace it with something better, not to fight the problem. So with food: Don't just fight food; find a fitting alternative.

TAME IT

It is always a good idea to consult with your primary care physician to make sure there are no endocrine imbalances that are working against you. If there are medical complications, be sure your PCP approves your weight loss plan.

In order to lose weight, we have to have hope that we will be successful. This is especially important if there has not been success in the past or if weight has been lost then gained back. If we succumb to food, we reinforce our weakness and tolerance is encouraged. We need to plan our work carefully and then work the plan. It'll work if you work it. We need to believe we have a choice. Some people decide there are zero alternatives and make change impossible.

After we have clearly stated the problem and the consequences, after we have stopped denying or wishing it weren't so, after we have taken responsibility for our action, we need to take a tough-love approach. Love yourself and do what you need for health and well-being. Losing weight is no easy matter and a no-nonsense attitude is necessary to achieve weight loss goals. Losing weight is not for the faint hearted. There are two main issues to consider about weight — health and self-esteem. If what we weigh is healthy and we feel good about our weight, the rest of the world can get over it or die irritated. Decide what you want and go for it. Change your mindset.

"Facing" (James 1:2) is necessary with the knowledge that you will not be overwhelmed (1 Cor. 10:13). Armed with the information that is gathered from the Name, Claim, and Blame steps, the power needed to Tame is usually available. There is no failure in this process. Even a day's setback with your ASR is a success in finding a way that doesn't work. Use that to help clarify things that need to be adjusted for further success. If you falter, use the Four-step Rule Process.

1. What is my rule? Don't consume senselessly.

2. What did I do? Drank a calorie-laden beverage.

3. How did it work out for me? I shot 200 calories and am disgusted with myself.

4. What did I learn that will help my next decision? Drink water.
   Then *do it*.

Don't get caught in the 2-3 loop — do it wrong, not work out, do it wrong, not work out, etc. Always include step four, "What did I learn about next time," and adjust your rule as necessary. Don't let one transgression throw you into a defeatist course of bingeing. Just start again from where you are. The urge to eat usually diminishes in a few minutes, especially with the use of an alternative ASR. It'll work if you work it. Choose your pain; choose your joy.

The difficult part of losing weight is making the Gethsemane decision and sticking to it; the rest is process. We truly need "godly sorrow." "Godly sorrow brings repentance [a change of behavior] that leads to salvation [deliverance] and leaves no regret, [like most failed attempts at losing weight] but worldly sorrow brings death" [from excess weight] (2 Cor. 7:10). Worldly sorrow, as it applies to food, is a sorrow that wishes we could maintain unhealthy eating habits and still be healthy and feel good about ourselves. The passage goes on, "[W]hat earnestness, what eagerness to clear yourselves, what indignation, what alarm, what longing, what concern, what readiness to see justice done" (v. 11). In order to lose weight we need to be earnest, eager, indignant, alarmed, filled with longing, concerned, and ready to stay the course. We need to be indignant with those who would tempt us to overeat. We need to be alarmed about the results of overeating. We need to be filled with longing for a weight that will promote health and self-esteem.

True repentance is a 180-degree turn. Some people say they make a 360-degree turn. Unfortunately that puts them right back on the course they were following. Some people make a 179-degree turn. There is just enough variance to throw them off course. That is worldly sorrow. If we're going to cut the tail off the dog, don't cut it off an inch at a time. It hurts every time. Cut it where you want it.

Healing of excess weight requires attention to a host of different mindsets dealing with the whole person. For proper use of food we need to be "transformed by the renewing of our minds" (Rom. 12:2) in many areas. *$$ CHEESE/SPICE APPROACH TO THE ANALYSIS OF EXCESS WEIGHT$$*

We need to change our minds about the way we look at food. We need to see food in a different "weigh." Definition of a weed — an undesirable plant. That makes a petunia a weed in an orchid patch. Definition of poison — something that we ingest that is detrimental to health. That makes that extra helping of delicious food poisonous. We need to see eating unhealthy food as an act of consuming poison. We need to see a skull and crossbones on any food that is detrimental to our health or self-esteem. That includes quality and quantity. Get some rocks that weigh what your extra weight is. Look at them; don't hurt yourself by carrying them around. Throw one away when you lose that much weight. Put 20 pounds of lard in the refrigerator; take out a package each time you lose a pound. Have someone take a picture of you from behind when you are bending over and put a copy on every food storage area. Whatever it takes!!

We need to monitor what goes on in our minds. Watch your self-talk. As the going gets tough you will recognize little messages whirling around in your mind. "I deserve it." "It's only one pizza" (extra large). These may flash back to when you first self-medicated with food. If these messages sabotage your efforts, replace them with positive thoughts. Don't fight the bad thoughts; replace them with positive mindsets. When the going gets tough, the tough starve.

We need to change our minds about what is going on in our stomachs. When our stomach grumbles and growls we need to adjust our thinking. Instead of thinking we need to eat, we think of an imaginary crew of food distributors — fat farmers farming fat. Unfortunately, our fat farmers are a lot like we used to be. They would rather have someone shovel down a bunch of calories instead of having to work for them. They would rather store food than harvest fat. Don't throw food to them; encourage them to farm fat. Cheer them on, realizing that every growl represents skinnier fat cells.

We need a mindset that helps us handle the emotions that often surface when weight is lost. If food has been a cover for emotional distress, the distress will be uncovered in the weight loss process. The reason so many people gain weight back is they do not take care of the emotions behind the weight. One of the worst culprits in this area is lack of forgiveness. It is amazing how many instances of abuse come to mind as weight is lost. Use the ASR of forgiveness for each issue that comes to mind. Consider it pure joy when you re-experience the stuffed emotions that emerge when the covering weight is lost. Those emotions can now be handled appropriately, which increases mental well-being significantly. If eating has been an emotional matter, we need to find comfort in God, not in food. "Praise be to the God and Father of our Lord Jesus Christ, the Father of compassion and the God of all comfort, who comforts us in all our troubles, so that we can comfort those in any trouble with the comfort we ourselves have received from God" (2 Cor. 1:3-4).

> "Harvey" said, "I didn't realize how much I had replaced God with food. I had found comfort in food instead of God. I ate when I was angry instead of seeking solutions with the help of the Holy Spirit. As I began to lose weight, I found the emotions that I had stuffed with food were exposed and I needed to seek God's help to resolve them instead of regaining the weight the way I used to."

We need a realistic mindset about exercise. Exercise is good, but don't reward a two-mile walk with a 300-calorie candy bar. It takes two thousand steps or about a one-mile walk to burn off one hundred calories. Exercise helps but we can't always exercise. However, we can always eat less. We can avoid one hundred calories by not eating a slice of bread. It's easier to keep it off than take it off. When feeling hungry, use an alternative behavior. The hunger pangs usually go away in a few minutes. Have a sticky pad full of alternative choices on the refrigerator door and do one of them instead of eating. It'll work if you work it. Reward yourself with something other than food. It often helps to journal when, where, what, why, and how you eat. Patterns will emerge. Having to write down indiscretions may be a deterrent to eating. Remember, nothing satisfies like our cherished ISR. Alternative X Desire is necessary. The desire to lose weight has to overpower the desire to eat.

In order to understand another challenge in the weight-loss process let's take an example of a two-hundred-pound man who loses forty pounds. Suppose he has chosen to eat four tablespoonfuls of food instead of five. Further suppose he has decreased his body mass by 20 percent. Now he weighs one hundred sixty pounds and needs even less food than before because there is less of him to maintain and haul around. Instead of four tablespoons of a food, he now needs only three to continue losing weight. Unfortunately, we have established a mental image (mindset) of the amount of food that is satisfying. We need to get over the shock of being able to exist in a healthy manner on so little food. Our mindset has to be on weight control, not on the amount of food we are used to eating. Use a saucer instead of a plate. Grieve the loss using NCBT.

Choose your pain. There is pain in losing weight. There is pain in being overweight. Choose your joy. There is joy in eating. There is joy in being trim and healthier. Make your own pain/joy T-chart.

THE JOHN CHAPTER 15 DIET PLAN

In the fifteenth chapter of the Gospel of John, we find a wonderful passage that can be used to structure a plan for weight loss. First we need to experience a strong new mindset with adequate preparation. Then we accept God's promises to help. Then we work the diet. It'll work if you work it.

THE PREPARATION

CONVICTION: If the Holy Spirit is convicting you of the need to achieve a healthy body, God will empower you to do it. (John 16:8)

SORROW: Godly sorrow is required for weight loss to occur. (2 Cor. 7:10)

GETHSEMANE: A heart-mind-body-soul-wrenching decision has to be made (Luke 22:42). First the decision has to be made. The rest is process.

GOLGOTHA: That part of us that misuses food has to die. If the root is in a lack of forgiveness, we need to forgive. "Father, forgive them for they do not know . . ."what they caused me to eat (Luke 23:34).

GARDEN: There will be a resurrection into a new life of better health and all that goes with it (John 20:14).

THE PROMISE

John 15:3—"You are already clean because of the word I have spoken." Remember, God loves you regardless; He won't love you more if you weigh less but you will feel better and may be a more effective vessel if you care for your body. "Remain in me and I will remain in you" (John 15:4).

THE PLAN

John 15:2—"Cut off [prune] every branch that bears no fruit." Eliminate the obvious junk from your diet. Most fats, oils, dressings, sauces, sugars, and starches must go. Eliminate between-meal snacks. Eliminate sugared beverages. This step will usually stop the weight gain and may even initiate weight loss. After a while, you may hit a plateau. Then comes step two.

John 15: 2—"Prune every branch that does bear fruit." Cut back on portions. Eat a balanced diet from all the food groups but eat less. Choose lean meats and protein-rich vegetables. Let your scales tell you how much to eat. If you aren't losing about a pound a week, cut back on food intake. This is not a calorie-counting plan. This is a weight-driven plan using appropriate alternative behaviors. Choose your pain; choose your joy. As you lose weight, you are hauling less poundage around so you will need even less food. Adjust by eating less so you continue to lose a pound a week. The emotions that have been hidden by the weight will surface so don't be surprised about being angry and irritable. Use your skills to handle emotions. Quite often, the self-talk that has faded will come back with the emotions. Redirect the response to an ASR. Remember — gurgling and hunger pangs are fat farmers farming fat. They won't starve. They work for food.

John 15:4—"Remain in me" — part of the "in Christ" relationship. Remember, when we are in Christ we have the fruit of the Spirit, which includes self-control. WE HAVE SELF-CONTROL. We just need to use it. Plan your work and work your plan. It'll work if you work it. What have you got to lose?

Anger has a voracious appetite. The causes, affects, and management of anger are considered next.

$ $ $ 🔑━━🔑 $ $ $

Treasure Chest #15
Resources for Losing Excess Weight

JOKES ABOUT WEIGHT

The scope of a problem can be measured by the number of jokes devoted to it. There are whole books of jokes about weight.

- My doctor told me to watch my weight so I'm getting it out where I can see it.

- I use the seafood diet. I eat whatever I see.

- I tried the lite diet; I ate whenever it was light.

- My grandmother was so fat it took her two trips to go upstairs.

- Sin tastes good.

- If you lose weight, don't look for it; someone else will find it.

186 T H E   C . H . E . E . S . E .   F A C T O R

WEIGHT GAIN/LOSS DIAGRAM

Emotional hunger is hunger for comfort or some other reason to ease emotional pain. The following diagram helps demonstrate the dynamic of food as the satisfier of an emotional problem.

B_____
    Emotional Hunger
A_____
    Physical Hunger   C_____
No Food _____

Horizontal line A represents the amount of food we need to meet our physical needs and maintain a healthy weight. Horizontal line B represents the increase over our physical needs — emotional hunger — that is meeting some emotional need. Unfortunately, emotions have a voracious appetite. Line C represents the decrease in food intake from line A that is required in order to lose weight. We literally cannibalize ourselves. There are two challenges to losing weight. First, we have to deal with the emotions that require food. Then we stop the excess intake that supports our emotions. We have to face the challenge of eating less than our body normally needs in order to continue reducing body weight. When we reach an appropriate weight we return to A and eat in a controlled fashion. Most of the pain and difficulty in losing weight is in step C, reducing food intake to less than what is required for an appropriate final weight.

CHEESE/SPICE APPROACH
TO THE ANALYSIS OF EXCESS WEIGHT

There are both contributing and healing factors to the problem of excess weight. Most weight problems result from roots in our CHEESE Factories and violation of God's purposes in one or more of the SPICE areas. It follows that healing comes from correction in the affecting CHEESE/SPICE areas. Remember the CHEESE/SPICE matrix from Chapter 4. Use of the matrix gives a thorough examination of any ISR, including food. As this chapter deals with weight, contributing and healing factors applicable to excess weight will be inserted in the matrix. Each person can do an analysis of his or her individual situation. Some combinations may not apply and are left blank.

CHEESE/SPICE FACTORS MATRIX

Remember—each item from CHEESE is paired with each item from SPICE to fill that particular cell. How do Choice and Spiritual factors Contribute to my use of food? How do Choice and Physical factors Contribute to my use of food? and so on.

	C	H	E	E	SE
S					
P					
I					
C					
E					

FACTORS CONTRIBUTING TO WEIGHT GAIN

CHOICE - CONTRIBUTING

Choice/Spiritual — We have a natural inclination to choose evil instead of good.

Choice/Physical — Many lifestyles lack physical exertion that burns fat. Many jobs are sedentary. We may be afraid to have our children walk any distance because of possible harm. Some people's exercise is a hurried walk from a vehicle to work or to their residence, where they quickly lock the door. A large portion of many people's entertainment is watching TV. Food has become a source of physical and emotional comfort. Food tastes good. It is fun to eat.

Choice/Intellectual — Many people choose sugared drinks in place of water, not realizing that six twelve-ounce cans of soda contain a day's limit of calories. Control is an issue in some cases of over- or under-eating. Eating is one of the few areas where children and teenagers have a measure of control. We may believe that food is one of the few ways we can get enjoyment out of a humdrum life. We can be subject to stinking thinking.

Choice/Community — Quite often, social is spelled f-o-o-d. Many weight loss plans are wrecked at social gatherings. After all, we have to be polite. The road to weight is paved with good conventions.

Choice/Emotional — The emotional sector has many traps for the susceptible person. Many of my overweight clients say weight causes them to disappear socially so food enfolds them in a cocoon that protects against social pain. Some people eat when they are anxious. Some people find eating to be a relief in the process of grieving. Some use eating to punish themselves or others. Sometimes we eat simply out of boredom. We want something to do and find ourselves in front of the "fridge."

HEREDITY — CONTRIBUTING

Heredity/Spiritual — There is something inherently perverse about human nature.

Heredity/Physical — Our basic metabolism is probably inherited. We may be thriftier, getting more out of the food we eat. Some may see this as a blessing because their food bill is lower.

Heredity/Intellectual —

Heredity/Community —

Heredity/Emotional —A stomach full of fatty foods has a calming effect and reduces depression. A full stomach leads to a feeling of contentment. Our mindset may allow food to relieve stress.

WHY WEIGHT?

ENVIRONMENTAL — CONTRIBUTING

Environment/Spiritual — The church potluck is a big downfall for many Christians. Paula brings pecan pie, which is her specialty; Barb brings double fudge cake, which is her specialty; Martha brings her fourteen kids, which is her specialty.

Environment/Physical — We are changing our environment so it is more and more comfortable to use machines to do our work instead of burning calories. Food companies and restaurants pander to our weaknesses. The food industry likes fat people; they are, shudder, their bread and butter. Food companies load up food with fat and sugar to cater to our tastes. They make food convenient and easy to access. Restaurants give large portions, you can even "supersize" them. The many smorgasbord-type restaurants permit us to eat several days' worth of calories in one sitting. Restaurants aren't legally responsible for providing unhealthy food. We live in an environment that is saturated with saturated fat.

Environment/Intellectual — The American mindset is "bigger is better." We also like a good deal, so getting twice as much food for the same price is a temptation. Buffet restaurants are very popular. One time I was sitting in a restaurant and people kept taking food off my plate. I complained to the manager and she told me not to sit at the salad bar.

Environment/Community — Family patterns are difficult to break. Family gatherings often offer a rich variety of fattening foods with wonderful cooks who are hurt if every dish isn't "finished off." In Joan's family we got to kiss the cook if we cleaned up a dish. We need to change so the cook slaps us if we clean up a dish. Probably not. The cook might kiss us if there is food left. If food has been used in punishing or rewarding, bad habits may be formed. If a child is sent to bed without any supper, he or she may gorge out of resentment. Coffee breaks — "Whose turn is it to bring the donuts?"

Environment/Emotional — Food if we're sad. Food if we're mad. Food if we're glad. If food is used to raise our spirits, it may also raise our weight. We may seek food any time we feel down.

EVENTS — CONTRIBUTING

Events/Spiritual — Potlucks

Events/Physical — Much of our lifestyle is centered on food. Even if we exercise, we often follow a bit of exertion with a celebration of calories that far exceeds what was burned off. The best exercise is to push away from the table.

Events/Intellectual — We strive to create the most attractive, most delectable dishes. Do this, but keep portions small.

Events/Community — Holidays, anniversaries, birthdays, funerals, weddings, office parties, going away, coming together, winning, losing — on and on. Our social lives contain a constant bombardment of calories. Most of these are added to our regular diet and, over time, add up to extra pounds. A cookie a day adds pounds in a month. We even have eating or drinking contests where people are encouraged to consume death-defying amounts of food or alcohol. In these instances, people take pride in eating and drinking beyond reason.

Events/Emotional — During social events the presence of other people may create a crowd psychology that encourages us to eat more.

SELF-ESTEEM — CONTRIBUTING

Self-Esteem/Spiritual — Many leaders, including spiritual leaders, seem to feel that a large body makes them look more powerful in the hope of having more influence on those who hear and follow them. (Not by might, but by My Spirit, Zech. 4:6). Too many chicken dinners. Did you hear about the hen that was a poor lay member so she was put into the ministry?

Self-Esteem/Physical — The widespread fascination with body parts may encourage some people to gain weight in certain areas. Unfortunately, it leads to furniture disease where our chest falls into our drawers. Some people have been violated and gain excess weight in order to become unattractive.

Self-Esteem/Intellectual — The brain is the most important weight organ. If our mindset is that we have to eat inappropriately, we will eat inappropriately.

Self-Esteem/Community — Some see excess weight as a sign of success. Others see excess weight as a sign of weakness.

Self-Esteem/Emotional — Behind every pound of emotional weight is the attempt to solve an emotional problem. If the problem isn't dealt with, it will call the weight back. I met a man who said he had lost one hundred pounds. When I looked at his stomach, he grimaced and said it was the same five pounds twenty times. The emotional issue is a combination of SPICE items with our CHEESE factory. Quite often overweight people are called lazy or stupid. Often they have fewer friends. There are employment and social biases. It costs more to ride in some planes. We may dislike our bodies. All the stated problems are depressing and may lead to giving up and further eating. A feeling of entitlement often leads to overuse of food. I deserve it, I work hard, and I don't have any other pleasures or vices. It's better than _____ (fill in the blank).

FACTORS INVOLVED WITH LOSING WEIGHT

CHOICE — LOSING

Choice/Spiritual — Our first choice, on our way to a healthy weight, is to be "in Christ." Some choice, or mindset, that is contrary to God's plan, led to inappropriate use of food. Food may have been an Inappropriate Stress Reliever (ISR) or whatever item(s) you checked on the "Eatercise" list. However, we can be "new creations in Christ"; "we are purified of all unrighteousness"; "there is now no condemnation." We can be "transformed by the renewing of our minds." Being "in Christ" eliminates a lot of bad reasons for misusing food. Our body is a temple of the Holy Spirit. We want our bodies to be as effective as possible for God's work. Consider John 16:8. The Holy Spirit "will convict the world of guilt in regard to sin and righteousness and judgment." If you feel the Holy Spirit is convicting you to lose weight, then know that God will give you strength as you follow His leading. Again, you may need a Gethsemane experience. "Father, if it be possible, let me eat this food, however, not my will, but thine be done."

We may have to scream and cry as the decision to lose weight is made. Once the decision is made, the rest is process. Gethsemane is followed by Golgotha. Part of us has to die to excessive food. Then comes the Garden where we resurrect in a healthier body.

In 1 Corinthians 6:12-13, "Everything is permissible for me but not everything is beneficial. Everything is permissible for me but I will not be mastered by anything." To be mastered by something is to be addicted to it. The question is, do I own my food habits or do my food habits own me? If we pursue an ISR long enough, it will possess us.

Choice/Physical — It takes muscle to carry that weight around. If a person is sixty pounds overweight, think of what it is like to have a sack of cement around his or her neck every time he or she stands up, every time a step is taken. No wonder he or she is tired! We eat more just to get the energy to cart ourselves around. My doctor told me to walk five miles a day. After a week I called him and said, "I'm thirty-five miles from home, now what do I do?"

Get a Body Mass Index chart. Weigh yourself each day and let the scales be your guide to food intake on the next day. Set a reachable goal. If too high a goal is set, another failure will be added to the weight loss saga. Remember that it took a long time to get to where you are. It will take a long time to achieve your desired goal. If you have been overweight you have developed some muscle to carry the weight around. Muscle is hard to lose. Legs, especially, may remain large because they have had several weight lifting reps.

You may vary several pounds due to fluid loss from perspiration. Don't shirk on water just to get a fake weight loss. The brain is sensitive to water loss and there can be serious consequences to forsaking fluid intake. Drink a glass of an appropriate fluid before eating to fill the stomach. Fluid retention may depend on the time of the month. Overall, you should be going downhill.

We usually lose one to three pounds a night through respiration, perspiration and urination. Weigh just before going to bed and just after morning urination to estimate average fluid loss. If you eat a lot of spicy food, your body will retain fluid to dilute the spices. You will notice an increase in urination and weight loss as the spices are eliminated from the body.

It seems to take a few days for the body to shift over from living off food to living off self. Think of two gangs of little people in the stomach. One group is yelling, "I'm dying, feed me," while the other group is saying, "Enough already." Help the good guys win. Don't eat so fast that you run their STOP sign - Stop Taking on Pounds! Instead, Start Taking Off Pounds! At first, the fat farmers will be screaming for food but let the stomach shrink. They will work for fat. Never eat to discomfort. If you have been on a weight gain you will need to cut even more.

Only take on your plate what you want to eat, no seconds. Only eat at the table. Only eat during mealtime. Put your tools down between bites. Chew slowly. Slow down and enjoy the flavor. Don't "wolf your food." Dogs "wolf" their food. (I wonder if wolves "dog their food.") Don't insult the cook by choking it down. Chew food until the flavor is gone, and then swallow. You will enjoy it more and have less chance of eating past the point where the "good stomach crew" can tell you that you are full. It also helps prevent acid reflux. Don't clean up the last bit of food in the dish. If it has to go to waste, don't let it go to your waist. It's the little things, over the long run, that make a difference. Whole milk, over a year, adds weight. A box of cookies, over a month, adds weight. Hold down sampling while cooking. As the old lady said when she threw her husband into the river when the boat was stuck on a sandbar, "Every little bit helps."

When you eat out with a spouse or friend, order one meal for two people or ask for a bowser bag when you order. You can usually make two or three meals out of one order.

Choice/Intellectual — There are dozens of diets that will work if you work one of them. In place of a diet, there are alternatives of medication and surgery. If medications and surgery are what it takes, then that is what it takes. Medications and surgery are not cure-alls. Medications have side effects. Surgery is just an enforced diet and people can gradually enlarge what stomach they have left. It took awhile to put the weight on so be patient and take awhile to get it off. Loss of a pound or two a week is reasonable and gives the body time to adjust.

You can count calories if it helps (five hundred fewer calories a day is a pound a week), but let your scales be your guide. If you are not losing weight, you need to eat less. You HAVE to eat less to lose. Keep cutting back until you are losing one or two pounds a week. Check with your doctor.

Allow desire, determination, and control factors to bring positive results. Be strong in a positive direction.

Choice/Community — Avoid wet places and wet faces. You may need to change your social life. If you have to be where there is a lot of food, force yourself to eat raw vegetables, no dip. How often have you decided to limit your food intake only to be in a situation where there is a celebration or some event accompanied by large amounts of fattening food? It is acceptable to simply refuse the piece of cake being shoved in your face by saying, "No thank you; I'm on a diet." Or, "I can't; I'm a foodaholic." It is cruel to push food at a person who is trying to lose weight.

Choice/Emotional — See yourself as a thinner person. Don't identify yourself with fat. Delight in a healthy body. Choose Appropriate Stress Relievers (ASRs). Choose your pain; choose your joy. There is the pain of hunger and there is the pain of low self-esteem and damaged health. There is the joy of eating and there is the joy of improved self-esteem and better health. There will be pain and joy either way.

HEREDITY — LOSING

Heredity/Spiritual —

Heredity/Physical — If we eat less and don't lose weight, the body must be getting more out of what we eat. Sometimes we have to eat less and less. Like a grasshopper hopping half the distance to a fence, successive jumps don't accomplish as much. The loss curve generally flattens out as we try to lose more. We need fewer calories for a lighter body. Muscle mass is the hardest to lose because the excess food intake has been changed to protein. Many people who have lost a lot of weight find they have large muscular legs. The reason is that many repetitions of standing and lifting have occurred as the person stands, walks, climbs stairs, etc. Body builders shape their muscles through hundreds of repetitions of lifting weights. The same thing happens when a person lifts thirty to two hundred or three hundred extra pounds several times a day.

Heredity/Intellectual — Hopefully, you have inherited some strong willed genes. The way to tell a girl baby from a boy baby is that girl babies have pink genes.

Heredity/Community —

Heredity/Emotional — Usually, urges for food pass after a few minutes, especially if an ASR is used.

ENVIRONMENTAL — LOSING

Environment/Spiritual — Spiritual leaders should lead by word and by example.

Environment/Physical — If you live in an area where safety or weather precludes outdoor exercise, get some good indoor exercise equipment and use it. It'll work if you work it.

Environment/Intellectual — Weight loss begins at the grocery store. Don't put it in the cart. Don't let it in the house. If it gets into the house, it will probably get into you. Eating out? Keep it out. Use dense foods thoughtfully. Things like cheese and nuts should be used wisely because they pack a lot of calories in a small space. Lettuce, on the other hand, requires more calories to chew than you get out of it. Honeymoon salad is good — just lettuce alone. No dressing.

Environment/Community — Get a buddy who will help you with "accountabudability." Allow your buddy to ask the tough questions. Look into food traps and talk them through. Don't be a fish that takes any bait. Get professional help if you seem to be stymied. Weight loss groups are helpful for some people. The more social support and accountability you employ, the better your chances are of losing weight and keeping it off. We'll never succeed in any effort we don't try so make resolutions — Four-step Rule Process. We miss 100 percent of the shots we don't take.

Environment/Emotional — Rejoice in the Lord! His elevator always takes us up.

EVENT — LOSING

Event/Spiritual — Be strong-willed at potluck dinners.

Event/Physical — Consider your events. Are they primarily activity or food-oriented? Go heavy on the activity, easy on the food.

Event/Intellectual — As a man thinketh in his stomach, so is he. If you are a gourmet cook, make delicious meals that are low in calories.

Event/Community — At parties use a game or a toy in place of a food tradition. At least replace the fat and sugar with something healthier. Make social events a time of victory over food. This may require a huge change in mindset.

Event/Emotional — Don't let food be an emotional factor during celebrations. Control your soul.

SELF-ESTEEM — LOSING

Self-Esteem/Spiritual — "Therefore, since Christ suffered in his body, arm yourselves also with the same attitude, because he who has suffered in his body is done with sin. As a result, he does not live the rest of his earthly life for evil human desires, but rather for the will of God" (1 Pet. 4:1-2). Being able to control our fleshly appetites has a marvelous effect on our self-esteem. Armed with that feeling, we are more able to resist other temptations. In order to gain this esteem we must have the same attitude that Jesus had. He "set his face" to go to Jerusalem. He said, "Not My will but Thine be done." We really don't want to live the rest of our lives for ISRs.

Self-Esteem/Physical — What panders to the "world's" tastes is usually meaningless or an affront to God. People usually look at the outside and make assumptions while "God looks at the heart" (1 Samuel 16:7).

Self-Esteem/Intellectual — When you do choose to lose, flail against failing as failure may foil further fights. When you lose a pound, do everything possible to keep it off. Don't be like the cleansed man whose demon came back with six friends.

Self-Esteem/Community — It helps to have people recognize and encourage you for your efforts at weight loss or staying trim. Seek out such people. Spend time with people who like you and will help you.

Self-Esteem/Emotional —THE JOHN CHAPTER 15 DIET PLAN

"EVERYONE SHOULD BE QUICK TO LISTEN, SLOW TO SPEAK AND
SLOW TO BECOME ANGRY, FOR MAN'S ANGER DOES NOT BRING ABOUT
THE RIGHTEOUS LIFE THAT GOD DESIRES" (JAMES 1:19-20).
"IN YOUR ANGER DO NOT SIN . . . DO NOT GIVE THE DEVIL
A FOOTHOLD" (EPH. 4:26-27). ANGER IS A GOD GIVEN
EMOTION. WHAT WE DO WITH OUR ANGER IS A CHOICE.

CHAPTER 16

USE OF ANGER IS A CHOICE

GOD GETS ANGRY

Have you ever wondered if God gets angry about so much that is
going on that is outright displeasing to Him? Well, He does get angry.
There are hundreds of references in the Bible that tell of divine anger.
What does God get angry about? Many times in the Old Testament
we find that God was angry at His children's disobedience. He gets
angry when people pick on His kids. Jesus was angry when the temple
was profaned (Mark 11:15). Jesus was angry when laws were put before
the welfare of a crippled man (Mark 3:5). A GLOSSARY for anger is
at the back of the book.

Should we get angry? The fact is that we, at least most people, do
get angry. We are made in the image of God and anger is one of His
emotions. Therefore we will get angry. The question is, how do we use
our anger wisely? We don't have God's wisdom, or His overall plan,
but we can learn about anger and attempt to use it constructively. The

purpose of this chapter is to help understand the sources and expression of anger, then to have a mindset that will give control over this awesome emotion.

ANGER AS A RESULT OF OUR CHEESE FACTORY

Hereditary factors, environmental factors, and events form the mindsets we have about anger. In accord with the CHEESE factory theory, we are born with the ability to become angry. Without the mind of Christ, we have human anger. A recipe for human anger might well be a mold of heredity filled with an emotionally and economically deprived environment with a few negative events thrown in to add flavor.

Anger is marked by psychological and physiological responses to threats (boundary violations). Threats include a raft of things that cause anxiety. A threat, like a loud sound, causes anxiety, or in more extreme cases, fear. Anxiety and fear are psychological responses to threats that trigger adrenaline. Adrenaline causes physiological changes that enable us to exercise great power, a God-given ability to either face a threat or flee from it. Anger is a face-or-flee emotion. If we face the threat, we grow; if we flee from the threat it grows and we stagnate or we may find an ISR. We need facing tools.

It is helpful to recognize the first signs of anger, whether they are emotional or physical responses. Tightness in the chest, a queasy stomach, a clenched fist, a flushed complexion, an increase in blood pressure, shortness of breath, or whatever — the quicker we recognize the emotional/physiological signals, the more we can set in action our responses to control anger. $$ MY ANGER PATTERN $$

If the hereditary mold is filled with an environment of hostility and hurtful events, it may produce a person who acts out inappropriately when angry. Anger reactions are also learned from witnessing what works for others and from what has worked for us in getting our perceived wants/needs met. If someone has a quick temper and it seems to work to an advantage, that behavior may be copied. Children take cues from their parents on how to handle situations that involve anger. The way children react to a boundary violation is more often caught than taught. If we grow up in an environment of harmful uses of anger, our mindsets will reflect that environment.

ANGER AT VIOLATION OF THE SELF

Neglect and/or abuse will cause a justifiable anger reaction, especially among children who are powerless to defend themselves. Using the SPICE acronym as a guide we can see how different areas of their lives are affected. Spiritually, their concept of God is distorted. They cannot see how a loving God can allow damage to their beings. Physically, they may have developmental deficits or scars that affect them throughout their lives. Intellectually, they do not understand the effects of neglect and/or abuse or they may be misled by false information. Socially, the neglect and/or abuse may inhibit their ability to establish positive relationships. They disrespect their parents and act out socially. Emotionally, they question their value and may develop a sense of guilt and/or shame as they try to make sense out of why they were violated.

The realization that they were not respected as human beings, created in the image of God, generates deep feelings of anger that some people find extremely difficult to overcome. They either spend their lives in the victim stage, constantly reliving the neglect/abuse, or they barely survive by fighting to push memories into the background.

An anger reaction that starts in childhood may become a conditioned mindset over the years. If anger is rewarded, it will be repeated. That doesn't mean someone is given $10 for being angry; it just means the result of the anger expression seems to be in the angry person's best interest. The rewards strengthen the person's natural mindset that their behavior is acceptable (to them). Inappropriate uses of anger are reinforced by self-serving rewards. When we have the mind of Christ, alternative, appropriate responses to anger are rewarded by love, joy, and peace. *$$ ALTERNATIVE ANGER ACTIVITY $$*

GENDER DIFFERENCES IN EXPRESSING ANGER

No generalization is totally true, including this one, but sometimes they are helpful when exploring mindsets. One generalization is that men and women respond differently to boundary violations — men get angry; women get depressed.

While anger in a man may be a symptom of depression, men usually mask their inner emotional states and express anger outwardly. A man may have common physical or emotional states such as hunger, loneliness, or exhaustion, but display anger because anger is one of the few ways men are conditioned to express emotions. If there is an anger expression for an emotion, men will find it. Some men develop anger as a fine art. They will find a way to translate almost any negative emotion into an anger response. Quite often, men get loud and break things or people. Generalizations.

Women often deal with loss by pushing anger inward, leading to depression. Be sure to note that loss, not anger, lays the foundation for depression. A great loss for women in our society is a loss of empowerment. The incidence of depression for women is far greater than for men. One of the main reasons women are depressed is that they are taught that it is "unladylike" to express anger outwardly. Generalizations.

Men are providers so they express anger by withholding and controlling money. Women are nurturers so they may consciously or unconsciously express anger by withholding emotional support. Men are physically stronger and emotionally weaker so they strike out physically. Women are physically weaker and emotionally stronger so they strike out emotionally.

Women use a large range of emotions; men get mad. Women cry; men get mad. Women get jealous; men get mad. Women share with each other; men get mad, etc. Generalizations. But there is enough truth in the generalizations to see a pattern that may exist in your life.

A combination of CHEESE factors leads to a mindset of how anger should be expressed. We need to realize that while the ability to be angry is innate, the way we express anger is learned. What is learned can be replaced with an alternative. The bottom line is, regardless of our CHEESE factory, the use of anger is a choice.

ANGER AND CONTROL

The word violent, which is defined as uncontrolled force, is often used in reference to anger. But, think about it. Natural storms can be violent. For instance tornadoes and hurricanes are out of our control and leave random, capricious damage, hitting one thing and leaving another untouched. However, a problem with defining a response to anger as a violent, i.e., uncontrolled act, is that it raises questions about the target of the anger and responsibility for the results. That which is uncontrolled is random in nature. If a person is out of control, he or she may fall down, or hit a tree, or babble incoherent sounds. However, when a specific thing or person is targeted, control is evident. A person may say, "If such and such happens, I won't be responsible for the consequences." But, if a specific act is performed, a choice was made and responsibility is attached.

A person who does damage during an episode of anger may plead, "Not guilty because I lost control." We find it difficult to put the anger of a person in the "uncontrolled" category because the damage inflicted is most often directed. Incidents like hitting someone in the nose, destroying an object, or shooting someone are specific and intentional. "Out of control" anger is an emotion that almost always results in specific harm to ourselves, others, or property.

To become angry over what someone else does or says is to allow them to take control of your life. Anger should not be dependent on another's actions. As long as you are "driving your bus" (passengers and baggage included), you'll usually go where you want to go. Giving the controls to someone else allows them to decide where you go. Choose not to give control to another person or circumstance. $$ RUBBER/GLUE INTERVENTION FOR ANGER $$

DIRECTIONS ANGER TAKES

We often choose to react to irritants, threats, pain, or frustration with anger. Our anger can be expressed in a variety of ways. We have taken the word "passes" from Paul's letter to the Philippians to help understand different directions that anger may take. "Don't be anxious about anything, instead, make your requests to God with thanksgiving and the peace that passes understanding will keep your hearts and minds in Christ Jesus" (Philippians 4:6-7, KJV). The word "passes" provides an acronym for Passive aggressive, Acted out, Somatic ailments, Self-harm, and, Evaluate and Solve.

ANGER TURNED OUTWARDS

Passive Aggressive Anger

Passive aggressive people are an irritant to others. They may deny, or not even realize that they are expressing anger. They are late for meetings, stall, object, "forget," make empty promises, hold back favors, and/or manipulate people by undermining others' plans. They may act in ways that irritate or hurt relationships. They may call people names and say, "just kidding." A lot of negative humor is actually an expression of passive aggressive anger.

Acted Out Anger

Angry people who act out have anger that is easiest to detect. They yell, break things, threaten, and manipulate by causing fear.

ANGER TURNED INWARDS

Somatic Problems

(Soma — Greek for body.) Some psychosomatic problems are from anger turned inward. Somatic problems include illnesses such as irritable bowel syndrome, backaches, headaches, depression, and/or anxiety. Obviously, not all the maladies mentioned are always a result of anger, but anger has to be examined as a possible contributing factor.

SELF-HARM

Some people express their anger by putting themselves down. They use negative self-talk to beat up on themselves. They may abuse substances. They may cut themselves. They may attempt or complete suicide. Anger has a voracious appetite and some people use food to sooth their emotions, thus having a problem with weight as well as anger.

ANGER USED CONSTRUCTIVELY

EVALUATE AND SOLVE

The appropriate use of anger is to channel it so some good is accomplished. Anger can be used in a controlled fashion to motivate action. Evaluate and solve using a problem solving strategy — state the problem clearly, brainstorm possible solutions, choose a plan of action, and implement it, being careful to monitor and adjust as necessary. Taking responsibility for positive change will help in using anger appropriately. Stubborn anger requires the NCBT — Alternative approach.

Stuffing, or attempting to hide anger, is like credit card debt. Pay now or pay later with interest. Stuffing anger may result in depression or physical ailments. If the problem is not solvable, the reality of the circumstances needs to be accepted; let it become an old stray cat — don't feed it, don't pet it, and don't chase it around with a broom. If your anger reaction to circumstances is minor, you may be able to acknowledge it and, through awareness, replace the reaction with an appropriate stress reliever. *$$ BALLOON INTERVENTION FOR ANGER $$*

Anger can be a great motivator for change. When we, or others, are oppressed, harassed, or abused, anger can motivate us to take steps to change the situation. When our children openly disobey us, the adrenaline rush can motivate us to learn positive parenting techniques and spend the time necessary to train them properly. Anger is inappropriate when its expression causes more stress. Anger is appropriate when it motivates positive change and relieves stress. An appropriate response to anger is to let the anger motivate resolution of the problem. *$$ STRING INTERVENTION FOR ANGER $$*

ABCs OF ANGER

Anger is a confusing emotion. We may have been told, "Don't get angry." But, we often feel angry. Ephesians 4:26-27 is helpful — "Be angry but do not sin; don't let the sun go down on your wrath; don't give the devil a foothold." Our anger must be changed from human anger to anger that is useful for God's purposes. We can, "be angry" but how do we handle anger so it doesn't, "give the devil a foothold?" We need to know that repeated use of an inappropriate anger reaction becomes a mindset by means of an ABC process. Antecedent — Belief — Choice. (It is helpful to learn new words. If antecedent is new for you, it means a preceding event — something that comes before. To fit the ABC acronym, mindset is changed to belief.) Understanding the ABC process will help make the use of anger constructive.

A is for an Antecedent that brings an anger reaction. Something "makes" me angry. Actually, I choose to express anger because I want to do something I can't, I can't do something I want, or someone (something) I love is threatened or hurt, etc.

B is for the Belief (mindset) that leads to a choice of behavior. What is my perception of the antecedent? What is my self-talk? Why do I feel an anger response is appropriate? If I believe I should tailgate if someone cuts in front of me, I will tailgate. If I believe the other driver is stressed and preoccupied, I will have compassion and back off. It is not the event that brings the anger response; it is the perception of the event. It's not the Antecedent but the Belief that shapes the response to anger. In the ABC of anger, the Belief quite often becomes ingrained so thought is no longer used. The Antecedent is immediately followed by a negative choice we may regret. AC-DC, Antecedent Choice, Dire Consequences.

C is for Choice of behavior. How we respond to an event is our choice — our response-ability is our responsibility. It may be helpful to think of a reaction as being different from a response. Reaction may be thought of as impulse-driven while response is thought-driven. Either choice is directed by mindsets. We train ourselves, or have been conditioned, to react in a certain way. We may be genetically inclined to have a quick reaction to events. We may have adopted reactions as a result of modeling after a significant other. Our reactions may have become habits. But our response is a choice. We can learn to choose a different response. *$$ DOMINO INTERVENTION FOR ANGER $$*

"Roger" was enthusiastic! He exclaimed, "The ABC of anger worked like a charm. Simply adjusting my belief about my boss' attitude, and what my response should be, I made the choice to change my whole approach to things that used to irritate the heck out of me." Mindsets.

CONTROL OF ANGER AS A MINDSET

A mindset of control of anger can be achieved in a variety of ways. We can maintain a mindset of calm by deciding not to get angry. We can consider the possible consequences of anger and question whether or not its expression would cause regret. We can ask questions: Why am I angry? Should I be angry? What good can anger do in this situation? We can think of anger as water in a tub. If the tub is almost full, it doesn't take much to splash over. The trick is to take some of the water out of the tub. If you adopt a mindset of control, your anger can be desensitized in much the same way as relieving anxiety by using relaxation techniques. Use meditation, muscle relaxation, humor, deep breathing, counting, imaging, empathy — whatever it takes, to keep the tub as empty as possible so it takes more to push you over the top. *$$ TUB INTERVENTION FOR ANGER $$*

Only as we come to understand that God's "grace is sufficient," even for our pain and anger (2 Cor. 12:9), only when we believe that "God works for good in all things" (Rom. 8:28), only when we firmly believe that His judgments are "true and just" (Rev. 19:2), will our mindset be that we can be released from the bonds of anger over past abuses. Only when we are able to forgive as we are forgiven (Eph. 4:32) can we release ourselves and the perpetrators from the legacy of anger and become "more than conquerors through Christ who loved us" (Rom. 8:37). We do not have to bear the weight of judgment for those who wronged us. We do not have to live in the garbage dumps and sewers of our past. Our use of anger can be transformed by the renewing of our minds. $$ FORGIVE $$

ANGER IS NEUTRAL

Some final thoughts about anger: Anger is neutral. Use of anger can be positive if it motivates constructive action, or negative when it is destructive. Use of the emotion of anger is a choice. It isn't an event that provokes anger; rather, it is the perception of the event that directs our reaction. If our mindset is that we should act out in anger, we will find supportive evidence. We decide what response a situation warrants. Nothing "makes" us angry; we choose to be angry. We choose whether or not to let an outside influence control our lives. When we react, we place our life and emotions in the hands of another or circumstance. In controlling anger, eliminate as many anger-provoking events as possible and choose not to react to the rest in harmful ways. ACT — DON'T REACT! Rather, RESPOND — DON'T REACT.

All of our reactions and responses are a form of communication. Unless these forms of communication are brought under control, harm can be done to relationships. Appropriate communication can be a valuable stress reliever so we go there next to tap into this God-given resource.

$ $ $ &— $ $ $

Treasure Chest #16
Resources for Controlling Anger

A psychoceramic is a cracked pot.

MY ANGER PATTERN

We all have our MOs — Methods of Operation that flow from our mindsets. Write down events leading up to the last few times anger was felt. Identify what triggered the anger reaction. Think about each trigger. Is there a pattern that identifies a mindset? Try to identify the roots of the triggers. Can the roots be dug out and discarded if the anger reaction is inappropriate? Can the reaction be changed to a new mindset that is thought-driven?

Consider the events that were listed. How did my body and mind demonstrate emotional reaction? It is important to identify the first signs of anger so any domino effect can be interrupted. Using the same list of anger events, list the actions that followed the physical and emotional reactions. What is the pattern to my actions? What new pattern can be established?

ALTERNATIVE ANGER ACTIVITY

Let's consider an Alternative Anger Activity (AAA). For each episode, list a preferable AAA response that will lead to a positive outcome. It is helpful to have alternative actions planned in advance so old patterns of behavior don't take over in the heat of the moment. Your list represents a golf bag full of different clubs for different anger situations. Identify long-term anger as your driver. Identify a short burst of anger as your putter. Identify the holes as goals and hazards as buzzards that should be avoided. Work on your game. Practice these alternatives just as you would practice golf.

RUBBER/GLUE INTERVENTION FOR ANGER — NONSTICK SUITS

An old playground chant goes, "I'm rubber and you're glue. What you say bounces off me and sticks to you." Trade in your Glue suit for a Rubber suit. Most of us wear Glue suits and the sandburs of life stick to us until we are a prickly, irritated mess. With a Rubber suit's nonstick surface the sandburs bounce off. Use a Rubber suit response when someone throws a sandbur. That way, we reflect their thoughts. For instance, if someone says, "You always exaggerate!" You can answer, "You think I always exaggerate?" We bounce it back to them to do with as they wish. Of course we say this in a very compassionate way. RESPOND; DON'T REACT. Give <u>them</u> ownership of the statement. It's their thought. You don't have to buy into it. If they repeat the accusation just smile and be silent or give a broken record response. The Rubber suit response is one of the few times that "you statements" are appropriate. What comes out of their mouth doesn't always go past their ears. When you reflect, it gives them a chance to hear what they said. Practice responses with another person. Practice that is done in a calm state can be used during a state of stress instead of reverting to old habits.

I've told you a million times not to exaggerate.

BALLOON INTERVENTION

Use a balloon to represent anger.
Pop a balloon if it won't cause a problem. Do you pop?
Release a blown-up balloon to represent chaos.
Let air out gradually to represent control.
Tie off a blown-up balloon to demonstrate stuffed anger vulnerable to being poked.

STRING INTERVENTION FOR ANGER

Get a piece of string about two feet long. (Thread is too light. Rope is too heavy.) If you want to shorten the string it doesn't matter which end you cut off. There are two ways to reduce the negative effects of anger — don't get angry or, handle anger constructively — two ends of the string. List ways not to get angry: mindsets, mottoes, and meditations. Cut a representative length of string off one end of the string for each. List Alternative Anger Activities — ways to handle anger when anger occurs: walk away, exercise, work, etc. These reroute anger and get us out of trouble. Cut a representative length of string off the other end for each. Keep going until the string is gone. Now practice in real life.

While we're on strings — A string went to an ice cream parlor and ordered a chocolate ice cream cone. The clerk said, "Are you a string?" The string admitted it was. The clerk said, "We don't serve strings here." So the string mussed one end of itself up, tied itself into a bow, went back and ordered a chocolate ice cream cone. As the clerk gave the string a cone she said, "Aren't you a string?" The string said, "No, I'm afraid not."

DOMINO INTERVENTION FOR ANGER

Choose a representative example of an anger event from your list. Using dominos, identify a series of steps in the anger episode with a domino for each step. Try to get six to ten steps. When set up, discuss the line. Push the starting domino. Discuss the trigger, the physiological reaction, and the acting out. Now, set up the dominos again. Discuss at what point the sequence could have been stopped. Set up a fork in the chain of dominos to demonstrate an alternative response. Push the dominos over so the alternative response is activated. If the reaction side goes down, discuss what may sabotage the new response.

TUB INTERVENTION FOR ANGER

Draw a tub. Draw a line near the top to represent your anger level. Draw some exposed things floating around in the tub that raise the anger level. Draw some submerged things that don't show on the surface. Label each thing as an anger issue in your life. Discuss ways to lessen or remove the anger-causing agent.

FORGIVE

FORGIVE self — others — God. Mentally kicking ourselves around the block does no good. Letting self-reproach rule prevents the joy and peace of the Holy Spirit from ruling in our lives. Forgive everything. Give it to God. Ill feeling eats me up; it usually doesn't bother the person who offended me. It makes me live in the past, the garbage dump of my life, and prevents healing. Assume a positive slant on everything — mindset — Romans 8:28. Forgiveness is the ultimate step in getting past the past.

RECYCLE the garbage. What is the benefit? Find some use for the event.

GRIEVE the loss. Depression comes from the loss of something. Identify and admit the loss. Allow yourself to process the grief with tears, talk, and transformation of your mind. Use NCBT – identify, accept, assign responsibility, and redefine your relationships with self, others, God, and the world.

VERBALIZE the problem. Use self-talk, talk with others, talk with God — and listen for His answers. He will answer.

"In the beginning was the Word, and the Word was with God, and the Word was God" (John 1:1). Jesus Christ continues to be the most precious of all communication forms as He speaks through us in all our thoughts, words, and deeds.

CHAPTER 17

COMMUNICATION

One of the great differences between humans and animals is the extensive ability to communicate verbally on a level where it is possible to have an idea of what is being communicated and whether or not it has been heard and understood. This is a God-given talent that is meant to be utilized constructively. We suggest there is a difference between simple talking and verbal communication. Two people can be talking to each other when neither is listening or a person can be talking without understanding. Verbal communication involves both talking and understanding. It certainly is in our best interest to utilize the gift of communication in the process of developing and applying ASRs.

When asked what they feel is the most important need in their marriage, most couples say they want to improve their communication skills. Neither one seems to have problems talking in given situations but neither feels that communication is occurring between the two of them. What is the problem? Neither feels heard.

This chapter about communication is written primarily with married couples in mind. However, it is critical that those planning to be married, or who are dating with marriage as an eventual goal, develop communication skills as they learn about each other. In addition, all human interaction is communication of one form or another and the skills and understanding discussed apply to all relationships.

One of the first interactions recorded between God and humans was speech. Adoration, Confession, Thanksgiving, and Supplication (ACTS) are communication issues with God and with our spouse. If we are sending a message to God by withholding prayer, we are saying the relationship is broken. If a spouse is sending a message by withholding speech, the relationship is impoverished.

We need to remember that the majority of communication is non-verbal; it includes body posture and facial expressions. In addition, there is verbal communication and, within the verbal realm of communication, the meta-verbal — HOW we say what we say. Often, silence is a strong communication but the message isn't always clear. It would be interesting to know how much of the non-verbal is an expression of the emotional self and how much of the verbal is an expression of the intellectual self.

COMMUNICATION WITH GRACE

Many people do not talk because they, and/or the listener, lack specific skills. Fundamental requirements for communication are: Grace, Respect, sAfety, Clarification, and Empathy (GRACE).

Grace is necessary in communication because there is usually a multitude of past and/or present insults that need to be forgiven. We find in 2 Corinthians 12:9 that God's grace is sufficient. Nothing else is sufficient. Grace is unmerited, unearned, and undeserved love and forgiveness. Grace is forgiving the unforgivable. Grace should be extended to forgiving ourself. God extended His sufficient grace to us so that we could extend this grace to others. Often, undeserved grace is necessary to allow communication to continue. We may have to take up our cross and forgive. Two people can't spend ten minutes together without grace being needed for commission or omission of something.

Grace communication generates a feeling of trust and safety, both extremely necessary in promoting intimacy (into-me-see). We must allow each other to begin in an imperfect state and to grow in a non-threatening environment. While we were yet sinners, Christ died for us (Rom. 5:8). While my spouse is yet imperfect, I can submit to him or her in conversation. While I don't communicate perfectly, I can start and improve with practice.

Mutual *Respect* is needed so that communication is up-building, not demeaning. Respect is esteem for, validating, or giving a sense of the worth to, another. "The fear [awe, reverence] of the Lord is the beginning of wisdom" (Ps. 111:10). We are to stand in awe of God. We are to have reverence, regard, respect, and esteem for Him. The beginning of true self-esteem is reverence for God Who formed us. The regard, respect, and esteem that begin with God are to be extended to our spouse.

Do you balk at talk? Check your respect level. Love communicates. When we love God, we respect Him and interact with Him. If God's mind and mine are going separate ways, there will be little communication and it will indicate I do not care for His opinion, likewise with my spouse. In 1 Peter 3:7, men are commanded to "be considerate as you live with your wives, and treat them with respect . . . so that nothing will hinder your prayers." In Ephesians 5:33, wives are encouraged to respect their husbands. If pornography is being viewed, respect for the spouse is not being shown and that is one reason prayer life is faltering or nonexistent. As it is in our relationship with God, a lack of respect will undermine communication in our marriage and rob it of intimacy.

An incredibly important requirement for open communication is a *sAfe* environment. In order for a person to talk, he or she must be able to speak in a non-threatening environment and feel he or she is heard. If people are repeatedly shot down or ridiculed, they soon retreat into silence. Many quiet people can recall a Significant Emotional Event in which they were ridiculed or embarrassed for something they said.

The listener is required to be receptive and use *Clarifying* and reflective skills. Many arguments would be cut off before they begin if only people would clarify before they go off on a tangent.

We need to have both sympathy and *Empathy* for each other.

Sympathy — I feel sorry for you; empathy — I feel your sorrow. Empathy validates the speaker's feelings and encourages further discussion. We may not agree but we must do everything we can to feel the other's feelings. Remember: his or her perspective is his or her reality. When the speaker knows that the listener is earnestly interested in understanding the speaker's point of view, he or she is enabled to share. Don't take offense. We need to listen in rubber suits because much verbalization is in the form of sandburs. We need to put on the whole armor of God as we communicate with each other.

THE ABCs OF COMMUNICATION

Work on the ABCs of communication. With a given *Antecedent* (act, event), *Believe* the speaker has his or her own mindset and the right to express feelings. *Choose* to listen with care without letting emotions squelch the exchange. Differences in opinions are joyful gifts from God to be used to weld people together. Issues are intended to increase intimacy.

CARING SKILLS

An underlying premise in conversation with God is "Cast all your anxiety upon him for he cares for you" (1 Pet. 5:7). If God does not care for us, there is certainly no reason for us to talk to Him. But He does care, for each minute item, and desires fellowship with us. If I care for my spouse, we will be able to talk about "all," each minute item. Do you care about all things about your spouse? If not, ask God to create that care in you. Marriage is one of God's relationship gifts to us. Do you suppose He would give us relationships and not give us the abilities to communicate and rejoice in them?

Many people find it difficult to pour out their hearts to God. Do these same people suffer a communication block with others? Probably so. How can this be overcome? It requires trust, practice, and a willingness to make and forgive mistakes. The most meaningful prayer life is not formal, nor stereotyped in format and place, but is a continual thought stream to and from God. We are to pray constantly and instantly. Likewise with our spouse. Don't worry about form; simply share and reflect.

Realize that God knows our hearts so we can discuss everything with Him. Any thought or act, good or evil, can be discussed. If we reveal something that makes us ashamed, vow not to repeat the act. Why jeopardize your relationship with God or others by doing things that beget problems? THINK ABOUT IT!

LISTENING SKILLS

In GRACE communication, the focus is on listening. Very few people have listening skills. Mom brags about Johnny's first words but she doesn't call Grandma to report that Johnny listened. When one is listening, one is not to think, one is to radiate warmth, absorb information, clarify, reflect, and ask — wear the other's moccasins. Reflection does not necessarily mean agreement. It means the listener is trying to understand the speaker's message and mindset. Respecting the other's mindset is a grace gift and a mindset in itself. Once the mindset is determined, problem solving can take place if needed. A huge amount of miscommunication would be avoided if we would attempt to determine what is being said before we "shoot from the lip."

There are three timing elements in the empathic listening process. When to talk, when to listen, and when to use each mode. The person with the greatest need should be able to initiate the communication process. Select the proper mode, empathic listening or expression, depending on the need. Shift back and forth as the flow suggests. If you are emotionally unable to communicate constructively at a given time, call a time-out and set a specific later date to continue. Discuss issues at the earliest possible time you are emotionally able to do so. The longer the delay, the more anger and distrust can arise.

Two basics of relationship communication are: 1) recognize a concern, and 2) talk about it. Underlying problems in a relationship that are not exposed and discussed become termites that chew away at the foundation of the relationship. Communication does not have to be profound. If we are loved, everything communicated has relevance and will be accepted with kindness.

If communication is breaking down or drying up, it can get started again if each person makes a list of ten things he or she would like to talk about. We need not agree with each other but we do need to share and allow sharing. We often think more clearly when we see the list and hear the words. Good communication requires the listener to reflect and clarify before passing judgment. Find common ground.

If you withhold conversation from your spouse you will not enjoy the fullness of marriage. If there is disagreement over a critical matter, count it as joy, an opportunity for growth. As you work out consensus, compromise or concession, your relationship will mature.

GROUND RULES FOR COMMUNICATION

1. The purpose of communication is to build relationship and increase intimacy. Each person must care for and be willing to be subject to the other. Each person must understand the physical and emotional capabilities of the other and work within those limits.

2. Perception is reality. To set this concept in the mind, place an M in the middle of two or more people. They may see an M, a W, a 3, or an E depending on their perspective. Note the difference in perspective. "The way I see it . . ." Everyone is right. Each person must be willing to "hear" what the other person "sees."

3. Agreement is not necessary. Every difference will result in consensus, compromise, or concession. Each person must recognize that reflection is not agreement.

4. Each person must be willing to let the other have the opportunity to communicate. A soft stuffed animal can be held by the speaker to signify that he or she is speaking and the other is listening, clarifying, and reflecting. (Don't use a rock.) Having the stuffed animal allows a person to take time to consider what is going to be said. There is no hurry to say something

that may bring regret. The speaker holds the stuffed animal while the listener responds. Trade every few minutes to balance the conversation. Use a kitchen timer if someone talks too long.

5. Speak in short sentences. This gives the reflector the ability to respond without undue memory strain and helps prevent the mind from wandering to a rebuttal.

6. Truth and trust are essential. Always tell the truth; always trust what is said to be the truth. Lies, unspoken lies, and half-truths will erode intimacy. Truth is freeing (John 8:32). A wonderful life rule is, "Don't do anything you have to lie about." There should be congruence between your feelings and your communication. If you are frustrated or angry, admit your feelings and mention the specific behavior that has elicited those feelings. What event do you want to use to describe your emotions? Are there any descriptors you wish to substitute?

7. Use "I" statements as much as possible. "You" often builds defensive walls. It takes practice but almost any statement can be made without using "you" or "your." Instead of, "You are confusing me with your yelling," try, "I feel confused when I'm yelled at." We have a right to our feelings. We need to express our differences and emotions. Our CHEESE factory formed them. Examine motives that you value. Allow yourself to express yourself. "I think." "I feel." "I want." "I wish." You are the world's leading authority on your felt needs. What do YOU want? How do YOU feel? Abandon the futility of talking about how things should be, how most other people do things, what is correct, productive, or even how good-intelligent-perceptive-sensitive-normal people do or see things. Work on the needs of your individual marriage. Always use issues to build relationship. Relationship is more important than issues. Relationship rules! Concentrate on specifics and

behavior (what can be done, seen, heard), not on motivation or character. State as hypotheses not as unshakable convictions. Wonder a lot. "I wonder if . . ."

8. No mind reading is allowed. Ask or tell. To think, "If he really loved me, he would know what I want," or, "If I have to tell her, it doesn't mean anything," is stinking thinking and sets up opportunities for failure. It creates "outimacy." Have a Love List for your relationship/marriage (Ask in the nature of Christ and you shall receive (Matt. 7:7). List things you want your partner to do for you. Your partner isn't a mind reader; he or she doesn't know what itch you want scratched.

9. Keep on track. Stick to one issue. Keep a list of bunny trails for future reference if necessary.

10. Stay in the present. Yesterday's stuff should be old stray cats.

Review these rules often until they become an unconscious part of your communication pattern.

WHAT TO TALK ABOUT

Look for and discuss positive things. Instead of talking about what is wrong, talk about what will make it right. Find out what works and do more of it. This is very important; a great emphasis should be placed on positive attitudes. One important thing to remember is that the human mind cannot think of two things at once. We cannot be positive and negative at the same time. We get to choose what is in our minds. Choose positive things. There will always be plenty of negatives but we get to choose. Isn't that great? So choose positive things! If we fight with the enemy, the enemy gets stronger. A better way is to make the enemy a spectator and replace it with a "friend," i.e., a positive alternative.

Ask questions together. Wonder, i.e., "What is the wisest way to spend our money?" If you don't cultivate your garden, weeds will grow. Recognize and work to eliminate weaknesses in your communication skills. If you are not finding time to talk, plan a time each week for communication, and while you're at it, plan a time for recreation.

Life is filled with problems. Choose a good problem-solving method and use it. A good problem-solving method suggests alternative solutions. A good problem-solving method is better than screaming, hurt feelings, and doors slamming. The Four-step method described in this book applies to hundreds of situations. Briefly:

What is the problem?

Brainstorm alternatives.

Form a solution.

Try it for a while.

LOVE LIST

Your fiancé, spouse, or children may need to be taught to receive and express love. We learn to love from example, by observation, by reading, from experience, and by trial and error. Guess how love is taught? By actions! Each person should make a love list of things they want to do for each other person in the family. List everything you can think of. Get in the habit of sharing at least one a day. Emphasize the "being" aspect. When remarking about the "doing," link it to a "being" attribute, using items from the love list. This listening skill should not be too difficult as it is usually pleasant to hear someone say something nice about us. At all times remember, we are sincere and forgiving. Also remember truth and trust. Always tell the truth; always trust.

$$ FAMILY COMMUNICATION EXERCISE $$

Two other means of communication you might consider having are: 1) writing sticky notes, and, 2) by having "caring weeks." Sticky notes: "What I really would love to have you do for me today is ____." Place it on the bathroom mirror or refrigerator door. Or, you could just write something nice and stick it in the underwear drawer.

"Caring weeks": Each week will have five caring days. Choose five wishes that you want your partner to fulfill during that week. The next week, your partner chooses five wishes to be fulfilled by you. Continue this process until caring becomes a habit. What we do should not be dependent on what the other does. If we worry about who is getting the most, we then resort to bartering and manipulation. We should not wonder if we're getting enough back. The happiest relationship is when we strive to out-give each other.

Some people find it easy to satisfy each other. Others are willing to do things for their loved one but are in a fog (they really are in a fog) as to what to do from day to day or on a given day. Very few of us are mind readers, yet, if we only knew what was wanted, we would be happy to do it. Soooo — communicate! Let's make it easy to love each other. $$ REFLECTIVE LISTENING/SHARING EXERCISE $$

FORGIVENESS AND COMMUNICATION

"Whatever you ask in my name . . ." (John 14:14), that is, according to the nature of Christ, will be given. We can expect only that which is in the nature of our partner. If one has not yet received the nature of Christ, the other's requests are severely limited. However, if our partner has accepted Christ and is empowered by the Holy Spirit there is much more that we can ask.

Forgiveness is a prime example. If he or she has asked for and received the forgiveness of God, the Spirit of love and forgiveness is present and forgiveness can be given. If forgiveness is not given, forgiveness has not been understood. *IF YOU CANNOT FORGIVE, YOU HAVE NOT UNDERSTOOD FORGIVENESS.* Lack of forgiveness is a deadly cancer. It eats its way through relationships, changing what is good into bad.

Is there something that you are doing, or planning to do, that you are ashamed to discuss? Do you see what this does to your prayer life/relationship? (1 Pet. 3:7) How can you talk to God in loving relationship when you are considering evil? Likewise, in your marriage relationship. After Adam and Eve disobeyed God, they attempted to hide from Him (Gen. 3:8). Then God asked, "Where are you" (Gen. 3:9). When we know we have done wrong, we do not joyfully enter the company of our spouse. If the relationship bond is to be strong and nourishing, don't do anything you can't talk about! If you have to keep

it a secret from God/your spouse, don't go there. Where are you?
God searches our inner thoughts. Anything we think we are withholding from Him eats away at relationship. Please understand, He
does not seek to blame or continually hold up our sins before us to
shame us. He seeks to have all things forgiven so we can be "new
creations." If communication has broken down, ask some questions.
"Why aren't we talking?" Is someone or something on your conscience
that needs to be discussed and forgiven? Take it first to God and clear
up the situation with Him. Then clear it up with yourself. After being on speaking terms with God and yourself, take it to your spouse,
another one of God's forgiven children. He or she, too, will forgive
— must forgive. It is not enough just to admit our sin. We cannot say,
"I did it; so what?" We must confess, with remorse, and commit to the
resolve not to repeat the error. We need godly sorrow (2 Cor. 7:10). We
need the mind of Christ and His mindset in our relationships. That
mindset provides open and trusting communication with any person
coupled with forgiveness as experienced and shown in the "in Christ"
relationship.

COMMUNICATION AND SOCIAL SKILLS

Obstacles to change often stem from personality patterns. Some
personality patterns are mindsets or habits and can be replaced by
alternative behaviors. One approach to personality analysis is to list
three basic styles of interpersonal behavior: passivity, aggressiveness,
and assertiveness. In general, passive people take things, aggressive
people break things, and assertive people make things. In a normal
distribution, or bell-shaped curve, passivity would tail off one way, aggressiveness would tail off the other way, and assertiveness would be
middle ground. You may see yourself using a different style in different
situations. Sometimes it is expedient to be passive; sometimes aggres-
sion is required but usually, the assertive style is best.

PASSIVE

The passive style of interaction is characterized by allowing others to push you around or make decisions for you. Passive people do not stand up for themselves. They usually do what they are told, regardless of how they feel about it. When using this style, you will rarely experience direct rejection. On the other hand, you may feel that others are taking advantage of you and the result may be resentment and anger. Examples of passive behavior are: low voice, eyes down, slumped posture, unhealthy submission, guilt, and apologies. "I don't count."

AGGRESSIVE

Fighting, accusing, or threatening behavior typify the aggressive style. In general, the person using this style bullies others around without regard for their feelings. Aggressors use anger to manipulate. This style has its advantages, since aggressive people often get what they want. On the downside, other people may avoid their company. Examples of aggressive behavior are use of: loud voices, sarcasm, threats, negative attitudes and statements, profanity, you-statements, absolutes, and physical gestures.

ASSERTIVE

The assertive style allows you to stand up for yourself, express your feelings, and tell what you want. You can do all this without feeling guilty or being inconsiderate of other people's feelings. You can be direct in asking for what you want or saying what you don't want. Examples of assertive behavior are: a calm demeanor, good eye contact, clear communication, specific requests, a non-hostile approach, use of I-statements, respect for others, and a desire for equality. See Matthew 18:15-20 for help in dealing with disputes.

Assertiveness can help deal with everyday stressors. Assertiveness will help you express anger, say no, stop being used, express affection, act with choices, etc. Be careful to realize that assertive people do not expect others to change, nor do they always get what they want; they simply fulfill expectations of themselves not to be passive and swallow anger, nor to be aggressive and offend people. The world isn't going to ask, "How high?" just because you say, "Jump!" Be assertive but have realistic expectations.

An assertive statement has three components —

1. Your perception of the situation — *I think* —
2. Your feeling about the situation — *I feel* —
3. What you want in the situation — *I want* —

WAYS TO HANDLE AGGRESSIVE PEOPLE

Ask the aggressive person to slow down, request a time-out, probe for what is happening, acknowledge if you are at fault, agree in part, keep on track, discuss one thing at a time, stay in the present, or use a broken record by stating again and again what you wish to communicate.

Slow down: understand, process, and become aware of your feelings and thoughts. Eat angry words, by saying, "This is too important . . . That's interesting . . . Wait a minute . . . Do you mean . . .? I'm not sure I understand . . ."

Use a time-out: the other person may need a time-out but you will have to recognize it and say, "I need a time-out." That avoids the dreaded "you" word and forces the other person into a time-out. An essential element of a time-out is to state when the time is in again so the other person does not have to struggle with feelings of anxiety and abandonment. During the time-out, go off the defensive and allow a solution mode to go to work.

Probe: Listen carefully. Consider whether or not the other person is trying to use, hurt, or deceive you, or is she or he poor at communicating? "Help me understand what you are saying." Wonder a lot.

Acknowledge: Don't accept criticism unless it is warranted. However, if you agree with the criticism you may need to apologize. Then ask, "How can we get past this?"

Agree in part: Avoid absolutes. Choose a statement you can partially accept. Say, "You are right, pink doesn't go with orange but I just felt like dressing weird."

Keep on track: Say, "That is another interesting issue. I'll write that down for later discussion. Right now we are discussing . . ." Stick to one thing at a time: Continually refocus to the issue at hand.

Stay in the present: Don't rehash unsettled problems. Make them a separate issue.

Use the broken record: Decide on a statement, rehearse it, use positive body language, repeat the statement, and don't get distracted. For instance, say, "That act is out of character for me." Say it over and over until the aggressor sees there is no future in pursuing the issue. If you change your record they will get a "mouthhold" (kind of like a foothold) and continue to argue.

If you see yourself as aggressive and want to change, you can apply these modifications to yourself by putting the problem-solving process in action.

Picture in your mind the most aggressive, most passive, and most assertive persons you know. Compare the different styles. How do you want to respond to people using each of them? What is your general style? Compare assertiveness at home, work, leisure activities, different times of the day, month, etc.

The goal of communication is intimacy. Intimacy is much misunderstood. The next chapter will shed light on this important topic.

$ $ $*   🔑   *$ $ $

Treasure Chest #17
Resources for Improving Communication

REFLECTIVE LISTENING/SHARING EXERCISE

GRACE is essential to helpful communication. The following process may seem stilted at first. Use it until you are comfortable and then adjust to your own needs. Don't reject this process unless you have something better that does not include anger and wall building. Statements are based on YOUR desires, values, perceptions, and feelings. The speaker holds a soft object so there is no confusion about who is talking and who is responding. The Speaker, S, talks, and the Responder, R, listens and reflects.

S: "One of the things I love about you is _____."

R: "I understand that one of the things you love about me is _____."

S: "Something that I would appreciate is _____."

R: "I understand that _____ would be appreciated."

S: "One of the gifts I have that I would like to extend to you is ___."

R: "I understand that one of the things you would like to give me is _____."

Continue the exchange, using short sentences until dialogue is complete. When finished the speaker should say, "That's all I want to say about that at this time."

The reflector should use the standard hardware store question, "Is there anything else you need?" Sometimes, this will bring out additional important information. Then pass the animal or soft object. When you become skilled in reflective communication, the skills can be used for areas of disagreement.

FAMILY COMMUNICATION EXERCISE

Communication skills of Grace, Respect, sAfety, Clarifying, and Empathy (GRACE) need to be learned. Family groups can work on communication. One uses speaking skills, one uses reflective skills, and the rest serve as observer coaches. Change roles to give each one practice at each station. At any time the coaches can call time-out and give instruction in GRACE communication. Practice by saying positive things — warm fuzzies.

Do you know what I herd? Sheep.

"I HAVE GIVEN THEM THE GLORY THAT YOU GAVE ME, THAT THEY
MAY BE ONE AS WE ARE ONE; I IN THEM AND YOU IN ME. MAY THEY BE
BROUGHT TO COMPLETE UNITY TO LET THE WORLD KNOW THAT YOU
SENT ME AND HAVE LOVED THEM EVEN AS YOU HAVE LOVED ME" (JOHN
17:22-23). JESUS' INTENT IS THAT WE SHARE THE SAME CLOSENESS
WITH HIM AND EACH OTHER THAT HE SHARED WITH GOD.

CHAPTER 18

INTIMACY

THE GOAL OF COMMUNICATION

The GOAL of communication is intimacy. In order to move
towards this goal we must seek to understand each other's mindset
— bias — perception — reality. We must accept the fact that others
have their own reality based on their CHEESE factory, as we do ours.
They have a right to their reality. We agree to start apart and purge to
merge. Remember that God wants us to be individuals but to be "one"
in harmony and intimacy (into-me-see).

Intimacy is the most precious of all human experiences. Intimacy
with God is a powerful aid to becoming intimate with our spouse. Before
one can achieve intimacy with another person, he or she must learn to
have an intimate relationship first with God and then with his or her
self. God-esteem leads to self-esteem. One characteristic of the mentally healthy person is agreement or congruence between the perceived
self and the actual self. Agreement between these aspects of a person's
life indicates a maturity that allows a person to "enjoy life more abun-
dantly." The lack of agreement in these areas will cause conflict that

erodes self-esteem, which essentially is intimacy with the self.

In the American culture, the word intimacy has frequently been used as a more "delicate" way of saying "sex." This is indeed unfortunate because it adds to the myth that intimate relationships are always sexual relationships. Also, it is not necessarily true that a sexual relationship is intimate. While sexual involvement may be one dimension of an intimate relationship, the mere presence of sexual activity is neither a substitute for, nor a guarantee of, intimacy.

The definition of intimacy is not when "two people become one." In fact, an individual must be able to maintain his or her identity in order to function in an intimate relationship. Togetherness is not necessarily intimacy, not even togetherness over an extended time period. Many married couples who have raised children and remain together were never intimate.

Intimacy requires time and interaction to resolve issues. Among other things, true intimacy requires the total involvement of each facet of several unique godlike and human qualities among which are a SPICE rack of: 1) spiritually based truth and trust, 2) physical (nonverbal) communication, 3) intellect — the will to submit, 4) social agreement about issues of friends and activities, and 5) the emotion of love. These five components have no priority. A single missing one will decrease the level of intimacy. Let's consider the SPICE of intimacy as it flavors our relationships.

SPIRITUAL — Truthfulness and Trust

Truth has a strong spiritual component. Jesus said, "I am the way, and the truth, and the life" (John 14:6). The way to life is truth. Lies bring destruction and death to relationships. God will give us the "Spirit of truth" (John 14:16-17). When we are "in Christ" and have received the Holy Spirit, truth will be a foundation stone in all our relationships. Always tell the truth; always trust (Eph. 4:25). Don't do anything you will have to lie about. RULE FOR LIVING: If you are thinking of doing something you will have to lie about — DON'T DO IT! If you do, don't lie about it. Lies are termites that destroy the foundation of intimacy. We can work with truth. Lies are vapors that permeate and rot the foundations of an intimate relationship. Lies destroy trust. Lies call for deceptive miscommunication in many forms.

Honesty is an expression of our spiritual health. If we lie, we are infected with sin. Honesty is the ability to be truthful regarding inner thoughts and feelings. Honesty is not a fruit of the Spirit; it is our responsibility. Truthfulness in a relationship goes deeper than the words we speak. We live truthfully so we don't have to remember what we said or did. Lies require a tremendous amount of energy to maintain — energy that is much better spent on enjoying relationship. Disclosure + acceptance + forgiveness = greater intimacy.

Many people are dishonest when they date. They give a false impression of themselves and their wants and needs — campaign promises. After the marriage vows are spoken, lies come back as termites to chew away at the relationship. Both marriage partners have to live with them. The liar either has to continue to live the lie or expose the truth and the other feels betrayed. A classic example is the one who is sexually provocative before marriage but turns it off afterward with resulting bitterness on the other's part. Faked foundations feature future failure.

PHYSICAL – Nonverbal Communication

Intimacy requires communication. We need to remember that the vast majority of communication is nonverbal. Therefore, we must recognize that intimacy depends largely upon our physical activity and presentation. Lack of physical communication, i.e., actions, should be considered a crisis condition. It is necessary to do whatever it takes to restore it. Lack of behavioral communication with a spouse is like not being on behavioral terms with God. It needs to be fixed.

The communication forms of talking, giving, acting, non-sexual touch, and sexual activity need to be considered. Note: Only one of these communication forms is verbal. Withholding any form of love language is a strong form of communication, i.e., "To heck with your needs." Recognize your own primary communication form, and the other's primary language, but develop skills in all the areas. You need to love your spouse in the language he or she understands, not necessarily your "native" love language. Make every effort to communicate your love expression to your spouse's primary receptor. Don't play nasty guessing games like, "If you really loved me, you would know what I want." Or, "If I have to tell you what I want, it doesn't mean anything." Heavens above!! Tell what you want and your lover will be thrilled to meet your need.

God loves to love us. We need to love to love our spouse in her/his love language. If one spouse's love language is verbal communication and the other hates to love by communicating verbally, the one who desires communication will pick up on that and it will become a termite, chewing away at the foundation of the marriage. If one spouse's love language is sexual intercourse and the other hates to love in that fashion, termites, etc. Loving to love calls for humble submission ala Ephesians 5.

We need to be multilingual in expressing love. The assertive communicator makes thoughts, desires, and feelings clear but does not set him or herself up for disappointment with unrealistic expectations. Be absolutely clear. Don't just hint around and then feel badly that your message wasn't understood. Make sure your partner receives and clarifies what you have communicated until you both are clear on your intent.

If you came from a family where expression of emotions was a no-no, you will need to work hard to learn to communicate your feelings. If you came from a family where lack of verbal communication was a rule, you will have to work hard to express yourself verbally.

One of the main reasons people don't share is often because they have been shot down or ridiculed in the past. Don't think for your spouse; instead allow your spouse the chance to tell her or his side of the story. Many misunderstandings are started, or made worse, when we think we know what the other is thinking. The mindset must be that all forms of communication are done with construction, not destruction, in mind. This mindset applies to giver and receiver. With that mindset, the receiver is given a chance to clarify, if necessary, and look to find positives in the message. In any communication, there is the possibility of error so the grace of clarification must be extended. A good example is the way we interpret Scripture. We accept a passage to be true and helpful. Any interpretation that appears to be a contradiction is discarded and a helpful interpretation is found. Mindset.

INTELLECTUAL — Submission

Submit means to yield in surrender. We are to "Submit to one another out of reverence for Christ" (Eph. 5:21). Submission is an act of the will. As a relationship moves towards marriage it should be realized that the primary force that holds a marriage together is the mindset "I WILL." Given all the self-help books and counseling in the world, nothing makes the success of a marriage more likely than "I WILL." It comes back to the two rules for marriage — 1) The marriage is more important than the individual. 2) If at any time the individual seems more important, see rule number 1. We give up nonessential needs for our spouse.

When we are committed to, and submit to, our spouse, the possibility of trashing the relationship by involving a third party or other ISR activity is eliminated. We just don't go there. DON'T EVEN THINK ABOUT IT! It is absolutely amazing how many troubles we avoid simply by being committed to our spouse. We can eliminate a tremendous amount of self-induced stress by our commitment. Any sacrifice we feel we make to ensure our commitment is far less than the grief caused by breaking that commitment. Submission provides stability and security. Submission allows us to use our time and energy building instead of salvaging wreckage. We come from sin, to righteousness. It is difficult, but not impossible, to get past the past and have a meaningful relationship. However, bad decisions that violate submission can leave deep scars and wounds from which some people never recover. Remember that God does not require us to submit to ungodliness.

COMMUNITY — Family and Friends

Most people enter their pre-marital relationship with a variety of past and present friends, some close. A huge part of coming together is dealing appropriately with those social ties. Some activities and bonds may have to be adjusted, discarded, or forgiven. While consideration has to be given to individual relationships that are constructive, common interests supply a framework for the social activities of the emerging couple. Overlapping rings demonstrate the he-we-she framework of marriage. Once the framework is in place, different aspects of individual personalities and interests can be expressed. Both what we do together and separately can build intimacy. Common interests allow mutual sharing and exert a power that is greater than the sum of the two. Separate interests allow involvement in personal interests and contribute material to share that enriches the other's life. But, separate interests should never decrease the "we." Togetherness gains meaning as energy is directed toward the goal of intimacy. God has purposes for us as individuals, as well as couples.

EMOTIONAL — "The greatest of these is love" (1 Cor. 13:13b)

Love is a verb. Love is giving. God so loved that He gave (John 3:16). Husbands are to love their wives as Christ loved the church and gave Himself for it (Eph. 5). Love makes the loved one feel validated and esteemed. Love gives the assurance that nonessentials are less important on the mental scale balance. Love reinforces the feeling of being a human being as well as being a human doing. Love is making a person feel good about him or herself. Love transcends shortcomings and deficiencies. Love is a filter that blocks out small stuff. Love is wanting to be together. Love is feeling incomplete without the beloved. If two people try to out-give each other in love, their relationship will be blessed.

As a parent loves a newborn and develops an unbreakable bond, so should spouses honor the "I do." The "you" in "I take you" is accepted as the "you" that really exists. If we love an ideal you instead of the actual you, the other will sense this and intimacy is compromised.

The love that is defined in 1 Corinthians 13 permeates the marriage. Love is patient, kind, protective, trusting, hopeful, and persevering. As we get to know each other through conversation and experience (into-me-see), love grows. Love is an infinite emotion and increases throughout a relationship. Love extends grace when nothing else can serve as reasonable atonement (at-one-ment) for hurts that have been rendered. Love thrives on giving and receiving forgiveness. Love deepens as the heat of trials serves its purpose in welding two souls together.

God's original and continuing intent is a love relationship with His family. That love is the "glory of God" (Rom. 3:23). When we enter into that relationship we rise to the fullness of His glory. His intent for marriage is that two should become one in love and reflect "the glory of God."

Christ's prayer (John 17) was that the Father, the Son, and the church would be one - intimate. Intimacy is the ultimate result of the fruit of the Spirit in action (Gal. 5:22-12). Love builds bridges instead of walls out of the materials that life gives us. In the plus/minus charts of life, love lives on the positive side. Grace given from God is extended through the relationship.

In summary, we are spiritual, physical, intellectual, social, and emotional beings. Each area provides opportunities for intimacy. Of the five areas, it is mostly in the spiritual realm that we need a solid core of agreement. A deeply shared sense of spiritual agreement will complement the other areas of relationship. "Do not let any unwholesome talk come out of your mouths, but only what is helpful for building others up according to their needs, that it may benefit those who listen" (Eph. 4:29).

As God desires intimacy with us, He desires a similar intimacy for us in marriage. He has provided a bride and groom relationship for the church and Christ and He provides for us a relationship that is unique in human relationships. We explore that relationship in the next chapter.

"HOW BEAUTIFUL YOU ARE, MY DARLING! OH, HOW BEAUTIFUL!" (SONG OF SOL. 4:1). "MY LOVER IS RADIANT AND RUDDY, OUTSTANDING AMONG TEN THOUSAND. HIS HEAD IS PUREST GOLD" (SONG OF SOL. 5:10). CHERISH AND NURTURE YOUR "FIRST LOVE"; "REPENT AND DO THE THINGS YOU DID AT FIRST" (REV. 2:4-5, APPLIED TO MARRIAGE).

CHAPTER 19

CHOOSING A MATE AND ON TO MARRIAGE

"Sue" and "Tom" had dated for only two months and he was pressuring her hard for sex. She had held on to her virginity until her freshman year in college because of her commitment to God and her respect for her parents. But, she had already lost two other guys by refusing their advances and didn't want to lose another. As her mind was twisted into the thought patterns of her dormmates, who derisively called her "Virginia," she believed his promise that he was experienced and knew how to practice "safe sex." Now she was pregnant, he had left her for another conquest, and she was getting all kinds of confusing advice from her "friends."

This scenario is played out all too often. Many young people, female and male, who ignore God's protective rules, find that a pregnancy, felony conviction, or some other impulsive choice throws their educational, vocational, and social plans into the dumpster. Prudent planning and deliberate decisions help fend off future failure.

Relationships are important. That is why God has given such clear directions for establishing and maintaining healthy human interaction. Second to our choice to allow God and His plans to be number one in our lives, is our choice of whether or not to marry and whom we marry. In the majority of relationships in the United States, we will marry someone with whom we spend time. That means we should not date someone who does not meet God's requirements. For those of you who know something about welding, preparation for marriage is quite like the process of preparing two surfaces for welding. Use the following requirements for welding to examine your premarital companions.

WELDING INTERVENTION

- The two surfaces must be compatible. Wood cannot be welded to metal.
- Do not be unequally yoked. 2 Corinthians 6:14
- The two surfaces must be free of dirt, oil, rust, and other interfering substances.
- We are purified, as He is pure. 1 John 3:3
- There should be a flux to remove oxidation and improve fusion.
- The Holy Spirit will convict of sin and righteousness. John 16:8
- There has to be an outer source of heat to fuse the two surfaces together.
- Consider it pure joy when you face various trials. James 1:2
- The two surfaces must be in contact. If one draws away from the heat, a weld cannot occur.
- If any person is in Christ, that person is a new creation. 2 Corinthians 5:17

We would be welded to God. It is His action that makes us pure and compatible with Him. If we are welded "in Christ" AND Christ is welded in us before we are welded together in marriage, a lot of problems will never arise. In both relationships we are more likely to be compatible, we avoid sinful practices, we are forgiven of past sin, we have the mind of Christ, we are filled with the Spirit, we face trials with joy, and we are empowered by God. God's rules are to protect us, not to ruin our "fun." A huge trial, in our loose culture, is appreciating God's protective rules about premarital sex. If Sue had considered the joy of facing trials she would have saved herself from the sadness of caving in. That fraction of an inch of her yardstick would have made a huge difference in the rest of her life. One of the most appropriate stress relievers is following God's guidelines and *not getting into trouble in the first place.*

If we marry and have children, and raise them "in Christ," their lives will be radically, wonderfully different because they will tend to avoid bad choices. We know the problems we avoid when we obey God's rules because we can clearly see the problems of those who have disobeyed them.

If we have grown up in an intact family where love was expressed and received, we have mindsets and coping mechanisms for loving and receiving love. Unfortunately, those families are in the minority. More than half of the children in the United States will be in a one-parent family at some time in their lives. Among those marriages that stay together, a significant portion do not experience appropriate giving and receiving of love. That leaves many of us with the task of learning these skills.

Some people believe love exists and they are able to give love, but are not able to receive it. Their CHEESE factory has conditioned them to feel that they aren't worthy, that there are strings attached, or that they will be hurt if they entrust themselves to another person. The Bible, other books, sermons, seminars, and a host of other resources are available to help us develop the giving and receiving of love.

MARRIAGE WORK

They hadn't worked at their marriage. They had just drifted along. Now, after seven years and three children, they realized they had drifted apart. She had overheard two older women at the salon talking about "empty nests" and asked him, "What will we have when the children are gone?" He retorted, "What do we have now?" The chilling answers led them to my office.

A MORE EXCELLENT WAY - (1 Cor. 12:31)

What a delightful thought. There is a more excellent way. You might be saying, "What does that mean?" Well, unless you have one of the few marriages that is totally on the correct path towards God's plan for marriage, there is a more excellent way.

We need to pause here and paraphrase 2 Corinthians 5:17. "If any MARRIAGE is in Christ, it is a new creation; the old has gone, the new has come." Every mindset, every challenge, every loss, in every circumstance we, and our marriage, can be made pure and new by being placed "in Christ."

Paul says the "more excellent way" is the way of love and gives several descriptors of love in 1 Corinthians 13:4-8a. Love is patient, kind, does not envy, does not boast, is not proud, is not rude, is not self-seeking, is not easily angered, keeps no record of wrongs, does not delight in evil but rejoices with the truth, always protects, always trusts, always hopes, and always perseveres. Love never fails. We would add, love forgives. Marriage partners should meditate on each of these factors and discuss them with each other.

LOVE IS ACTION

What is love? Love is action. Love is mutual ideals, dreams, sharing, trust, loyalty, devotion, single-mindedness, and, often, sheer determination in action. Be wary of the worldview of love that is strongly physical, Hollywoodish, with fireworks, bells and whistles. Seek an all-SPICE love relationship: Spiritual, Physical, Intellectual, Community (Social), and Emotional, that is based on God's plan. We are to love as ". . . Christ loved the church and gave himself for it" (Eph. 5:25).

Some marriages are sick because the couple's actions are the opposite of the elements of love listed above. One or both partners is mean, selfish, easily angered, keeping a list of wrongs, not trusting, not protecting each other, and so on. Some marriages are sick because of a lack of hope. Some are sick because of a lack of perseverance. The 1 Corinthians 13 passage is a prescription that helps cure the ills of sick marriages. Love, patience, and kindness are fruit of the Spirit (Gal. 5:22). If we have the Spirit of Christ, we have an infinite supply of love for a rich and fulfilling marriage. Being filled with His Spirit is ours for the asking. Do you think that God would give directions to us without empowering us to achieve His plans?

Hope and perseverance are essential characteristics of love, especially in the formative stages of the marriage relationship. God gives us hope: "I know the plans I have for you, declares the Lord, plans to prosper you and not to harm you, plans to give you hope and a future. Then you will call upon me and come and pray to me, and I will listen to you. You will seek me, and find me, when you seek me with all your heart. I will be found by you declares the Lord" (Jer. 19:11-14a). Note that perseverance is required to "seek me with all your heart." He has promised that when He begins a good work in us, He will carry it on to completion until the day of Christ Jesus (Phil. 1:6). This applies to each person and also to marriage. Have an intense desire to allow God to do His work.

Establishing the relationship that God wants us to have in marriage requires love, skill, hope, and perseverance for we have hereditary, environmental, and eventful flaws from our CHEESE factory that need to be corrected. These flaws should be faced with joy. When we are "in Christ," flaws can be used as stepping-stones towards maturity and completeness that lacks nothing. James 1:2 says, "Consider it pure joy . . . whenever you FACE trials . . ." — just as Jesus set His face to go to Jerusalem.

Trials provide the heat that welds two into one. If we are made of wax, heat will dissolve our marriage. If we are made of steel, we will be welded together and the weld will be stronger than the original two pieces. God has promised never to give us a trial beyond our ability to endure but will give a means of growth (1 Cor. 10:13). Note very carefully that this passage says we will have trials. By the way, we have enough trials without doing stupid things that create trials. Following God's loving guidelines reduces the number of trials and makes them easier to solve.

LOVE IS A BASIC NEED

One of the greatest drawbacks in marriage is when one or both partners lose the desire to give and receive love. Love is a basic need. We know love is a basic need because it is a gift from God and He doesn't waste gifts on unnecessary stuff. Many people grow up in homes where little love is expressed. They cannot become as little children and love simply, fully, and freely. There is too much fear of letting go and being hurt. Many people withhold love for fear of not getting love in return. Agape love does not expect a return.

We need a proper understanding of God's love for us, that it is ofttimes undeserved and that it continues even when we are unlovable. We need to love each other in the same manner. God loves us as human beings. The world loves us as human doings. God loves us for who we are. The world loves us for what we do. When we are loved as human beings, our purpose is to BE — to be "in Christ" and to be filled with His Spirit. Then we are promised that we will bear fruit. The doing is an outpouring of love in response to being loved as beings. When the actions of love are present, the emotion of love is present. If the action dies, the emotion dies.

We are to love our neighbors as ourselves. Our self-love can be positive because we are to love what God loves. He loves us so we know we are lovable; however, self-love is incomplete. We thrive if someone else loves us. It is such a good feeling to know that some other person sees us as a worthy, lovable person, that is, deserving of the actions of love. Our relationship with God allows us to know that our Creator finds us worthy. The activity of Christ is evidence of this. The need for a right relationship with God precedes, and is necessary for, a right relationship with our own self and with our spouse. Once we have this experience with God, we are able to enter into our marriage relationship with the depth and meaning that will give us the fullness of marriage to pull through the rough places.

In life, as in death, Jesus entered before us and showed us the way. So many people mistake Christ's mission as preparing us only for death. We need to see that He also prepared us for an abundant life so that our joy would be full. We are to love God with our whole heart, mind, soul, and strength, and our neighbors as ourselves. The former is necessary and preparatory for the latter. Remember, Ephesians 5 tells us a man is to love his wife even as he loves and cares for his own body. This certainly parallels the second summary commandment (love your neighbor as yourself) which is a powerful model for marriage. If a marriage partner is to have the fullness of marriage, he or she must love in the same way.

THREE KINDS OF LOVE

Marital love is a special kind of love that should include a combination of three Greek words for love. Philios in marital love is when our spouse is our friend. Any courtesy that would be afforded to strangers or coworkers (or our dog) should be given him or her. Agape in marital love has no strings attached. "I don't love you because I need you or what you do for me; I love you because I love you." Love is not bartered. Love is a gift, not a manipulation. We are to love with a love that wants all good things for our spouse, so that everything God intended can be realized. Eros in marital love is sexual love and should be exclusive with only, ONLY, our marriage partner to fulfill the joys of procreation, re-creation, and recreation that God has given us.

Marriage is more than the sum of philios, agape, and eros. It is the personification of Christ as the husband and the church as the bride. It is a metaphor of the love story of God for His people. Foundational to marriage is an accurate understanding and acceptance of God's place in the relationship — the three-stranded cord (Eccles. 4:12). We cannot braid two cords. But, if we accept God's grace gifts we are new creations in Christ (2 Cor. 5:17) and have the ". . . mind of Christ" (1 Cor. 2:16). In this, we gain the third strand. This gives us the ability to think under the guidance of the Holy Spirit and puts our relationship into the capable care of the Founder of marriage. When we give our imperfect marriage/self to God, we get a perfected (not perfect) marriage/self back (1 John 3:3) with power, gifts, and fruit.

Love in marriage can be almost explosive as we extend it to our beloved. We can love our best friend and others with philios and agape, but only our spouse with philios, agape, and eros. The combination of philios, agape, eros, and the much more of God, is the ideal marriage. If you do not have it, ask for it. God will bless you with it. Once you have all three kinds of love in your marriage, give them freely because loving is the best way to sustain love. We gain love from our spouse by giving love to our spouse, not as a purchase price but as a reciprocal gift.

The ideal marriage relationship described in the above paragraphs is somewhat like the birth of a child. There may be years of gestation. During this period different problems will arise; solutions bring fusion to the marriage. *$$ OVAL INTERVENTION $$*

EROS IN MARRIAGE

Sexuality is probably one of the most perverted activities in life and often far from God's intent. Let's face it. Our culture is preoccupied with sex. Satan has taken a God-given creative experience and turned it into an obsession. Satan's lies and twisted truths have led many people into a cesspool of mistakes, many of which have lifelong effects. Life is more than sex. Marriage contains many other elements that bring happiness and fulfillment. There are, therefore, many things that must be clarified before we can have an understanding of what He wants for us to have in the sexual aspects of our marriage.

We need to put the sexual relationship in perspective. Of the one hundred sixty-eight hours in a week, the average couple spends one hour making love. The physical act of intercourse takes less than 1 percent of our relationship time. That means 99 percent of our relationship time is other. Some people spend 99 percent of their time worrying about the 1 percent. Think about it.

PENNY ILLUSTRATION

There are seven days in a week, twenty-four hours in a day, hence one hundred sixty-eight hours in a week. Put one hundred sixty-eight pennies in one side of a container with two sides. The average married couple has intercourse twice a week, one half hour per time. That represents one penny. Take one penny and drop it in the empty side. That's our sexual experience. There are 167 more hours to fill with meaning. Those hours should be discussed before and during marriage.

We are created in the image of God and God is a creative being. Therefore, we are creative beings. This creative function covers many areas, one of which is creating human beings — procreation. However, intercourse is not just an act of procreation; it is also re-creation, each time an opportunity to re-create our marriage and ourselves. And rec-reation — we are to enjoy this subset of an intimate relationship. God has given to us the ability to create new life. Just as we go forth from the communion table with newness of life, we go from intercourse with newness of marriage. "This is my body which is for you" (I Cor. 11:24) can be applied to the holiness of the sexual relationship in marriage. If any person (marriage) be in Christ, she or he (the marriage) is newly created, the old is gone, and the new has come. Even so, God planned the sexual relationship for His children. In the oneness of marriage, the old is gone and the potential for new life is present — procreative and/or re-creative. Sex outside of marriage is a perversion of God's intent. Adultery is a gross form of idolatry, one of the worst inappropriate stress relievers.

THE MARRIAGE PASSAGE

Ephesians 5:21-33, combined with 1 Corinthians 13, gives further guidelines for a godly marriage. In Ephesians, two instructions are given to women: submit to your husband as to Christ, and respect your husband (vv. 22 -24, v. 33b). Four instructions are given to men: love your wife as Christ loved the church, love your wife as your own body, feed and care for her, (nourish and cherish, KJV), and leave your parents and cleave to her (vv. 25, 28, 29, & 31). More instructions are given to men because of the shameful ways women were treated in the time when the Bible was written. Hopefully, the situation has improved in your house.

It will be helpful if you get your Bible out while reading these instructions. While verse 21, "Submit to one another, out of reverence for Christ," sums up the previous verses, it also sets the stage for the "marriage passage." Note: the marriage relationship considered in Ephesians 5 was an arranged marriage. Many times, the couple didn't even see each other until the wedding ceremony. It should be clear, then, that marital love is more action than emotion.

Many men's marital growth gets stuck at verse 24, ". . . wives should submit to their husbands in everything." And their mindset ignores the rest of the passage. They think, "Wives have to be subject in all things so men are off the hook." Husbands can do anything they want and wives have to put up with it. They filter out the rest of the verse: "Now as the church submits to Christ . . ." It is important to remember that Christ does not abuse. Men need to meditate deeply with loud cries and tears if necessary, and love their wives as Christ loved the church. They need to follow the instructions in verses 25-33, to progress to marital maturity.

As was said before, men get stuck on verse 24. For purposes of emphasizing the husband's responsibilities, we'll consider them first. Begin at verse 25. Husbands are to love their wives as Christ loved the church, which is His body. It doesn't say that we are to love our wives IF they act in a certain way. A man's actions towards his wife are not dependent upon her actions. It is obvious from this passage that he who does not love his wife does not love himself. *An abusive husband hates himself.* If a husband loves his wife as Christ loved the church, he will have the same care, devotion, and love for her and will give up parts of his life for her. Christ loves us even when we aren't lovely.

Husbands are to ". . . nourish and cherish . . ." (KJV) their wives. This refers to physical and emotional support. "After all, no man ever hated his own body . . ." (It is insightful to see the "man" as Christ and the "body" as the church.) As Christ gave Himself up for the church, husbands may need to experience a Gethsemane, a Golgotha, and the Garden for their wives.

Now, for the wives: "Wives submit to your husbands as to the Lord." Many women who are married have experienced at least one divorce. When a wife has experienced any or all of the three A's — Adultery, Abandonment, and/or Abuse, verse 22 carries a lot of baggage. Definite intention of forgiveness for the past and hope for the future are required in order for wives to respond to the directive to submit.

"As to the Lord" means husbands are to be as Christ towards their wives. Christ would not abuse and neither would a godly husband. Wives are not required to submit to ungodliness. If a wife is to submit in "everything" the husband must be sure all things are in and from God. Obviously, this applies to those who marry "in Christ."

OTHER BIBLE VERSES APPLIED TO MARRIAGE

As we enter the challenge of achieving maturity in marriage we want to be appropriately armed with the knowledge and strength of God's word. We cannot expect to walk in darkness and be filled with light. In Isaiah 55:11, God promised that His word would not return to Him empty, but it would accomplish what He desires and achieve the purpose for which it was written. His word, then, tells us that, "You will go out in joy and be led forth in peace; the mountains and hills will burst into song before you, and all the trees of the field will clap their hands" (Isa. 55:12). So, "Make level paths for your feet (in marriage), so that the lame may not be disabled, but rather healed" (Heb. 12:13). Don't make stupid decisions and make a crooked path for yourself that will injure your relationship.

"Take captive every thought to make it obedient to Christ" (2 Cor. 10:5). "Submit your bodies as living sacrifices, not being conformed to the world but being transformed by the renewing of your minds" (Rom. 12:1-2). "Don't be anxious about anything but, with thanksgiving, make your requests to God and the peace of God that passes all understanding will keep your hearts and minds in Christ Jesus" (Phil. 4:6-8). "Let your faith be refined by your trials so that the result will be praise, glory, and honor when Jesus Christ is revealed" (1 Pet. 1:6-7). "And whatever you do in word or deed, do it in the nature of the Lord Jesus, giving thanks to God the Father through Him" (Col. 3:17). Be slow to take offense and be quick to forgive.

THE MARRIAGE GARDEN

There may be times when we experience a Gethsemane and a Golgotha before we obtain victory in the garden of our marriage. In a godly marriage there will be Gethsemanes of Decision, ". . . not my will but yours be done" (Luke 22: 39-46), where we will struggle and come to a decision. There will be Golgothas of Death where a desire or choice needs to be subjected to God or our spouse. Few relationships enter the Garden of Direction without life-changing decisions and death of selfishness. Marital gardens, like actual gardens, require a great deal of cultivation, weeding, and watering. We cannot just sow seed and expect to collect the harvest without a great deal of work. Once the decision is made, the rest is process. *$$ GARDEN INTERVENTION $$*

If there are problems in marriage, they need immediate attention. One weed begets others. Weeds can't just be broken off at the surface; they need to be dealt with at the root level. The roots of the problem were most likely in place before the marriage.

One of the "weeds" that can undermine a marriage is undesirable baggage from previous relationships. If that baggage is not recognized and processed, it will most likely repeat damage in the new relationship. The baggage may have come from the family of origin, from dating, or from a previous marriage. In the case of serial marriages, whether they end by death or divorce, the baggage may increase in volume and intensity.

Baggage is funny stuff. It's like a grudge, after a while we don't even remember we are carrying it. Baggage is like weeds. It can't be ignored or eventually it will take over the garden, or at least, reduce its productivity. The baggage needs to be brought to the surface and sorted. Keep the good and junk the rest.

When challenges arise in a marriage, there are different directions that can be taken. Many people seek relief with another person, substance, pornography, food, or other ISR. As a result, the opportunity to achieve the intimacy of a mature marriage is lost. Issues are intended to increase intimacy. Destructive ISRs are termites that eat away at the foundation of a marriage. Resistance to change is a huge termite. *$$ TERMITE INTERVENTION $$*

CHANGE IS POSSIBLE

In the chapter on change, the difficulty of making changes is explored and methods to effect change are suggested. The material in this chapter will help married partners discover tools that can help change a shaky marriage into one that is fulfilling to both parties. If your marriage is not fulfilling most of your marital needs, take hope in God's promises, utilize His power, gifts, and fruit, and work towards the relationship He desires for you to have.

Two mindsets that allow the renewing of our minds are the mindset of wanting to change and the mindset of giving God permission to help us change. We can't change if we won't. CAN'T CAN'T! and WON'T WON'T! Can't and won't are words of unwillingness. If I feel I can't accomplish a task, I won't even try. Can't and won't need mindset adjustments.

We should enter the "in Christ" relationship with thought. We need to count the cost. We should measure the worth of the world against the worth of our soul. It only makes sense that we should enter marriage, the "one flesh" relationship, with the same thoughtfulness. The "in Christ" relationship not only gives us eternal life but also abundant living (John 10). The "one flesh" relationship is a rich and fulfilling marriage.

ONE PERSON CAN CHANGE A MARRIAGE

As the saying goes, "It takes two to tango." But, does it take two to have helpful marital therapy? Usually two is better; however, if your spouse does not want counseling, it often is beneficial to start by yourself. Even in couple's work, one may falter for a while. The other can keep on going, giving the faltering one time to adjust and get back with the program. The response should not depend on the spouse's actions.

Stress in the marriage could reach a disastrous level if either of the couple takes a "you go first" attitude. Help may be too late in coming. It may be a long wait if one expects the other to change first or to co-operate in getting help. It is helpful to remember — If you always do what you have always done, you'll always get what you always got. We can't keep on doing the same thing and hope for a different outcome. Quite often, one spouse is obsessively worried about what the other is doing. The "other" is usually content to let the worrier do the worrying, that is, "If she is worried about my behavior, I don't have to worry, so I won't." This is a very subtle, but all too often present, dynamic in a dysfunctional relationship.

Problems in a marriage can be resolved but no resolution can come without action. If YOU are the one who is motivated to change your marriage, YOU can change it by changing yourself. Remember that we can't change others but we can give them something different to react to. Change in marriage is like a set of gears; if one gear reverses direction, the other has to change or the gears strip.

Someone has to get on the try-cycle. We miss 100 percent of the shots we don't take. If I wait for my spouse to act and no action is forthcoming, then is it my spouse's fault? Not really. "We love because he first loved us" (John 4:19). Someone has to act in love first. Sometimes we think placing the blame on the spouse takes away responsibility for behavior and then there is no need to change. Instead, we could ask questions like, "What affect am I having on the relationship?" or "How is my behavior contributing to the problem?" I might ask, "What am I doing differently when things go well?"

The wife may say, "My husband is so predictable." But, if one spouse is being predictable that means the other is being predictable. After a while a dance begins. One retreats, the other advances; one backs up, the other approaches, and on and on. (Predictable can be good if good is happening.)

If 50 percent of the marriage is good, feed and water that half so it will grow. There will always be negatives. Every marriage is a throw of the coins. We can dwell on the heads or we can dwell on the tails. It is our choice. If we focus on the negative, the negative will take center stage. Do more of what works and stop doing what doesn't work!

A competent therapist can help sort out the helpful and unhelpful interactions of a marriage. If one of the partners changes behaviors there is a good chance the other will reciprocate. If nothing else, the person getting help will usually feel better about herself or himself.

MARRIAGE WITHIN THE IMAGE OF GOD

Marriage is God's invention. As He wants enjoyable fellowship with us, His intent is that we should enjoy each other, nourish, and cherish each other. In Genesis 2:24, God stated His intention that a man and a woman should become one and be complete in their marriage. Both Jesus and Paul reiterated this statement. In Jesus' prayer in John 17:11, He prayed that God, He, and we should be one. This state of intimacy (into-me-see) is achieved only if we actively pursue that oneness. When we accept Christ we have all the resources, rights and privileges of being a child of God and we spend the rest of our lives working out our salvation. When we say, "I do" we are immediately married but we spend the rest of our lives maturing in that marriage. In either case, the candle gets lighted and continues to burn throughout its existence.

God's Spirit is the source of power, gifts, and fruit. When we have His Spirit, we have tremendous resources that are ours for the using. We have, ". . . love, joy, peace, patience, kindness, goodness, faithfulness, gentleness, and self-control" (Gal. 5:22-23). We need only to allow the attributes of the Spirit to be active in our lives. We need to understand and apply to our marriage the relationship that Jesus has with the church. Husbands are to love their wives as Christ loved the church (Eph. 5:25). This applies to wives in a reciprocal fashion.

God so loved that, "[He] gave his one and only Son, that whoever believes in him shall not perish . . ." He didn't say, "I love you," and then wander off. Love is giving, not getting but it needs a receiver. The best marriage is when each person strives to out-give the other. EACH ONE STRIVES TO OUT-GIVE THE OTHER. It is good and proper to say the words, "I love you." We must also show, "I love you."

THE LOVE RELATIONSHIP

One goal in marriage should be to put relationship before issues. RELATIONSHIP IS MORE IMPORTANT THAN ISSUES. We should want our marriage relationship to work, more than we want our personal needs to be met. Resolving issues is a task that is necessary for the building of relationship. One of the mottoes for road rallies is, "Press on regardless." This mindset is often necessary in the making of a marriage. Once ground has been gained, ". . . let us live up to what we have already attained" (Phil. 3:16). We must always strive not to lose what we have gained.

Love is neither bartering nor compromise. Love is neither negotiation nor manipulation. The bedroom is not an extension of the stock exchange. My actions towards my spouse should not be conditional on his or her actions. Marriage is not a 50/50 relationship. It should be 100/100. In a 100/100 marriage there are two rules:

RULES FOR MARRIAGE

RULE NUMBER 1 — My marriage is more important than my individual needs.

RULE NUMBER 2 — If it ever seems that my individual needs are more important than my marriage, see rule number 1.

Challenges that God gives are a gift but can be lost in the process of protecting the "self" from change. In the power struggle that results from efforts to control, couples typically get caught up in task issues, assume the worst about each other, and neglect the goal of relationship building. Our coping style, developed in our family of origin, will be replayed in current marital interactions. *$$ BUILDING TOYS INTERVENTION $$*

MARITAL NEEDS

Some examples of marital needs are: connection, understanding, trust, intimacy, respect, admiration, and sexual fulfillment. The order of stated needs is intentional but not absolute. Intimacy is in the middle because it is the goal of the other needs. Some spouses go from the connection end to intimacy. They need trust before the door to intimacy is opened. Others go from sexual fulfillment to intimacy. Each one needs to learn to understand, accept, and work with the spouse's mindset about intimacy. Each spouse must speak the other's intimacy language. STOP! Think about that. Speak your spouse's intimacy language as an act of love. If she is speaking acts of considerations and you are speaking thoughtful gifts, you may both be loving but neither feeling loved. You may not think putting your socks in the hamper is a big deal but you may lose connection if you don't. *$$ MARITAL NEEDS CIRCLE $$*

Problems mandate change. Feelings of anger, resentment, and resistance may surface and expose growth areas. Remember, we can't keep doing the same thing and expect a different result. We must agree to make known and discuss our marital needs. *$$ RINGS INTERVENTION FOR MARRIAGE $$*

Two important ingredients in a happy marriage are sympathy and a forgiving spirit. We should be sympathetic in regard to our spouse's needs. We need to satisfy him or her even if it takes sacrificial love. If the desires of either the husband or wife are outside of Christ, adjustments need to be made.

Mistakes are made in the marital growth process so there has to be forgiveness. Ask if needs are being met. Tell how needs can be met. God intends for us to meet each other's marital needs. If we withhold a marital need, we are robbing our spouse of God's intent for us in marriage. Withholding stops marital flow. *$$ FAUCETS AND DRAINS INTERVENTION FOR MARRIAGE $$*

One of the most powerful things we can do for our beloved, our marriage, and ourselves is to pray aloud together. This is more than autosuggestion. A power is released that is far more than either person or the couple can muster. Ask your spouse what he or she needs and what he or she feels will be helpful for your relationship. Pray specifically for these things. Pray that each of you will be unto God and unto each other what will fulfill His intentions for your marriage.

If something has become more important to you than your marriage, read the following vow to your spouse:

RENEWAL VOW

I do not want my relationship with you to be ruled by anything other than what will nourish and cherish you. If my heart is ruled by any selfish desire, I know I will manipulate you to meet my needs instead of loving you. If you are giving me what I want, I'll reward you but if I feel you are not meeting my expectations I will show anger, frustration and discouragement when I am with you. My problem is not you or the situation, but that I have pursued an inappropriate goal in our relationship and now it owns me instead of my owning it. I have left God's desire and direction for me in our marriage and have given myself to less than what we can have together. Please feel free to point out such areas to me and forgive me. Love me, pray for me, and work with me so that God's perfect will is active in our marriage.

Examine your relationship style. Analyze what patterns there are in your conversations and activities. What issues come up again and again? In a 100/100 relationship, each person is committed to solution-focused harmony. Solution-focused harmony is a relationship that works towards answers rather than dwelling in the negative. The marriage is more important than the individual. Working on relationship issues serves to aid in the growth process.

The first commandment requires, "You shall have no other gods before me" (Exod. 20), and the first requirement of marriage should be to have no other person before your spouse. In marriage we must be careful that some aspect of marriage does not become a god that is more important than the spouse. If we cease to act in a godly manner because a desire is not satisfied, that desire has become our god.

Throughout the teachings in the Bible, the relationship between God and humans is likened to the marriage relationship. Israel was the wife of God. The church is described as the bride of Christ. The sacraments express the relationship between God and humans and are powerful analogies for marriage. Marriage is a gift to us from God (Gen. 2:24, Matt. 19:5, and Eph. 5:31). It follows that we will enjoy marriage to the fullest when we have a growing relationship with God and each other. Both relationships require love that is demonstrated in forgiveness, submission, obedience, sacrifice, giving, and grace.

$ $ $ ⚷━★ $ $ $

Treasure Chest #19
Resources for Improving Relationships

GARDEN INTERVENTION

Draw a garden with crops and flowers. Label them as what you want in your marriage. Draw things that negatively impact a real garden — weeds, bugs, rocks, critters, etc. Label them with attitudes or activities that can undermine a marriage. Draw things that are necessary to make a garden flourish — good soil, fertilizer, water, sun, etc. Label them with attitudes or activities that promote a healthy marriage. Discuss each item using communication skills of respect, safety, and clarification.

TERMITE INTERVENTION

Material: six to ten rubber or plastic ants and some fake pesticide containers. Label different ants as issues that are undermining the marriage. Label pesticides as ways to eliminate the issues. Discuss, using communication and problem-solving skills.

BUILDING TOYS INTERVENTION

Materials needed: some type of building set. The pieces represent
challenges that happen in life, seemingly good or bad. We can use
the challenges to build a wall or a bridge. Exactly the same challenge
can be used to make a wall or a bridge. It is our choice. Use construction pieces to build a wall between yourself and your spouse — name
the parts with negative aspects of the relationship. Why are these bad
things? What is the wall? Tear down the wall and use the same material for a bridge. Reframe the parts so they help fuse the marriage.
How can the bad things be used to make good things?

MARITAL NEEDS CIRCLE

Write the marital needs in the shape of a circle. The circle can be
entered at any word and go either way to intimacy or beyond to any
other word, not necessarily in any given order. We can zigzag around
the points of the circle. Remember that God's desire is for oneness (one
flesh), another word for intimacy. Identify areas of interest and verbalize how the circle can be traversed. Discuss roadblocks, detours, and
side trips. "I would trust you, but . . ." Where does the "but" come in?
Discuss ways to get on track.

RINGS INTERVENTION FOR MARRIAGE

Two overlapping rings represent the "he-we-she" needs in a marriage.
List positive and negative factors in each area. As the marriage area
increases, the individuals decrease. Agreement in the "we" area brings
intimacy and adds to each individual. Caring for individual needs
strengthens the "we." Neither is ever to detract from the other but all
aspects should build towards maturity in marriage and in Christ. Be
careful that an increase of the "he" or "she" does not decrease the
"we." Neither the "he" nor the "she" should include an "other."
Using the rings in a different way, label the overlap as attempts to control the other partner that bring resentment and entrenchment. Label
the area that is left for the controlled person as to how he or she is decreased in self-concept and relational power. Add the area of overlap
to the area of the controller and discuss how more has been taken on
than can be handled. This can result in burnout of the marriage.
Discuss the passive-aggressive actions that result. Discuss how responsibility is shifted to the controller and how the controlee no longer
takes responsibility for his or her own actions. After all, if the controller is calling the shots, it is his or her fault if anything goes wrong.

Another subtle area of control is exercised when an ISR is being used. The dependent person will consciously or unconsciously find or contrive a relationship where the spouse becomes an enabler in order to be absolved of the responsibility to change. It is amazing how people become set up by their CHEESE factories and are attracted to a codependent, even when it was not obvious during courtship.

FAUCETS AND DRAINS INTERVENTION FOR MARRIAGE

Visualize a large tub with many faucets and drains. Have the couple draw a picture of the tub with many faucets and drains. Have them label the water in the tub as what is appropriate for their marriage. Have them draw a line to represent the fullness of the tub. We need to keep positive SPICE faucets open — communication, dating, caring. We need to keep negative faucets of resentment, abuse, unproductive anger, pornography, and third parties, etc., shut. We need to keep our forgiveness and resentment drains open so any sludge can run out. Otherwise we become like the Dead Sea; our environment becomes polluted and very little life exists. Close up any drains that are losing positive things.

OVAL INTERVENTION

Draw a two-by-four-inch oval in the middle of a sheet of paper. Label the oval "The image of God" for your marriage. Inside the oval write down what you feel God wants for your marriage. Take turns. Then go around the outside of the oval, drawing polyps, cancerous things that are eating away at the image where we are living, for each thing that is not right in the marriage. Examine what resources are in the oval and gain new ones if necessary to block out each polyp. The object is to stop living in the polyp and move into the "oval" of God. Find out what is good and do more of it.

"PUT OFF YOUR OLD SELF, WHICH IS BEING CORRUPTED BY ITS DECEITFUL DESIRES; TO BE MADE NEW IN THE ATTITUDE OF YOUR MINDS; AND TO PUT ON THE NEW SELF, CREATED TO BE LIKE GOD IN TRUE RIGHTEOUSNESS AND HOLINESS" (EPH. 4:22-24). NEWNESS IN CHRIST MEANS A NEW ATTITUDE (MINDSET) THAT IS A RADICAL DEPARTURE FROM OUR OLD MINDSET.

CHAPTER 20

GETTING PAST THE PAST

OUR MINDSET IS A CHOICE

Many topics have been addressed in this book. There are many more outside its scope. We have discussed many negatives and many positives in personal, marital, and community life. In order to move from the past into a present that is fulfilling God's desires now and building for a bright future, we need to follow the Apostle Paul's example stated in Philippians 4:13-14, "Brothers, I do not consider myself yet to have taken hold of it. But one thing I do: Forgetting what is behind and straining toward what is ahead, I press on toward the goal to win the prize for which God has called me heavenward in Christ Jesus." Thus we come to the final chapter of this book, which we pray has contributed to a foundation for the continuing chapters of your life.

We all have bad experiences, unmet expectations, losses, and grief to deal with, in one form or another, from our past. It is important to our well-being that we choose the most productive and positive way in our approach to these negatives. While we may not be able to control the events, we can choose what effect they have on our lives. When we experience unmet expectations, losses, and grief, we can choose to be angry and to behave in a bitter, resentful, or defensive manner, and live in emotional, spiritual, and often physical pain. Or, we can adopt the attitude, that is, the mindset of Christ. "Therefore, since Christ suffered in His body, arm yourselves also with the same attitude, because he who has suffered in his body is done with sin" (1 Pet. 4:1). We can "consider it pure joy" (James 1), by tapping into our spiritual, emotional, and social resources, and move towards maturity. The listening ears and caring words of a trusted confidant can help us choose an attitude that lessens the damage and gives hope and peace in the situation. In more serious situations, professional help may be needed to work through hurt and disappointment. As the bumper sticker says, "Manure Happens." However, manure can help things grow.

We are spiritual, physical, intellectual, community, and emotional beings (SPICE). Each of these factors of our being needs to be fed and nurtured as we grow. Neglect or abuse of any of these components of our person will decrease our ability to have "the attitude of Christ" in the image of God. To promote the attitude of Christ, we need to continue to allow the Holy Spirit to guide and empower us.

A classic example of a positive attitude is shown by Joseph's experiences as recounted in the book of Genesis. As you consider the following events, think of his mindset. He was sold into slavery (Gen. 37:28). While in slavery he had success in everything he did (Gen. 39:2-6). He was falsely accused and thrown in jail for more than two years (Gen. 16-20). While in jail, his capabilities were recognized and he was placed in charge (Gen. 39:21b-23). Because he was able to interpret Pharaoh's dream (Gen. 41:25-27), he was made second in command to Pharaoh (Gen. 41: 39-40). All of Joseph's experiences were used by God to work His purpose (Gen. 45:5-8, 50:40). What was intended for evil, God used for good. Joseph's choices, during times of seeming defeat, allowed God's purpose to be fulfilled. God can see the end from the beginning. Praise be to Him that He is in control!

GOD WORKS FOR GOOD

There are those who say simply, "Get over it." This may not be the best thing to do. To get over it may deprive us of God's intention. Our desire should be to reap the harvest for which the past has prepared us. The process of dealing with the past requires identification of each issue and accepting its influence on our personalities and lives.

GETTING PAST THE PAST

There are four mindset stages involved in getting past the past — victim, survivor, conqueror, and more than conqueror. We need to move from the victim stage (controlled by and living in the past), through the survivor stage (just existing), through the conqueror stage (depending on our own devices), to the "more than conqueror" stage available in Christ (Rom. 8:37) — God's power, gifts, and fruit in action. When considering forgiveness, the more than conqueror stage is reached when we accept God's forgiveness for ourselves (forgiving ourselves) and extend it completely to others.

Some people are stuck in the victim stage. They forfeit happiness because they feel they have to prove to the world they were hurt. They live as if their pain is necessary to hold the aggressor responsible for the act. These people often hitch their wagons to abuse instead of to healing. They choose to live in the Frogdom of Curse instead of the Kingdom of God. They literally "hold it against them" instead of trusting the "true and just judgments of God" (Rev. 19:2). They "hold a grudge" so perp won't get off the hook. They don't realize that perp is still on God's hook. "The Lord, the compassionate and gracious God, slow to anger, abounding in love and faithfulness, maintaining love to thousands, and forgiving wickedness, rebellion and sin. Yet he does not leave the guilty unpunished; he punishes the children and their children for the sin of the fathers to the third and fourth generation" (Numbers 14:18). That should be enough for us. *$$ FROG INTERVENTION $$*

Holding another person's sins against him or her gives a feeling of great power — "wealth." As mentioned in various settings, power and control are hard to release. A victim may think that holding a grudge gives him or her an advantage over an abuser. This is a false sense of power that actually keeps the victim in bondage, re-experiencing the pain. Like the rich ruler (Luke 18:18), victims keep their "wealth" of hurt and pride and go their way sorrowing, continuing to live in the sewer of abuse. Have you turned away sorrowing because you have a great hurt you don't want to forgive? You need to flush your emotional toilet and don't live in the sewer. *$$ GRUDGE INTERVENTION $$*

Survivors are better off than victims but they lack any zest for life; they just exist. Like plow horses, they simply lean into the harness every step and move their legs to keep from falling down.

Many people get stuck in the conqueror stage, depending on their own devices. This stage probably represents the majority of people in the United States. They give an outward appearance of success, and even feel good most of the time but they miss the joy and peace that God intends for them. Pride and a false feeling of control maintain a façade of success but they fall short of the "glory of God." They lack the fellowship, power, gifts, and fruit of the Spirit He intends for us to have.

While, "The sins of the fathers are passed on to the children to the third and fourth generation," God has promised to ". . . show love to a thousand generations to those who love him and keep his commandments" (Exod. 20:6). He wants us to be "more than conquerors through him who loves us" (Rom. 8:37).

WE CAN BECOME MORE THAN CONQUERORS

The Apostle Paul said, "Forgetting . . ." While it may not be possible to forget totally, we can make bad memories old stray cats by not letting them trap us in the past. To become more than conquerors we must be able to use the past as a platform for the present and a stairway to the future. "Forgetting" (Phil. 3:13) suggests the acronym FoRGeT, which helps us remember four activities that are helpful in getting past negative circumstances of our lives. Forgiving, Recycling, Grieving, and Talking are necessary. Note: We have changed "Forgetting" to "Forgiving." While we may not forget negative experiences, we can forgive them. Forgiveness is such an important component of spiritual and emotional health that a step-by-step FoRGeT method is provided to assist in the process of leaving our negative past behind. In the rest of this chapter, we explore the four components of the FoRGeT process. Although there is nothing magic about the order, sometimes it works better to reverse the process by first talking, then grieving, recycling, and forgiving.

TALK

What we can't talk about controls us. If we don't talk, we spend our lives being held hostage by our feelings. It takes energy to stuff emotions, energy that is taken from effective living. It's like trying to swim while holding volleyballs under water. *$$ VOLLEYBALL INTERVENTION $$*

Talking can be any form of communication that helps us get the problem out instead of burying it inside ourselves. We can talk to God, talk to family, friends, or professionals that we know can be trusted to keep our confidences, use self-talk, or write to express our thoughts and feelings.

Why talk to others? Among the many practical things in the book of James is advice on easing the burden of the past. "Therefore confess your sins to each other and pray for each other so that you may be healed. The prayer of a righteous man is powerful and effective" (James 5:16). Sharing your burden cuts its weight in half. However, be careful that the person with whom you are sharing can handle your pain.

To move toward a more meaningful life, we need to examine thoroughly how trauma affected us and how it has changed our lives. Feeling and expressing different emotions is necessary in order to work through emotional pain. According to your personal style and need, you may cry, talk, write, review, and express your emotions as many times as needed, until you control the feelings. You may need to "talk it to death." Emotional therapy with a professional is needed if some, or all, of the characteristics of Posttraumatic Stress Disorder (PTSD) are being experienced. Look for signs of traumatic recall, avoidance, and tension. It is critical to recognize that different stressors affect different people in different ways. YOU know how YOU feel so YOU need to get help that is appropriate for YOUR needs. Those who experience PTSD need to recognize they now have, or can gain, sufficient resources to exercise control in their lives.

It is important not to attack the problem in such a way that more trauma occurs. Peripheral issues may be dealt with first in an onion-peeling process. Based on the example given in John 21:15-17 ("Peter, do you love me?"), we gently ask the same question over and over. Remember, sometimes onion peeling brings tears but with tears come the memories. You may need to discuss the issues in small increments. You must, however, discuss the issues or they will maintain control over your life. It is like being in a cage in the middle of a dungeon with monsters running all around us. The object of treatment is to exchange places with the monsters so they will be forever caged. *$$ MONSTER INTERVENTION $$*

GRIEVE

Grief is intense emotional suffering in response to a significant loss. Traumatic or tragic events in your life may bring on a grief reaction. Grief, or grief work, is a necessary part of dealing with events where there has been a loss. When an event causes grief, it should ultimately be handled with a mindset of thanksgiving and faith that God can bring good from any situation. This is not always easy. Remember that mindset is the key.

The need to grieve comes with matters of loss and those experiences that seem to defy meaning. Grieving is important, but we should control our grief and not let it lead us into inappropriate stress relievers. We need to define the loss, accept it, assign responsibility and process it according to our individual need (Name it, Claim it, Blame it, and Tame it).

Severe losses give us a feeling that life is out of control. A sense of control is a vital factor in mental health. Without a sense of control, we face anxiety and, in acute cases, panic. Our sense of the world becomes disturbed and resources seem inadequate. Our CHEESE factory may have given us an incomplete understanding of life. Therefore, a significant part of the grieving process is the restructuring of our relationships with God, others, and our environment. Emotions should be expressed, as often as necessary, followed by the discovery of healing resources, until a degree of mastery over our feelings and our environment is achieved. Those who deal with people who are working through the grief process need to understand and appreciate the need of the grieving person to go over and over the loss. *$$ EMOTION EXERCISE $$*

Expectations (mindsets) have a great deal to do with grief, anger, and depression. Many things in life are taken for granted and there are some things we wish would happen based on hopes and dreams. In those times when life does not work out as we had hoped or expected, we desperately need the mindset that we can have total expectations of God, only reasonable expectation for ourselves, and we must try to have realistic expectations of others and circumstances.

RECYCLE

Recycling is the process of finding some meaning or benefit from seemingly negative experiences. Sometimes there is gold in the garbage. (See the chapter on "Why Do We Have Trials?" for a more in-depth treatment of negative circumstances.) All of us have garbage in our lives, both physical and emotional. We need to keep current in sorting our emotional garbage, grieving the true waste, and recycling the rest.

The disposal of our household garbage is a metaphor for handling our emotional garbage. When recycling is available, the first thing we do is sort out that which can be useful. In our emotional lives we have to decide what is useful as a growth experience and what seems, at least at the time, to be pure garbage. A variation of the Serenity Prayer may help here. Help me to grow with what is helpful, help me to throw what is harmful, and give me the wisdom to know the difference. Take stock of your treasure and trash. For-give the trash away. Recycle anything that is of value. Stash the trash and take pleasure in your treasure. *$$ HOUSE CLEARING INTERVENTION $$*

Getting past our past has a lot to do with finding meaning in the bad stuff. This is a very personal endeavor. One person's pie may be another person's poison. As we mentally recycle events in our lives, we can usually find some way God is using the experience for His purposes. It may have been a learning experience, teaching us some way to be more empathic with others who are suffering. Sometimes we wouldn't wish it upon anybody else but it is part of who we are.

Appropriate humor can be helpful. The story is told of two boys who came home to find their toy room full of horse manure. One of the boys was devastated; everything was ruined. The other one said, "Give me a pitchfork, with all this horse manure there has to be a pony in here somewhere." Mindset.

As problems are a result of negative aspects of our SPICE rack, solutions come from opposite, positive actions in the same areas. Change of behaviors and forgiveness are usually required.

GETTING PAST THE PAST THROUGH FORGIVENESS

Forgiving others is one of the greatest things we can do for ourselves — *for ourselves*. We will continue to need to extend the grace of forgive for the rest of our lives. Forgiveness is of vital importance. Forgiveness is fundamental to spiritual, physical, intellectual, community, and emotional health. What we can't forgive controls us.

Upon hearing these words, "Dora" sobbed, "How can I forgive him? What he did to me changed the course of my life. Most of the garbage decisions I have made can be traced directly back to him. I still wake up screaming. My husband says, 'Get over it.' God may forgive him but I can't." Off to Gethsemane.

Sometimes forgiveness is necessary so that we can get past the past. We may be stuck in some terrible event. Either we have done something, or someone else has done something to us and that controls our mindset. Not being able to forgive keeps us in bondage to the memory. By not forgiving we choose to live in the garbage dumps and sewers of our lives and relive the insult over and over. Fortunately, we have the "in Christ" relationship thanks to God's bar of soap in 1 John 1:9. We can confess our sins and be purified (1 John 3:3). In addition, through the power of the Holy Spirit, we can be healed from the wounds others have inflicted upon us. And to top it off, we now have the power and ability to forgive those who have offended us. Forgiveness is our ticket out of the sewer.

Realize that forgiveness is not the same as reconciliation. We can forgive a dead person but that does not bring reconciliation. We find in 2 Corinthians 5:19 that God was "reconciling the world unto himself through Christ." In our forgiveness, God took upon Himself our sin so that, with our repentance, we could be reconciled to Him. Obviously, this was to bring about relationship. Note that in the prayer that Jesus taught, He did not say, "reconcile as you are reconciled," but "forgive as you are forgiven" (Matt. 6:9-13). Reconciliation requires cooperation from the forgiven. We must forgive but we are not bound by the past if they refuse to accept forgiveness. Forgiveness is primarily for the forgiver. It relieves the forgiver of re-experiencing the trauma. It relieves the burden of punishing the abuser. Forgiveness puts the offense in the past. Forgiveness prepares the forgiver for reconciliation if the abuser repents, asks for, and receives forgiveness. Then, reconciliation can restore relationship.

Change may be held up by a lack of forgiveness. Lack of forgiveness is an ISR. Like other ISRs, lack of forgiveness stunts growth. When we are not forgiving, we are not growing. An unforgiving mindset is an albatross around our spiritual necks. Just like any other mindset, we will find evidence that supports unforgiveness. Jesus taught us to pray, "Forgive us our debts as we also forgive our debtors" (Matt. 6:12). We get what we give. If I deny forgiveness to others, my own forgiveness is blocked. Thus, my spiritual growth is blocked. I am trapped in the bitterness of the past, living in my personal sewer. Yuk! Forgiveness of our sins is a great gift. The ability to extend forgiveness to others is an equally great gift. Forgiving is a weight off our emotional shoulders. God empowers us to forgive. He does not empower us to hold grudges.

When we have compassion for our offenders and check into their mindsets and CHEESE factories, we can often forgive them as Christ does, "For they know not what they do" (Luke 23:34). If *they* knew what they were doing, God also knew and He will repay. If they are "in Christ," He pays for the offense. If they reject Christ, the debt is theirs to pay. Unfortunately, many people choose to live outside of Christ and are not availing themselves of God's grace and healing power. In addition, many Christians hope that by holding a grudge, the perpetrator is living in misery. That is usually not the case. If you expect your offender to be losing sleep over the offense, you will probably be disappointed. If you expect to feel better by constantly reliving an event, you are giving the offender continuing power over your life. What DO you expect by not forgiving? One of the keys to vibrant Christianity is forgiveness. Some Christians, having the keys to the kingdom (Matt. 16:19), have locked themselves out of the abundant life that God means for them to have.

We may have to ". . . complete in our bodies the sufferings of Christ for the sake of the church" (Col. 1:24). Note: This suffering is not for salvation — it is for the body of Christ. Faith is needed to believe that God's way is better. Grace is necessary when nothing can be done to atone for the wrong that has been inflicted upon us. The forgiveness for wrongs is undeserved and cannot be earned. As for our suffering, we are to be like Christ and He suffered. Therefore, we may be called upon to endure hardship in the nature of Christ.

GETTING PAST THE PAST BY FORGIVING OURSELF AND OTHERS

It becomes more and more evident that what we can't talk about, and what we can't forgive, controls us. What we can't forgive will create a mindset, occupy our thoughts, and influence most of what we do. All too often, people sit on opposite sides of their church from those they won't forgive, violating one of the major concepts of their faith. Lack of forgiveness will split families. It is sad to see that happen. Many times the joy of a wedding is marred by a split in the family when a divided family tries to help unite a couple. Or, at a funeral, when families need to support each other, a lack of forgiveness impedes the comforting and healing that should occur. *$$ FORGIVENESS PIE $$*

To get on with our lives, we need to accept forgiveness from self, others, and God and realize we also benefit from forgiving self and others. We can be released from the prisons of our emotional pain through the power of forgiveness. Forgiveness is one of the major "keys to the kingdom" that locks out the past and opens the future. Lack of forgiveness for self and others is a major contribution to misery and a roadblock to joy and peace. Lack of forgiveness is a major issue that makes the dump of our lives a permanent address.

Only grace is sufficient to restore our relationship with God. Grace is a flat-out gift. It is not deserved; the wrong cannot be undone. But, God extends grace to us so that we can accept it and extend that same grace to others. We MUST extend grace. ". . . forgive him, so that your Father in heaven may forgive you your sins" (Mark 11:25). Our forgiveness is conditional upon our forgiving. There are times that this grace, extended to others, is the necessary and sufficient gift to restore relationships. Change of mindset requires us to be forgiving rather than vengeful.

Forgiving is instantaneous but it is also a process. Forgiving is like lighting a candle. It begins burning right away but sometimes takes a while to finish. The word forgive implies giving or a gift. When you forgive others, you give them the gift of grace. We are given grace that we might give grace to others — unearned — undeserved. If we do not give grace, it stagnates in our spirit and our emotions. Our spirit becomes a Dead Sea.

Sometimes the most difficult act of forgiveness is when we must forgive ourselves. Some people believe if God really knew them He wouldn't forgive. If the sinful act was willful or stupid, we know we should have done differently. However, if we don't forgive ourselves we place our fate in our own hands instead of in God's grace. It implies that we have knowledge superior to God Who is willing to forgive us. We need to know that we aren't smarter than God. "There is now NO condemnation…" (Rom. 8:1), including our own. We no longer have to be in bondage. We no longer have to serve sin (Rom. 6).

Trust God to deal appropriately with those who have offended you. God said, "Vengeance is mine, I will repay" (Rom. 12:19). You can bank on it. "True and just are his judgments" (Rev. 19:2). Your judgments may be neither true nor just. Vengeance is God's job. He empowers you to love and forgive. He will not empower you to exact vengeance. Why continue to give Perp control of your life?

Sometimes we feel we need to forgive God. This is a bit presumptuous. Instead, we need to come to an understanding and acceptance of how God works. He has causative and permissive will and we are subject to things caused and allowed. When we give ourselves to Him, what happens in our lives is according to His purposes and plan. Therefore, we do not complain but we rejoice when we face trials (James 1:2). The alternatives of arguing with God and bemoaning our fate are counterproductive and indicate that we do not feel that He knows what He is doing.

"Walt" had been told he was just like his father and in many ways he was. The history of alcohol and drug abuse, the failed marriages, and the legal problems — all were a haunting reproduction of his father's life. But now Walt was different. At least he thought he was, He had accepted Christ and was trying to be obedient to God but something kept pulling him back. There were times the old ways seemed less scary. At least they were familiar. It wasn't until after several sessions of counseling that he realized that he unconsciously felt that his ending had to be the same as his father's death — death while cursing God. His life was the same, why wouldn't his death be the same? A new understanding of forgiveness for his father and himself cut the cords that were binding Walt to the past and opened up the relationship with God that he knew was his real inheritance. We become "more than conquerors" when we forgive and place those who have sinned against us in God's hands.

If we are serious about forgiveness, we must investigate what God went through to forgive us, and often we must join with Him in His suffering as we forgive others. Jesus taught us that we are to forgive as we are forgiven. Christ suffered so that we could have complete forgiveness. It may take suffering for us to forgive. We receive grace that we might give grace. *$$ BIBLE REFERENCES REGARDING SUFFERING $$*

We are to FoRGeT what lies behind (Phil. 3:13). We need to *Forgive* everyone who has offended us and all that they have done to us. We need to *Recycle* negative experiences that help us grow in God's purpose. We need to *Grieve* that which is loss. We need to *Talk* about the bad stuff so that it doesn't control us. That is how we get past the past. Until the task of forgiveness is accomplished, we will be bound to the past, prevented from fully enjoying the present, and looking forward to a bleak future. Forgiveness releases us to gain God's gifts in greater measure as we ". . . forget what lies behind and press on toward the goal . . ." (Phil. 4: 13-14).

Our prayer for you is that you will yield to the Spirit's work in you that the renewing of your mind will be complete "in Christ." The next chapters are yours to write.

$ $ $ 🔑——— $ $ $

Treasure Chest #20
Resources for Living as New Creations "in Christ"

FROG INTERVENTION

Most people know the fairy tale of the prince who was cursed by being turned into a frog. He was condemned to a life in the "Frogdom of Curse." His "salvation" came when a princess kissed him. Too many people live in the Frogdom of Curse they have received by doing something or by having something done to them. The only release is accepting and extending the redemptive act of Christ so they can move into the Kingdom of God.

List abuses that have "cursed" you.

Describe an area in which you are living in the Frogdom of Curse.

Consider the application of 1 John 1:9 to remove the curse.

Back to the original situation in the Garden of Eden where it was not the apple in the tree but the pair on the ground that was the problem.

GRUDGE INTERVENTION

Material: ugly stuffed animal.

The animal represents a grudge about some event or person that has not been forgiven. Name the grudge. Hold the grudge in one hand and go through the day. Note how you fairly quickly learn how to operate even though you are holding a grudge. Note conscious or unconscious irritability. Note the decrease in productivity. Discuss how grudges bring emotional crippling with loss of energy. What grudge do you need to release?

FORGIVENESS PIE

Draw a four-inch pie circle in the middle of a sheet of paper. Cut the pie into twelve sections. The pieces may be of different sizes. Label the sections with the following requirements for forgiveness: grace, accepting forgiveness, forgiving others, forgiving myself, change of mindset, compassion with understanding, expectations, suffering, faith, and endurance. The other sections are for individual circumstances. Use the Name it, Claim it, Blame it, and Tame it exercise with each slice of forgiveness. Alternative X Desire > Problem.

VOLLEYBALL INTERVENTION

It will be a big help if you have a swimming pool and two volleyballs handy. Otherwise, draw a stick figure holding two volleyballs under water while attempting to swim. Label the volleyballs as events or emotions that are occupying your emotional energy and depleting your zest for living. Discuss the effect they have and how forgiveness will care for them.

MONSTER INTERVENTION

Materials: a small cage, rubber monsters, or a suitable drawing. Replicas of dinosaurs work well.

Label the different significant monsters (traumas) in your life.

Usually, this should be done with the help of a competent caregiver. Using the descriptors of Posttraumatic Stress, discuss the aspects of memory, avoidance, and arousal the "monsters" cause. Name the stressors. Claim them, as you feel competent. Place blame appropriately. In many cases you were powerless at the time. Don't think the child you were when the abuse occurred had the capabilities you now have. "I should have . . ." is futile and counterproductive. Recognize your present resources and learn new ones. Release yourself; tame the monsters and put them in the cage. (Forgiveness is a great monster tamer.) Lose the key so you can't open the cage again. You can't have a different past but you can now shape a new beginning for the future.

EMOTION EXERCISE

Use the following list to deal with emotions generated by past or present trauma. Consider the stated emotion, look for its source, determine the effect on your life, select a process to flush it away, and choose an appropriate alternative behavior.

Emotion	Source	Effect	Flush	Alternative
Guilt				
Anxiety				
Sorrow				
Depression				
Anger				
Frustration				
Pain				
Victimization				
Primary Loss				
Secondary Loss				
Unfinished Business				
Blame				
Mistrust				
Other:				

HOUSE CLEANING INTERVENTION

Draw a picture of your emotional and spiritual house.

Search through your house: all the rooms, the attic, the basement, the sub-basement, and the garage. Draw pictures of boxes. Label them with abuses, grudges, time wasters, bad habits, etc. Thank God for the good stuff. Ask Him if anything needs to be thrown out. These may be thoughts or activities that are good but not essential. Look for anything that is holding you back in your "in Christ" growth that needs attention. Put out the garbage. Leave it out.

BIBLE VERSES REFERRING TO SUFFERING

There are many verses that help us understand and deal with the process of suffering as it applies to forgiveness.

Hebrews 5:7-9 - "During the days of Jesus' life on earth, he offered up prayers and petitions with loud cries and tears to the one who could save him from death, and he was heard because of his reverent submission. Although he was a son, he learned obedience from what he suffered and, once made perfect, he became the source of eternal salvation for all who obey him." We are enjoined to be like Jesus.

Luke 22:42–44 - "'Father, if you are willing, take this cup from me; yet not my will, but yours be done.' An angel from heaven appeared to him and strengthened him. And being in anguish, he prayed more earnestly, and his sweat was like drops of blood falling to the ground." We sometimes need to get very serious in our Christian walk. It is comforting to know that God will not leave us alone during these times. Our "angels" may be people we know or a supernatural experience.

Philippians 3:10-11 - "I want to know Christ and the power of his resurrection and the fellowship of sharing in his sufferings, becoming like him in his death, and so, somehow, to attain to the resurrection from the dead." There are times we will suffer forgiveness. Suffering teaches obedience. Obedience bears fruit. The suffering of forgiveness is a very deep and intense fellowship.

Colossians 1:24 - "Now I rejoice in what was suffered for you, and I fill up in my flesh what is still lacking in regard to Christ's afflictions, for the sake of his body, which is the church." Remember: This suffering is not for our sins. That work was finished. But there are deficiencies in the church, especially in the area of forgiveness, that require suffering. There will necessarily be long-suffering on our part for the Body of Christ. We must identify with Christ in suffering.

BOOK QUESTIONS

CHAPTER 1: MINDSET

BIG IDEA: We filter life through, and act according to, our mindsets.

1. Why is it necessary that we understand the concept of mindsets?
2. Memorize Romans 12:2.
3. Explain how mindsets can be positive or negative.
4. Why does the mindset of a person outside of Christ need changing?
5. How are our minds transformed and renewed?
6. Why doesn't the man without the Spirit accept the things of God?
7. Explain how mindsets act as a filter for incoming information.
8. What do we hear when someone speaks to us?
9. Are words necessary in the formation of mindsets?
10. Why are mindsets necessary?

CHAPTER 2: WHY WE ARE THE WAY WE ARE

BIG IDEA: Choices, Heredity, Environment, Events, and Self-Esteem (CHEESE) develop our mindsets.

1. Why do many people want to explore issues from their past?
2. What is the importance of the CHEESE Factory in our lives?
3. Memorize the elements of the CHEESE Factory.
4. How does the impact of choice change as we grow up?
5. How does heredity affect our physical and emotional traits?
6. Explain how heredity is a mold that helps shape the influence of our experiences.
7. Give an example of how different environments can cause different traits.
8. How do significant emotional events affect our lives?
9. Name some significant emotional events in your own life.
10. What early factors shape our self-esteem?

CHAPTER 3: DEVELOPING SELF-ESTEEM

BIG IDEA: Our self-esteem is initially influenced by significant others and continues to develop as we experience life.

1. How is self-esteem validated?
2. What are the benefits of entering a child's world?
3. How do children feel when significant adults don't spend time with them?
4. How do parents sacrifice their children?
5. What are some reasons children don't tell when they are being abused?
6. How does the "scale balance" in our minds work?
7. Why must we first love our self?
8. Why is parental abandonment such a serious issue?
9. Why has God given us rules?
10. What is the best thing you can do for your children?
11. What do we get back from our children during our senior years?

CHAPTER 4: THE SPICE RACK

BIG IDEA: Spiritual, Physical, Intellectual, Community, and Emotional factors influence our CHEESE Factories.

1. Where did the idea of the SPICE Rack come from?
2. Explain how the S of SPICE flavors our CHEESE.
3. Explain how the P of SPICE flavors our CHEESE.
4. Explain how the I of SPICE flavors our CHEESE.
5. Explain how the C of SPICE flavors our CHEESE.
6. Explain how the E of SPICE flavors our CHEESE.
7. Why do the elements of SPICE need to be considered when a problem is to be resolved?
8. How do habits affect actions?
9. Why did the Corinthians think, "All things are lawful for me?"
10. How did Paul counter that way of thinking?
11. Explain how the CHEESE/SPICE matrix works.

CHAPTER 5: THE "IN CHRIST" RELATIONSHIP

BIG IDEA: The most delightful choice we can make is to enter a relationship with God through the work of Christ and the Holy Spirit.

1. What is the most delightful thing we can do in life?

2. What is the benefit of believing in Christ?

3. What is the benefit of confessing our sins?

4. What is the benefit of receiving Christ?

5. What is the benefit of obeying Christ's commandments?

6. What is the main reason people don't receive the benefits of Christianity?

7. What two aspects of sin need to be resolved in our confession and forgiveness?

8. Does becoming a Christian mean that we will never sin again?

9. How is becoming a child of God like lighting a candle?

10. How does God use Christians in the process of others' growth into Christ?

CHAPTER 6: ADVANTAGES OF THE "IN CHRIST" RELATIONSHIP

BIG IDEA: Life "in Christ" brings all the privileges of being God's children.

1. What does the statement, "We are no longer slaves to sin" (Rom. 6:17) mean?

2. What purifies us in God's eyes?

3. How are the truths about God discerned (understood)?

4. What are advantages of being in the family of God?

5. What are the three main thrusts of the Spirit in our lives?

6. How do we "bear fruit?"

7. How do spiritual gifts differ from talents?

8. How do we receive the fruit of the Spirit?

9. What does anxiety say about our concept of God?

10. Explain the two-lane path to peace given in Philippians 4:6-9.

CHAPTER 7: WHY DO WE HAVE TRIALS?

BIG IDEA: *The only way that we know that God's grace is sufficient is to experience the depth of pain.*

1. What does the natural mind think about God and suffering?
2. Which translation of Romans 8:28 do you prefer? Why?
3. How do we experience the depth of God's grace and comfort?
4. What method for handling "thorns" is given in 2 Corinthians 12:7-10?
5. What are some of the things we don't want to learn from experience?
6. What does Jesus teach about hardship being a payback for sin?
7. What is the danger of relying on people or things for joy and peace?
8. Describe the activity of our two Heavenly Intercessors.
9. Discuss reasons we receive comfort from God.
10. How do we gain contentment?
11. How do we know that being tempted is not sin?

CHAPTER 8: EXPECTATIONS

BIG IDEA: *We can really be disappointed by reasonable expectations.*

1. How are expectations like mindsets?
2. What are our expectations of God?
3. What kind of expectations should we have of ourselves?
4. What is the meaning of "realistic expectations?"
5. How do unrealistic expectations prevent change?
6. What is "unanswered prayer?"
7. How does control relate to expectations?
8. Why does God allow us to have negative emotions?
9. What is the source of reactive depression?
10. When do we feel anxious?

CHAPTER 9: STRESS AND INAPPROPRIATE STRESS RELIEVERS

BIG IDEA: Inappropriate stress relievers create more stress.

1. What is the definition of stress?
2. How does change relate to stress?
3. How is stress related to a perception of loss of control?
4. What is the effect of Inappropriate Stress Relievers?
5. How can pride lead to divorce?
6. What are some types of evidence to show that manipulation is being used?
7. Why might angry people misuse substances?
8. Why is casino gambling generally a losing proposition?
9. What are some inappropriate uses of food?
10. Why is viewing pornography contrary to God's intent for sexuality?

CHAPTER 10: ISSUES WITH DEPENDENCE

BIG IDEA: Knowing that a substance or activity is more important than you is devastating.

1. Describe tolerance and withdrawal symptoms.
2. How does denial inhibit the change process?
3. How does belief in choice affect the change process?
4. What definition of codependency to you prefer?
5. How might environment influence a person to become a caregiver?
6. How does a position of power affect the change process?
7. How do children connect punishment and blame?
8. What type of lifestyle might be generated by feeling shameful?
9. What lies behind a person's need to enable?
10. How does a codependent person lose his or her identity?
11. What happens when a person knows that a substance or activity is more important than he or she is?
12. Why might an enabler go from one dependent person to another?

CHAPTER 11: THE DESIRE TO CHANGE

BIG IDEA: *Change creates stress and requires an appropriate stress reliever.*

1.   What did it take for the opposing sides in Exodus to change?

2.   What mindsets did God instill in Moses in the wilderness?

3.   What is sometimes the only thing that causes us to accept the pain of change?

4.   Why do people hope that someone or something else will change?

5.   What is the basis of our hope in God according to Jeremiah 29:11-14?

6.   What makes it difficult for us to release a false mindset?

7.   Describe the three areas of the Holy Spirit's conviction.

8.   What type of sorrow leads to change?

9.   What characteristics of godly sorrow do you feel are important?

10. How does the Gethsemane/Golgotha/Garden experience play out in our lives?

CHAPTER 12: PROBLEM SOLVING

BIG IDEA: *The renewing of the mind requires the ability to solve problems.*

1.   How do verses in the Bible let us know there will be problems for Christians?

2.   When do we realize that we have a problem?

3.   What are the three possible resolutions to a problem?

4.   Briefly state the four steps of the problem-solving method given in this chapter.

5.   What is the importance of keeping notes during the problem-solving process?

6.   What is the rule about giving up on a solution?

7.   What is necessary if one person is always conceding?

8.   How are choice and responsibility connected?

9.   How does John 12:47-48 help parents with establishing rules?

10. What must children realize about choices and consequences?

11. How can our relationships become like the Dead Sea?

12. What is necessary to gain skill in problem solving?

CHAPTER 13: A PROCESS FOR DEALING WITH DIFFICULT SITUATIONS

BIG IDEA: *Alternative X Desire > ISR*

1. Who are the players in the process of renewing our minds?

2. What type of mindsets need strong treatment?

3. Memorize the Name it/Claim it/Blame it/Tame it poem.

4. How does the metaphor of peeling onions apply to examining mindsets?

5. What does an "I don't know" answer symbolize?

6. What is necessary for the "NAME IT" step?

7. What is necessary for the "CLAIM IT" step?

8. What is necessary for the "BLAME IT" step?

9. What is necessary for the "TAME IT" step?

10. Why is there a multiplication sign between Alternative and Desire in the change inequality?

11. How are the NCBT steps applied to healing from loss?

CHAPTER 14: APPROPRIATE STRESS RELIEVERS

BIG IDEA: *Appropriate stress relievers relieve stress without creating more stress.*

1. What do people without resources often do to relieve stress?

2. What was the Apostle Paul's stress reliever, according to Philippians 4:13?

3. Name and discuss two types of stressors.

4. How do secondary stressors come about?

5. Why do people hesitate to give up on ISRs?

6. What is sometimes required to endure the pain of change?

7. What does Romans 6 say about being slaves to sin?

8. What is one reason people turn to ISRs?

9. What is the difference between the accusations of Satan and

the conviction of the Holy Spirit?

10. What is sometimes necessary if alternative stress relievers don't seem to work?

11. Name and discuss three different ways God comforts us.

CHAPTER 15: WHY WEIGHT?

BIG IDEA: Food is meant for the body, not for emotions.

1. Where does excess weight come from?

2. How do the authors describe the mindsets that deal with weight?

3. What is the purpose for having food?

4. What is the feeling that many people have when they see how little food they need to eat?

5. What emotion do we need in order to consider losing weight?

6. What kind of attitude is necessary in order to lose weight?

7. What are the two main issues to consider about weight?

8. Why are there no failures in a good weight loss program?

9. How do we prevent a "two-three" loop in the four-step behavior modification model?

10. How does "worldly sorrow" apply to losing weight?

11. How can rocks and lard be used as motivational tools when losing weight?

12. Who are the "fat farmers?"

13. Why do so many people gain weight back once it is lost?

14. How many steps does it take to burn off 100 calories?

15. What adjustment in food intake must be made after weight is lost?

16. Explain the John Chapter 15 Diet Plan.

CHAPTER 16: USE OF ANGER IS A CHOICE

BIG IDEA: The way we use anger is learned and is a choice.

1. Name some ways anger reactions are learned.

2. Why should we learn to recognize emotional/physiological signals of anger?

3. How might inappropriate anger be rewarded?

4. What are some generalizations about the different ways men and women express anger?

5. What is the problem with defining directed anger as "uncontrolled?"

6. What is an appropriate response to anger?

7. How is passive aggressive anger expressed?

8. What way, or ways, is your anger expressed?

9. What shapes our response to anger, the antecedent or our belief about the antecedent?

10. How does forgiveness tie in with anger control?

CHAPTER 17: COMMUNICATION

BIG IDEA: Many people talk; few communicate.

1. What is the difference between talking and communication?

2. Name three types of communication.

3. What are the components of the GRACE acronym?

4. Why is Grace important for communication?

5. Why is Respect important for communication?

6. Why is sAfety important for communication?

7. Why is Clarification important for communication?

8. Why is Empathy important for communication?

9. What are the ABCs of communication?

10. What does caring have to do with communication?

11. Name some basic listening skills.

12. What can be done if communication is drying up?

13. What is the purpose of communication?

14. Describe a procedure to demonstrate differences in perspective.

15. What are some dangers of "you statements?"

16. What should be done instead of talking about what is wrong?

17. How do evil acts disrupt communication?

18. Why does God encourage confession?

19. List characteristics of assertive people.

20. Describe some ways to communicate with aggressive people.

CHAPTER 18: INTIMACY

BIG IDEA: *People can be married for years and never experience intimacy.*

1. How important is it that we recognize another's reality?
2. Where does true self-esteem come from?
3. Compare *intimacy with the self* and *self-esteem*.
4. Why isn't intimacy two people becoming one?
5. How do lies destroy intimacy?
6. What problems does dishonesty in dating create in a marriage?
7. Why does intimacy depend so much on nonverbal communication?
8. Why is submission an intellectual act?
9. How do separate and common interests contribute to intimacy?
10. How does the definition of *love as giving* promote intimacy?

CHAPTER 19: CHOOSING A MATE AND ON TO MARRIAGE

BIG IDEA: *We need to communicate in the other's love language; they might not understand ours.*

1. Why do we have to be careful about whom we date?
2. Apply the welding analogy to relationships.
3. Why does God have rules?
4. Why do many children lack relationship skills?
5. What is the "more excellent way?"
6. Why are some marriages sick?
7. What plans does God have for us?
8. What is the difference between a human being and a human doing?
9. How does Ephesians 5:28 compare with Luke 10:27b?
10. Discuss three kinds of love.
11. Why is a three-stranded cord necessary?
12. Discuss procreation, re-creation, and recreation in the sexual relationship.
13. Why do men get stuck at Ephesians 5:24?

14. How should men treat their wives?

15. How is the marriage garden like a vegetable or flower garden?

16. Describe how "termites" can destroy a marriage.

17. What do "can't" and "won't" accomplish?

18. What happens in a "you go first" marriage?

19. What should we do if something isn't working?

20. Why must we speak our spouse's love language?

CHAPTER 20: GETTING PAST THE PAST

BIG IDEA: Forgiveness requires the action of only one person; reconciliation requires the action of two.

1. What can we choose about events?

2. Name and describe four stages of getting past the past.

3. What happens if we can't talk about something?

4. What does James 5:16 suggest as an aid to healing?

5. Define grief.

6. What restructuring does grief sometimes require?

7. What is the goal of the recycling process?

8. How do people differ in finding meaning in trials?

9. What does lack of forgiveness do to our freedom?

10. Compare forgiveness and reconciliation.

11. How might people with unforgiving mindsets find evidence to support their attitude?

12. What do you think about the idea of having to forgive God?

GLOSSARY

GLOSSARY FOR MINDSET – Chapter 1

Adapt—adjust or modify to fit

Deceit—the intent to mislead by the concealment or perversion of the truth

Habit—a way of acting—an ingrained mindset—does not require thought

Metaverbal—above or beyond verbal, HOW something is said

Mindset—the way we interpret the world and approach life

Perception—what we think is real. We act according to our perceptions, not reality

Reaction—a response that has become automatic through usage. MOTTO: Act, don't react. Better—Respond, don't react

Response—a thoughtful way to deal with an event

GLOSSARY FOR SALVATION – Chapter 5

Atonement (at-one-ment)—compensation for a debt, reparation

Grace—unmerited favor, an unearned, undeserved gift, forgiving the unforgivable

Salvation—salvation means deliverance—the opposite of perishing

Reconciliation—to bring into agreement, to make compatible

Redemption—to buy back—liberation—emancipation

Repent—to change one's mind—to feel remorse for a past action or attitude

Adoption—we obtain a new parent, a wonderful brother, and a host of siblings

GLOSSARY FOR DEPENDENCE – Chapter 10

Addict—someone who has lost control to an inappropriate stress reliever

Addiction—being controlled by a substance or activity that disrupts life factors

Antecedent—a prior circumstance, something that comes before

Boundaries—overt or covert mindsets that define personal and emotional space

Boundary Violations—irritants that cause depression, anxiety, frustration etc.

CHEESE—Choices (Character), Heredity, Environment, Events, Self-Esteem

Codependency—my sickness is that I need for you to be sick

Control—the area within our boundaries where we feel safe

Dependence—a new term for addiction—involves increased need and withdrawal distress

Enabling—helping people maintain dependence on a substance or activity

Irritation—a boundary violation that causes depression, anxiety, frustration, etc.

ISR—Inappropriate Stress Reliever—a substitute for God—the result of our best thinking

Lust—intense sexual desire or appetite

Maladaptive—incomplete, inadequate, or faulty

Mindset—perception—influences how we respond or react to circumstances

Prayer—ACTS—Adoration, Confession, Thanksgiving, Supplication

SPICE—Spiritual, Physical, Intellectual, Social, Emotional – areas of illness/cure

Stress—a force exerted by one thing upon another

Substance—chemical that alters the neuro-chemical balance in the brain

Tolerance—the need for more to have the same effect

Withdrawal—physical or psychological distress when returning to "normal"

GLOSSARY FOR ANGER–Chapter 16

AAA—Alternative Anger Activities

Anger—a strong feeling of displeasure aroused by a real or perceived wrong

Exacerbate – To increase

Mindset—Perception—accepts confirming evidence, rejects contrary evidence

Posttraumatic Stress Disorder—A set of behaviors stemming from extreme, accumulated, or prolonged threat

Psychological—emotional, having to do with the mind

Physiological—physical, having to do with the body

Rage—violent anger

Reaction—a knee-jerk result of a stimulus—habit-driven

Response—a thought-out result of a stimulus—thought-driven

Repression—an unconscious forgetting of something terrible that happened

Suppression—a conscious effort to block a bad memory

SPICE—Spiritual, Physical, Intellectual, Social, Emotional

Violent—acting with or characterized by uncontrolled, strong, rough force